Superannuation Can Be Murder

Other books by the author:

Non-Fiction

Two Climactic Invasions
A comparison of two amphibious invasions across the same English Channel, each of which changed the world. 1066 and 1944. Factual and exciting.

Fiction
Written under the pseudonym, Dudley Flint

Social Club Murders
A ménage a trios of sexy senior social club members uncover a duo of serial killers preying on club widowers. At gunpoint, the tethered male member of the trios faces death in a weird drug/sex ritual

Contempt for Caution
An ageing Private Investigator contrives to pit a sophisticated serial killer against a sexual deviant multiple murderer. An explosive nautical confrontation provides promotion for a bent cop, love for a straight one and vengeance for the Investigator

Superannuation Can Be Murder

Superannuation for Murderers,
Swindlers, Conmen, Cheats and Frauds
and Superannuation Fund Managers
and Trustees (Includes SMSFs)

PERCY COOPER

Copyright © 2015 Percy Cooper

All rights are reserved. The material contained within this book is protected by copyright law, no part may be copied, reproduced, presented, stored, communicated or transmitted in any form by any means without prior written permission.

Cover image by iStockphoto
Cover Design and typeset by BookPOD Pty Ltd
Printed and bound in Australia by BookPOD Pty Ltd
Typeset in Garamond Premier Pro 12/15

National Library of Australia Cataloguing-in-Publication entry:

Creator: Cooper, Percy, author.

Title: Superannuation can be murder : superannuation for murderers, swindlers, conmen, cheats and frauds and superannuation fund managers and trustees (includes SMSFs) / Percy Cooper.

ISBN: 978-0-9941519-2-6 (paperback) 978-0-9941519-3-3 (ebook)

Subjects: Fraud--Australia.
Pension trusts--Australia.
Retirement income--Australia.

Dewey Number: 364.163

This book is dedicated to my wife, Bev. Humility precluded her name being mentioned in the text. Defying her family, Bev married a former Ward of the State, a gas company employee and Army Reserve Sergeant, and helped him through many years of night school to gain the education that advanced his civilian and Army careers. We shared the sublime happiness of raising three wonderful children, suffered the gut-wrenching, lasting loss of two young ones and now rejoice with our seven grandchildren. For 55 years of marriage I can never fully express my thanks. The dedication of this book is but a tiny token.

Author's Credentials

PERCY COOPER HAS OVER 40 years experience as General Manager, Trustee and Consultant to Australia's top government, semi-government and industry superannuation funds. He served for 15 years as a Councillor of the Victorian Division of the industry's peak body, the Association of Superannuation Funds of Australia. During that time he addressed ASFA lunchtime meetings, seminars and conferences on technical aspects of fraud, disability swindlers, ramifications of murders of contributors, investment issues and the Limitation of Actions Act. He holds the prestigious ASFA Distinguished Service Award.

In the wider field of business, Percy served as a Director of a Bank, a Motel Chain and a joint semi-government/Bank multimillion dollar property trust and was Chairman of an ASX listed property development company. He was a member of a Victorian Government Advisory Committee, a position he held for 14 years being appointed by the Kennett Government and re-appointed by the Bracks Government. A foundation member of a Credit Cooperative and later its Chairman for 12 years, Percy was elected Chairman of the Victorian Council of Cooperative Housing Societies Inc. He was Chairman of the multimillion Latrobe Capital & Mortgage Corporation.

As a licensed Private Inquiry Agent he draws on decades of experience to detect and resolve, mainly by common sense negotiation, "irregularities" within the superannuation industry. Parallel with his business career, Percy served with the Australian Army Reserve rising from a humble National Serviceman to Officer Rank and receiving the ED (Efficiency Decoration). His last posting was as the 3rd Divisional Artillery Intelligence Officer.

Percy's qualifications and vast experience, civil and military, make him the only person capable of writing this unique "super" book.

Author's Note

IN AN INCREASINGLY LITIGIOUS SOCIETY, it is a prudent precaution to avoid mentioning the correct names of some actual people involved: even though the events related are matters of public record. Names in some chapters have been changed. In referring to reprehensible persons, the names of people I detest have been substituted. The names of decent folk are given names of people I respect. That should set some readers a puzzle.

To avoid any possibility of adding to the emotional distress of those adults who were innocent children at the time of the event described, I have tinkered with locales also. Over time, changes have occurred in various Criminal and Civil Laws and some Court procedures and penalty boundaries. I have chosen to retain in the narrative the law titles and Court peripheries in vogue at the time of each event.

Glossary

ACCC	Australian Competition &Consumer Commission
ACL	Australian Consumer Law
AFP	Australian Federal Police
AFSL	Australian Financial Services Licence
APRA	Australian Prudential Regulation Authority
ASA	Australian Shareholders' Association
ASIC	Australian Securities & Investments Commission
ASFA	Association of Superannuation Funds of Australia
ASX	Australian Stock Exchange
ATO	Australian Taxation Office
Austrac	Australian Transaction Reports & Analysis Centre
CSS	Commonwealth Superannuation Scheme
DIY	Do it yourself
PDS	Product Disclosure Statement
POCA	Proceeds of Crime Act 2002
RSE	Registrable Superannuation Entity Licence
SCBM	Superannuation Can Be Murder—this book
SCT	Superannuation Complaints Tribunal—Superannuation (Resolution of Complaints) Act 1993
SMSF	Self Managed Superannuation Fund
SMSFAA	Self-managed Superannuation Funds Auditors & Advisors Pty Ltd
SMSF-PAA	Self-managed Superannuation Funds Professional Association of Australia

Contents

Author's Credentials vi

Author's Note vii

Glossary viii

Chapter One
Murder and Mayhem in Superannuation 1

Chapter Two
Wrong Body 11

Chapter Three
"Sickie" Swindlers 23

Chapter Four
Swindled by a Psycho Manipulator 33

Chapter Five
Two Departures, Plaintive and Painful 39

Chapter Six
Dangerous Dependents 47

Chapter Seven
Successful Superannuation Thief 67

Chapter Eight
Contributor's Rorts 79

Chapter Nine
Diplomatic Complications 99

Chapter Ten
Soliloquy of a Superannuation Sleuth 113

Chapter Eleven
Saints and Conmen 123

CHAPTER TWELVE
The Gigantic Commonwealth Superannuation Fraud (That Wasn't) ... 135

CHAPTER THIRTEEN
Super and Illegal Gas 143

CHAPTER FOURTEEN
Stultifying Statistics 157

CHAPTER FIFTEEN
Caught by Statistics 183

CHAPTER SIXTEEN
Tainted Trustees 191

CHAPTER SEVENTEEN
Identity Theft, the Core of All Fraud 211

CHAPTER EIGHTEEN
Restitution or Retribution? 227

CHAPTER NINETEEN
Is Your Super Secure? 239

CHAPTER TWENTY
When Will Super Be a Terrorist Target? 255

Chapter One

Murder and Mayhem in Superannuation

SUPERANNUATION IS EXHILARATING! IT'S THE people. The contributors, beneficiaries, fund managers, actuaries and accountants, auditors, lawyers other service providers and administrators. It's also the hordes of the frauds, swindlers and the occasional murderer that makes superannuation exhilarating.

Recall how you felt during a spell of burning hot weather. Recall the towering humidity that saps all your vitality. Now picture a Monday morning in Melbourne in early February after four days of sweltering heat when the air seems so thick it's like breathing a warm milk shake. Everyone was moving S-L-O-W-L-Y this morning. Even sound seemed softer in the cloying air. Then bang, the Superannuation Fund office door was slammed open and a big sweaty woman with bare muscular arms and long, unwashed peroxide blonde hair rushed into the reception area where I happened to be standing.

In eardrum assaulting screams, with some of the most profane and obscene language that I have ever heard she shouted that her husband died on Friday. She demanded his superannuation. She wants it now and she wants it in cash. With a raised fist she warned me that if she doesn't get the money immediately then I might prematurely join her husband. To emphasise her point, this foul mouthed piece of repugnant femininity pushed past me to my Secretary's desk, heaved up her Underwood typewriter and smashed it against the brick wall.

I'm told that managers of some superannuation funds would treat such behaviour as just a routine Monday morning but I have reservations about that. I've only had this top job in a rapidly expanding fund a couple of weeks, so to me this initiation was a shock. Superannuation is supposed to be refined and sedate.

I tried to make allowances for grief, I really did because grief affects people and they perform strangely. Regrettably I had personal experience of strange behaviour within my extended family. Expressions of sympathy for the death of her husband were dismissed with a wave of a sizeable hand. Her aggression and abuse increased. Every diplomatic effort made to confirm her identity before details of the superannuation of our apparently deceased contributor were released, were rudely rebuffed. She pushed her way past the reception desk into the main office and started breaking it up. Attempts to reason with her were contemptuously ignored, bad language and threats continued as she tossed stapling machines, paper hole punches and papers on to the floor.

Had it been a man, my outraged staff and I would have subdued him. But we were all of that generation raised to respect women not to punch them, so we had a problem. My elder brother trains horses for a Gold Coast entertainment venue. He's suntanned, stringy and tough. I suspect that he uses the same criteria to judge people as he uses to judge horses. He reckons that his smaller, chubbier, young brother is too trusting and too soft. At that moment I felt that he was absolutely right.

The security man of the Fund's parent company was phoned and asked to come in a hurry. My Secretary, Gloria, laid out a tray of tea and biscuits. We hoped to keep the complaining woman quiet. We tried to consider the feelings of other visitors including an obviously ill contributor with an appointment to discuss a possible application for total and permanent disability retirement. Usually a large packet of biscuits was sufficient for a week of morning and afternoon teas/coffees for Gloria and me. This awful woman devoured an entirely new packet of Chocolate Ripples in under thirty minutes. And it was anything but quiet. Each biscuit was stuffed intact into the maw and crunched. The action reminded me of my Army

Reserve training where I saw bullets from a machine gun belt being fed into the gun's breech on automatic. The crunching paused only once when the frightful female demanded in a splutter of choc biscuit crumbs "Where's my fucking money?"

In a brief pause in her "I want my money" tirade she told us the name of her late husband. Our records showed that a man of that name was a 46 year old with 19 years of superannuation membership. He was a storeman at a technical materials depot in Rooks Road Nunawading. However I refused to give details of any beneficiaries' entitlements until given some proof that our contributor was dead and that she was indeed his wife (legal or de facto). The security man arrived and managed to calm her down. An ex-Policeman, he became suspicious at her evasive replies to his questions about how her husband had died. He arranged for the local Police to visit the family home at Tecoma, a sleeply village, between Upwey and Belgrave in the Dandenong Ranges. The local Police phoned back about forty minutes later to say that they had found a dead male. They found the husband's dead body easily; I won't elaborate the point but remind you that since Friday the weather had been torrid and it was now mid morning Monday. The two young Police Constables simply followed the buzz of the blowflies. Barely had the phone call ended when two plain clothed detectives arrived, cautioned the woman then arrested her on suspicion of being involved with the death of a male. Her bad language increased in vigour and volume. Her last words as she was wrestled through the superannuation office door were "I want my fucking money". Quiet at last.

Considering that this was the young Gloria's first job since graduation from Business College, she coped very well. As it transpired, the husband had been shot, point blank, five times, in the back, with a .303 bolt action military rifle. The body was left where it fell. Incidentally, later at the trial I felt sorry for the Defence Lawyer who, because of her repeated statements to the Police about it being an accident and that" The bastard deserved it," was forced to persist with a plea of accidental shooting. Five shots from a bolt action rifle accidentally? Impossible.

A senior detective assigned to the homicide investigation suffered a constant diatribe of bad language, threats and diabolically rotten body odour from the accused for some time before the ungrieving widow was charged with murder. After that experience he is said to have considered changing the charge of murdering her husband to one of mercy killing of him.

The assisted departure of the widow ended the involvement of the fund save that we were ordered to furnish the Court and the contesting Counsel with a statement showing the (normal) widow's pension benefit plus the pension payable to each dependent child Also the one off lump sum that could be paid if the Trustees permitted commutation of the total pension benefit. In this case the commuted sum would be $28,486 (1971 value). Evidently the self conferred widow fixated on that amount as being "her" money.

Her fixation obliterated any consideration of her adolescent three children. Her behaviour towards them became positively vile. One theory was that it was a convoluted way of protecting them by imposing a degree of distance but I couldn't accept that. She commiserated so much on her own situation that there existed no empathy for anyone else. She just wiped them. That action added to their trauma

But the Trustees and I had not forgotten the kids. They were effectively, orphans. Dad was dead; Mum faced the prospect of a long stay in prison. Invoking their discretionary powers under the Trust Deed the Trustees deemed the kids as orphans and paid a monthly pension to each at double the normal rate. The extra money significantly improved the welfare of the children who were in the care of loving and not too well-off relatives.

In the Supreme Court a guilty verdict was notified to the judge by the jury. The woman received a jail sentence of 25 years. Her legal aid financed appeals against both the conviction and the severity of the sentence failed. The superannuation death benefit of our contributor was paid to the three teenage children by way of a pension until the youngest child attained the age of 18 years, with the balance of the beneficiaries 'account being commuted to a lump sum that was divided equally and paid to the three children. The children were adults by now and they moved interstate to start new lives. Only the legal minimum amount required under the then operative Probate Duties Act was paid as a lump sum to a Trust Account on behalf of the convicted woman.

Up to this point I have painted an unattractive picture of this obnoxious murderess, but my wife insists that everyone has at least one redeeming feature. I'd feel uncomfortable if I didn't record this woman's good point.

Are you irritated by bad spelling? Are you annoyed to see errors in the newspapers, signs in shops and notes sent home by school teachers? You are? That's good because it allows me to tell you of the redeeming feature of this otherwise disgusting woman – the spelling was absolutely correct on every one of her many visible tattoos. I refrained from any attempt to check those not visible. I'm not suicidal. The correct spelling was no big accomplishment. Most of the tattooed words only had four letters.

End of story? No! As they say on the TV ad, "but there is more!" The convicted murderer was let out of prison on parole some years later. After serving less than half of her sentenced term the authorities decided that she posed no threat to society and should be given a rehabilitation opportunity. We, at the superannuation fund, were not warned that she was on the loose. What a surprise my Secretary Gloria and I got one Monday morning when she again slammed into the superannuation fund office, with more bad language and threats. Obviously she had not learnt any manners in the last few years, but I suppose you don't in prison. Gloria remembered her previous visit and quickly unplugged the brand new electric typewriter, carried it into my office and locked the door.

The woman's behaviour was just a little subdued this time, because one of our staff members at the Reception Desk was the first ruck for a local Aussie rules football team. He was too big for her to push around and when she threatened to hit him he didn't hesitate for a split second, but raised a big fist and said he would "flatten" her if she tried. Gee, how I wish I had thought of doing that years earlier. The ruckman was a younger "no sex discrimination" generation with none of the inhibition of my older generation. She had a Community Aid Lawyer trotting behind her. They really were an "odd couple". I played centre half forward in my school and local football teams when I was younger and in her grubby wedge heeled sandals the woman and I were eye to eye. The lawyer barely measured to her shoulder despite his platform shoes. If his weight and mine were added together, the woman still held the advantage.

Thankfully Gloria was still my Secretary even though she was married to an Engineer who worked in our building. Calmly she set up a tray with cups, saucers and a new packet of biscuits. The lawyer and I seemed to beget an instant mutual dislike. For my part it stemmed from annoyance at the perception that convicts seem to get priority access to free legal aid to use community money against the community to make life easier for them. It seems to me we are fighting ourselves with our own money and the convicts are laughing. The convicted murderess had already spent oodles of public money for her trial and appeals and here she was again being granted more public cash. The lawyer was one of those who thought his Certificate to Practice law was a licence to intimidate. By this time I had been manager for over six years, more experienced, more mature and we had better security. When he tried to "bounce" me into agreeing that his client was unfairly treated, and his client started to swear at my staff I told him to put his client's complaint in writing and promptly had them escorted out of the building by our security men.

Legal action was launched against the Trustees of the superannuation fund because, the convict claimed in a writ served on me by the lawyer, out of personal malice towards her ,we paid money to the three dependent children without putting aside sufficient money for her from her deceased husband's superannuation death benefits. Her allegations were subjective, totally unsubstantiated and malicious. This woman who conferred widowhood upon herself sought to destroy the reputations of the Trustees, both appointed and elected, of the superannuation fund. If your case is weak, you attack the people. It's like playing the man not the ball in football, or bodyline bowling in cricket.

Notwithstanding assurances from our legal team I was distinctly uneasy. Friends more experienced than I stressed that litigation should be avoided whenever possible because no outcome could ever be predicted with certainty. If this woman won her action, say on some obscure legal technicality, then I personally could be up for a big payment. The Trust Deed indemnity did not extend cover against a breach based on impropriety, ie, malice. As a young married man with a wife, three kids and a mortgage I could be ruined. And I was terribly indignant that the obnoxious female was using my tax money to attempt to ruin me. I was not a convict so funding to protect myself was not available for my family.

Within the fledging superannuation industry, any Trustee who breached the Trust Deed of the fund they were obligated to honestly serve through misinterpretation of an obscure legal point incurred no disapprobation. However a Trust Deed breach made in malice or self-interest incurred legal penalties and any such Trustee became an industry pariah, so the accusations of this convicted killer or the concoction of her lawyer had some sting.

Her assertion was that the superannuation fund Trustees and management that included me, were motivated by personal malice towards her. She claimed that the Trustees did not properly exercise the discretion allowed to them under the Trust Deed of the superannuation fund. Therefore they ought to be punished and the punishment should be in the form of a payment to her of a substantial sum. A Trust Deed is a legal document. It lists the rules that govern the set-up and continuing activities of the superannuation fund. The rules cover basic features such as Trustees duties, contributor responsibilities and entitlements, retirement and early retirement, disability and death benefits, pensions, etc. The people who are trusted to see that the rules are complied with are known as "Trustees". They have a responsibility to look after beneficiaries and so ought to have anticipated that one day she would be freed, she claimed. It must have been clear to them that she deserved more superannuation money to enable her to enjoy a suitable lifestyle because, she stressed, she was just a poor widow. How she attained the status of widowhood was deemed to be irrelevant.

The hearing was by judge alone, no jury. Her legal counsel tried hard but could not convince the judge in the civil jurisdiction of the County Court of any breach of trust by the Trustees. Nor did he succeed in his argument that the decision of the Trustees, to make the minimum payment, implied malice or neglect to exercise the discretion allowed under the Trust Deed. No evidence was given that malice existed. It was argued the making of the minimum payment was itself evidence of malice. That argument was rejected. As the Law then stood; Trustees were not required to explain or justify any decision. If they gave no reasons for a decision then they could not be challenged. However our Trustees chose not to avail themselves of that option and were prepared to openly argue that they had indeed exercised discretion. By allocating the minimum amount, as per existing Probate regulations, they were maximising the payout to the dependent children of the marriage and that the interests of the children were paramount. Growing children needed money, she didn't, she was being housed, fed clothed, medicated, etc., by the State.

However the claim of the murderess was not established and the Trustees were not required to enter a defence. In throwing out her case in a manner that made any appeal by Legal Aid improbable, the judge made a comment almost as an aside of which I, in my relief at the rejection of the claim, failed to assign any significance. However it clearly excited the lawyers for both parties. The judge said something along the lines that the Trust Deed of our superannuation fund offered to the Trustees the option of the use of discretion but it was not obligatory that it be exercised.

In my view at the time, and I still hold that view today, my confrontation with that disgusting woman was my first contact with a criminal who attempted to rob the superannuation fund of assets that properly belonged to the members. It would not be the last. At that time it was an axiom of law that you should not benefit from your own crime and that could have been a line of defence. Another possible defence could have been the Limitation of Actions Act 1958, commonly known as the "Statute of Limitations."

But she could not support her claim to grab the money so her community aid funded court case was lost. The woman had no assets, so the superannuation fund could not recover its costs. It cost her nothing to sue because prisoners are exempt from paying court fees, and she got out of jail during the case. Who won? I was told some time later that the judge commented to a lawyer that to find in her favour, and allow her more money, given the fact the she killed her husband, would be like declaring "open season" on all husbands in Australia.

Do you think about murder when someone mentions superannuation? Maybe the only murder you think about is the scale of the fees charged by some financial consultants? As an epilogue I mention that the woman was involved in a fight in a pub at Moreland and her parole was cancelled. A few years later she was granted another parole but again breached the conditions and went back inside where she died about two years later of natural causes.

As a reader you will have noticed that the crime was viewed specifically from the superannuation fund viewpoint. No attempt was made to explain every facet of the investigation as is done on TV crime shows. The superannuation fund perspective is unique and will be retained throughout. Note that at the time of these events the superannuation industry was truly a fledging. It had virtually no Law it could call its own. Today the events would be settled by The Superannuation Complaints Tribunal without recourse to a Court.

Chapter Two

Wrong Body

ALMOST WITHOUT EXCEPTION, THIEVES WHO steal or attempt to steal money from superannuation funds use some form of identity theft. Identity theft is predicted by a recently retired Commissioner of the Australian Federal Police to become the epidemic crime of this century. It happens when another person or an organised gang of people obtain sufficient information about your personal circumstances to create a twin or clone of you. Not actual, but virtual, to fraudulently raid all of your assets and credit facilities for their own advantage. And almost without exception, thieves steal or attempt to steal the identity of a living person.

Stuart (let's call him by that name) was a bit different. He reversed the swap. He gave his identity to a man who had recently died. Here are facts collected from court transcripts, published information in the media, reports of State Law Institutes, informal interviews with State and Federal Police, people who worked at Credit Unions, Banks, Insurance Company Investigators and from observations of the Manager of the superannuation fund. It is an account of a married couple and their immense vanity, greed, irresponsibility, and abdication of their duty to their children. It involved a superannuation fund in a situation unprecedented in Australian crime before 1980.

It posed the question "What must be done when superannuation Trustees are confronted with a death benefit claim on an already cremated body and evidence emerges about the alleged corpse still being alive?"

I'll paint the scene. In early 1985 Stuart, a superannuation contributor was 44 years old. Medium height, receeding red hair, married to a nurse who worked part time at the local hospital. Both were doyens of local society and fashion as were their three, rather snobbish, teenage girls. Stuart was the well academically qualified and well paid district manager of a sizeable regional financial entity. He had tried to grow a moustache to appear more debonair but the gingery fluff that resulted just made him look ridiculous so he shaved it off. Hair-wise his wife was the opposite with shoulder length dark brown tresses kept immaculately groomed. She looked glamorous even in her nurse's uniform.

Stuart's family lived on a 4-hectare (10-acres) hobby farm just beyond the urban area of a large inland city. In the three years since they bought the farm it was equipped with everything one could dream of, not necessarily for farming, but for luxury entertainment. Swimming pool, spa and tennis-courts, immaculate lush green lawn bordered by beds of pink azaleas and regularly replaced yellow and purple pansies. Along one side of the block were newly built brick stables and a saddling area. Despite his excellent salary and the wife's part time nurse's pay, the family was sliding ever more heavily into debt because of their extravagant life style. They were of the persuasion that the world owed them a living. Despite their alleged high IQ, their vanity blinded them to the reality that the world was here first. Expensive cars, extravagant first class overseas holidays, private schools for the children, state of the art home renovations, lavish entertaining, and incredibly expensive jewellery, clothes & shoes, kept Stuart and his wife continually, almost covertly, borrowing and juggling just to meet minimum payments on their ten credit cards. Maintaining a high profile social position as the elite in their provincial city was their obsession.

At the rear of their hobby farm were several large corrugated iron sheds. From the look of the gently rusting bottoms of the corrugated iron the sheds were probably once part of the original farm property prior to its subdivision into hobby farms for weekend "tax dodge "farmers. In one shed was an old caravan. An "itinerant worker" a "swaggie" (swagman), lived in the caravan when he was passing through the area. He was one of several homeless perpetual wanderers – the last of a dying breed – who incessantly trudged around the State. The "swaggie" paid for his keep with odd jobs, fixing fences and gates, adjusting the irrigation system, feeding the fowls and crutching the half a dozen sheep that Stuart kept as mobile lawn mowers. The "swaggie" was a very good handyman, when he was sober. That was about 50% of his waking hours.

The fowls were making a lot of noise. That usually meant that the feed had not been spread in the trough. The swaggie was not seen feeding the fowls so Stuart's wife went to the caravan one Saturday morning to find the "swaggie" dead. The wife, as a nurse, recognized the permanent condition and also recognised that bottles and cards of prescription pills nearby indicated the "swaggie" was receiving treatment for a heart condition. She read the label and understood that the dosage level indicated a serious condition. He appeared to have died peacefully in his sleep shortly before being found. The facial expression on the corpse was serene. He was still a bit warm and rigor mortis and post mortem lividity were only just beginning to stiffen the extremities and back of the corpse.

The wife walked slowly back to the house with little sympathy for the deceased. In fact any sympathy she had was applied to reflecting on the disastrous financial situation of the family. Debt and disgrace were imminent. Desperation became the mother of invention. The opportunity to use the corpse to provide a solution to the family's financial problems occurred to her on the 200 metre walk back to the house. She and Stuart calmly talked things over between themselves at first, exploring various scenarios. When a feasible plan was invented the couple called their teenage children into the house from the stables and presented them with the plan. They collected the body of the swaggie in a wheelbarrow, covered it with a horse blanket, cleaned it up, put a pair of Stuart's pyjamas on it and then put the corpse in the family double bed. An unbiased observer could make a case that Stuart and his spouse, Shelley, were conservationists in that they did not want to waste the opportunity to utilize such a convenient corpse. They acted with commendable alacrity.

Wearing a bulky coat, goggles and helmet as a disguise, Stuart rode off down back roads on a trail bike taking a basic minimum of travel items in the bike's panniers. As soon as Stuart was clear of the property his wife called an ambulance and a doctor in apparent panic. Ambulance paramedics arrived followed shortly thereafter by a Doctor from the hospital where the wife worked part-time. The Doctor's arrival was probably a concession to a staff member as home visits were rare in the area. She told the Doctor and the Ambos that her husband was dead. The visitors all agreed he was dead. Neither the Doctor nor the ambulance paramedics had met the husband before. Her identification of the corpse as her husband went unchallenged despite the fact that in death the husband must have appeared much older than photographs in the local paper. After all, what young Doctor would accuse a distraught widow, a high profile local identity, a fellow worker in the health industry of mistaken identity? Between them the wife and three children put on acts of grief that would have won truckloads of academy awards in Hollywood.

An autopsy was ordered by the local Magistrate, who also acted as District Coroner. Because Stuart had not been treated by a Doctor in the previous six months his death fell into the category of an unexpected death and therefore was a "reportable death" under the Crimes Act. The autopsy was promptly performed at the local hospital by the Senior Surgeon who was registered to do so under Coronial Regulations. Results were reported to the Coroner, who found in a formal hearing that death was by coronary occlusion – a heart attack, and therefore natural causes. As standard procedure, the report went to the Registrar of Births, Deaths and Marriages. A death certificate was issued in Stuart's name, based entirely upon the identification made by his wife – now his widow, or in superannuation terminology, the "relict" of the late Stuart. A Coroner's file on adult death becomes Public Domain upon completion of a determination and anyone is entitled to see that file. In the case of the late Stuart, no one thought there was anything suspicious because no one ever accessed the file.

Only a month prior to Stuart's "death", the superannuation fund had sent out its regular six monthly benefit statement informing Stuart of his benefits. A fortuitous event that clearly influenced the action that followed. Thus Stuart and Shelley were aware that a sizeable death benefit could become payable to dependants were he to "drop off the perch". Furthermore, the usual pension benefit could be commuted to a lump sum on a generous factor. Greed and the need for freedom from the remorseless pressure of overwhelming debt, debt which they were desperate to conceal, proved to be the motivation for the collusive illegal action of the husband

and wife. The children were made well aware of the parlous state of family finances and were just as appalled at the prospect of a moneyless future as were their parents.   No ponies, no swimming pool and yuk, a Public School. The girls had studied drama at their expensive Private School and it proved to be money well spent.

Upon being informed of Stuart's death, a superannuation representative was sent to see the widow with condolences in deference to his high ranking in company service. The offer of an advance payment on the sizeable superannuation fund death benefit, to help defray funeral and other expenses was accepted. On return to the Head Office, the superannuation fund representative told the fund General Manager that he thought the family exhibited more interest in the money and exhibited less distress than he expected. Shelley lost no time in telling him that she intended to apply for commutation of the pension benefits into a single lump sum payment.

The family's display of grief and mutual support at the specifically, indeed insisted, closed-casket funeral touched the hearts of all who attended. Sympathy from the rural community oozed protectively around them. The superannuation fund sent a wreath to the funeral in recognition of Stuart's brief service as a Trustee of the fund some years earlier. The body was cremated at the regional Crematorium.

Stuart's family began to reap a financial bonanza. The bank mortgage protection insurance began procedures to pay off the house first mortgage as soon as the Certificate of Death bearing Stuart's name was issued by the State Registrar. Loans secured by second and third Mortgages on the family home from several Credit Unions were likewise eliminated by insurance in accordance with the Credit Union practice of the debt dies with the borrower. These arrangements wiped out $290,000 of debt (in 1988 dollars). Sympathetic neighbours and friends provided free services to the sorely "bereaved" family. Their lawns were mown and their drive way was re-gravelled, the swimming pool was cleaned, cash donations covered the arrears and current Private School fees of the children. The contractor who supplied the LP gas to the property wrote off the few months' debt as a gesture of condolence. Other compassionate creditors did the same. Nearly $10,000 of other debt disappeared. The wife accepted the debt cancellations as nothing more than the proper respect that local yokels should show to the family of a superior personage.

The swindling family's undoing was the obituary that appeared in the quarterly staff magazine of Stuart's employer organisation six weeks after the burial. It was a beautifully written obituary. Around 2000 words penned by a staff writer from information gleaned out of personnel records. One could not be castigated for believing that Stuart was an angel incarnate so effusive was the prose.

An employee from a town in a Western Region about 240 kilometres from Stuart's Provincial City, who had worked for a time in a clerical position in the same financial service Department as Stuart, read the obituary and telephoned the magazine's editor to advise that Stuart was not dead. The employee was concerned that the city-based editor of the Department's magazine was confused. Most country employees believe that their city based colleagues live in a permanent state of confusion – something to do with inhaling too many car exhaust fumes is the popular concept. The concerned employee was referred to the superannuation fund Manager, by the magazine editor. Over the telephone and completely unprepared, the Manager did the best he could to extensively quiz the identification of a living Stuart but the country employee could not be shaken. He was adamant that Stuart, with whom he had once been at night-school, was alive and well and working in a far Western country town.

He mentioned that Stuart's usually rather long ginger hair was a different colour, he now had a black crew-cut and was growing a beard – but it was definitely Stuart. What would you do? The best the Manager could think of at short notice was to instruct the observant employee to keep well clear and to get another person, who also knew Stuart, to quietly confirm or deny the identification. It was thought that might take a day or so and give time for contemplation. After all, if the country employee was correct then some type of malversation was indicated. But the prospect of Stuart being alive seemed absurd. After all, the superannuation fund had seen an official death certificate. If the employee was not correct some embarrassment might occur and embarrassed people often seek compensation by litigation. Obviously the Manager had to act but the action must be cautious. He made a phone call to the Regional Manager of the employee and was given an unequivocal assurance that the employee was reliable.

To the discomfort of the Manager, early the next morning the observant employee phoned to confirm the additional positive identification by another former colleague of the presumed corpse and added that Stuart was working as a labourer at a Bulk Fuel Depot. Furthermore the employee had made discreet enquiries and found that Stuart was employed under a different name. He figured it was some kind of tax dodge, given that he always considered Stuart to be a bit shifty. The Manager did not believe in ghosts so gave serious consideration to a response. So serious that instead of the usual one cup of "on arrival" coffee he had two. The Manager consulted the fund's solicitors who gave rather sceptical approval to his plan to confirm the identification.

Early the following day a Union Representative and the Manager took a chartered light aircraft for a two hour flight west. By prior arrangement they met the observant employee at the local Police station with the Police Sergeant and a Constable. The Bulk Fuel Depot where the possible reincarnation of Stuart was supposed to be working was relatively close by. The group walked to the Fuel Depot and got within 30 metres of a person in overalls using a hoe to clean weeds along a chain wire fence before they were spotted. It was Stuart. He shouted a few rude words then sprinted off like a startled rabbit. The two Policemen and the employee dashed off in pursuit.

The next bit you may find difficult to believe, but the Union Representative, caught up in the excitement also sped off to join the chase without stopping to negotiate a special rate for the job. The Manager felt it essential that someone preserve the dignity of the superannuation fund so he declined to join in the chase. The chase was of short duration because the Police Constable who took off after Stuart played on the wing of the District premier footy team and in 300 metres brought a blown Stuart down in a classic tackle in the long grass and thistles. Handcuffs were clicked on.

Stuart and Shelley were arrested, charged, and categorically informed by the Police and members of the Public Prosecutor's Office that the law took a dim view of people conspiring to bury a body under an incorrect name. Such a disgusting deed would take an enormous amount of Public Service time to correct, they said. Worse still, they asserted, the Coroner would be exceedingly displeased and could impose a horrendous sentence as a warning to copycats.

Stuart and Shelley were initially charged with "Perverting the Course of Justice" to hold them in custody. Then were added various charges of fraud, including several charges of Obtaining Financial Advantage by Deception. These related to the insurance companies, the credit unions and other creditors and of course, the superannuation fund death benefit claim by the wife. Another charge under the Burial Grounds Act 1951 followed. The wife was granted bail because of the children, however Stuart was denied bail partly because of his flight and partly because the unusual nature of the charges against him motivated the Magistrate, in whose jurisdiction the case fell, who had been fooled once into issuing a Death Certificate, refused to assume the risk of Stuart absconding again.

A special Court hearing had to be convened in relation to the Registration of Births, Deaths and Marriages Act 1959 so the Court could rescind the previously issued Death Certificate in Stuart's name and later convict them both in separate hearings under Section 53 of the Act for "False Representation". The case created a superannuation precedent in Australia. It was the first time that a death benefit claim was withdrawn by the purported deceased.

Stuart and his wife each put up a spirited defense in their separate trials, firstly in the Magistrates Court then in the County Court against the insurance fraud and fourteen other charges. Their high priced legal eagle won an initial victory and each gained unfettered access to their extensive and expensive wardrobe. Every day they stood arrogantly in the dock in the Court as if they were models in a fashion show. Stunning clothes but no jewellery. All valuables were subject to a Mareva Injunction, a type of Court Order that temporarily freezes assets of an accused. Stuart's hair had grown long during his time in remand and the original ginger-red colour returned. "Full of conceit but without any trace of remorse" was the description written by a local newspaper reporter.

They were very lucky to have been charged only with Perverting the Course of Justice, etc, in relation to the false interment. At one stage a charge of murder was contemplated by the Police. The Swaggie's fingerprints in Police records and in the caravan, and medical records relating to his pre existing serious cardiac condition plus autopsy records helped Stuart and Shelley avoid more serious charges. Both Stuart and Shelley were of above average intelligence and were soured by the chance identification without which their plan would have succeeded. They were further soured, but not in the least embarrassed, when some of their most outrageous lies were exposed as such. Any sympathy they may have had was kept entirely for themselves. They had not one shred of it for the disconsolate family of the "swaggie" they unlawfully buried.

After the initial flurry of excitement the attitude of the superannuation fund Trustees was one of detachment. Not because of any inherent admirable attribute but simply because recent legislative changes imposed a heavy workload. It was felt it better to leave matters regarding compensation for the advance payment made to Stuart's family in the hands of the fund's legal advisors. It was close to a year later before the first trial. The Manager was called as a witness to give evidence about the superannuation benefits. The prosecutor and fund legal advisors simply wanted a certified written copy of a benefits statement to be lodged but the defence Counsel insisted that the Manager appear in person. To the Trustees it seemed as if Stuart wanted to cause as much inconvenience as the Court would let him get away with. In a corridor leading to the main Court room the fund's legal advisors unexpectedly met the legal team of Mrs "Stuart". Shelley spat at the Manager.

No charges were laid against the three children, the eldest of whom was now an adult, nor against members of Stuart's family who lived in the Western country town. The Manager believed then and still believes that the intentional degree of involvement of the teenagers and of Stuart's family justified criminal charges being laid. Perhaps the children did suffer punishment. During the series of trials Stuart and Shelley drifted apart. At their final appearance of another failed appeal they barely acknowledged the existence of each other. They had long since severed all communication with their girls.

The company formally dismissed Stuart. It may sound trite to say he was formally dismissed, however each move by the company and the superannuation fund was made as if under the microscope of his lawyers who were desperate to uncover any error, even nuance of an error, to use as a bargaining chip to assist their client in his predicament. His total superannuation dismissal benefit was $9,500 – a lot short of the $340,000 death benefit which his wife aspired to claim. By the end of the series of trials, the superannuation fund Trustees were incensed because Stuart's belligerent courtroom antics and false accusations caused the fund considerable expense. Stuart did everything to cause inconvenience and run up costs in the hope of blackmailing the authorities into negotiating lesser charges. He exploited the knowledge of the superannuation fund staff gained when he had served as a Trustee several years earlier.

He told outrageous lies about the Trustees and Managers in the hope that mud would stick and, at times, from the aggressive questioning of witnesses by his lawyers, it seemed as if the superannuation fund stood accused, not Stuart. The superannuation fund had to engage a Senior Counsel to protect Trustees and staff against his ceaseless tirade of allegations. A defendant inside a Court can make allegations with impunity which would be slanderous if made outside of the Court. Similarly Counsel for the defence can couch questions in such a way as to damage the reputation of any witness against his client. Sustained objections were frequent. Magistrates and Judges became exasperated. Several blunt warnings were necessary to keep the trials within bounds. Indeed Stuart and his defense team sought to lay the blame on almost every person that Stuart had ever met in the last 30 years. Many names were mentioned as persons who, in some way, influenced Stuart's behaviour, as if they should share the blame for his actions and thereby diminish the magnitude of Stuart's crimes.

The unfounded accusations of theft of contributors' funds by Trustees received considerable press coverage. Reports of statements in Courts allow the media great latitude in what they print, without fear of defamation. Those innocent Trustees and persons maligned by Stuart's unsubstantiated accusations bitterly resented the extensive reporting that some sections of the print press gave to Stuart's lies, but seemed not to be so free in column space when reporting that investigations revealed the accusations of Stuart to be totally without foundation.

In their justifiable anger, the Trustees questioned why they should make a $9,500 dismissal payment to Stuart when the superannuation fund and its contributors had been forced to incur costs and massive loss of staff time. Theoretically, the resignation benefit of a superannuation fund contributor is sacrosanct. If the contributor goes bankrupt, the superannuation benefit is unavailable to creditors. It is supposed to be untouchable during employment up to age 55. However the Trustees were so incensed that they decided to take a risk and test the law that protected

Stuart's own entitlements whilst his deliberate actions were causing fund expenditure thereby diminishing the potential future entitlements of other contributors. Superannuation fund expenses, direct and indirect plus verifiable other costs were totalled and the amount was $40 short of Stuart's $9500 dismissal benefit. The superannuation fund was about to send him a cheque for $40 when it was recalled that the cost of the wreath sent to his funeral was $40. An itemized list of costs was sent to him in prison, with the $40 cost of the wreath marked "paid" contra'd against his dismissal payout figure. He got no money at all.

The deduction by a superannuation fund of expenses incurred when a contributor attempted fraud against the fund was a precedent. Theoretically the deduction was a violation of the contributor's rights in a law that disregarded the rights of other fund members. The fund got away with it because in order to sue for his superannuation, Stuart had to go to the Equity Court. It was an axiom of law then, that Plaintiffs who complain to the Equity Court must have "clean hands". By the time his payment was seized, Stuart was legally tainted with eleven convictions. His hands were decidedly "unclean". What was pioneered became standard practice with all other funds as a deterrent. If it is not, it should be. Superannuation funds need more legal muscle to protect their members against the growing number of vexatious litigants.

Superannuation is like an iceberg. Most people only see the smaller pristine white top bit but beneath the surface superannuation funds are gigantic and powerful much like the iceberg that sunk the Titanic. Whatever happened to that iceberg?

I like a story that's complete and so another epilogue. Stuart was paroled after six and a half years. With the 18 months he spent in remand that totalled eight years behind bars. Shelley too was sentenced on a mixture of charges, only some of which were made concurrent. The total was ten years. Those sentences were deemed harsh at the time but they withstood several appeals so the moral is "Don't bury a body under a bodgie name". She was paroled in just under five.

Unsubstantiated rumour has it that Stuart and Shelley re-united and took over the Northern New South Wales boat hire business of Shelley's parents who retired. Nothing is known about the girls.

Chapter Three

"Sickie" Swindlers

A BRIEF INTERLUDE INTO TECHNICALITIES. Two main types of superannuation evolved in Australia. The most common titles used to distinguish each are Defined Benefit and Accumulation Benefit.

"Defined" derives from the promise by the fund to its contributors to pay a resignation, retirement, early retirement, disability or death benefit based on a defined formula regardless of the actual account balance of the contributor. Elements of that formula are the final or near-final salary, the length and magnitude of contribution service, actual or potential and a "percentage". The "percentage" is based on the contribution level of the contributor. In operation, the contributions of the contributor and the employer are invested. In the event that the sum of the two contributions plus investment earnings are determined by an actuary to be insufficient to fulfil the benefit promised to contributors, it is the legal responsibility of the employer to make good the deficit.

Defined puts all risk of a financial shortfall on the employer. Because of the formula including "actual or potential" years of membership, the contributor has an attractive disablement or death "insurance" cover, eg a contributor joining a fund at age 25 is disabled, the disability benefit is based on retirement age of 65. So even though the contributor has only, say, one year of contributorship when total and permanent disability retirement happens, the pension benefit level to be paid will be calculated to include 40 years, ie the total of actual and potential period of fund membership. If the fund permits a pension to be commuted to a lump sum, as was once the prevailing practice, a short term contributor may receive a cash payment with favourable taxation treatment, many hundreds of times the contribution made during the short period of fund membership.

"Accumulation" accurately describes the form of the second and simpler superannuation type. The employee contributes at a rate usually determined annually. The employer contributes at a minimum rate, determined by the Government, of the wage of the employee. Both amounts are invested and the earned rate is added to the employee's balance periodically, i.e., it is accumulated. All risk regarding the final payout rests on the employee. If investment returns are high then the contributor is advantaged. If however the investment yields should prove negative, and that can occur in volatile economic conditions, the contributor is disadvantaged. Payment for an early disability or death is only the balance of the account and that may be very low. Additional optional payments can be made by the contributor to insure for higher benefits against disability or death but these can be outside of the superannuation contract.

Minor variations to these two fundamental types exist. Note that the benefit for short service contributors in "Defined" almost always exceeds by a large sum the benefit of an "Accumulation" for disability and death. Those discrepancies fertilize the seed of the sin of greed.

I have seen most of the classic movies and been enthralled by magnificent acting performances that justifiably won Oscars for the actors. Notwithstanding that prize winning screen performances I hold those the greatest actors I have ever seen were some robustly healthy superannuation short term contributors trying to convince the superannuation fund doctor and myself that they were victims of serious illness or injuries, to obtain a large lump sum permanent disability benefit.

Despite clear details printed in the Members' Handbook applicants sometimes misunderstood the procedure. That was understandable. An application for something that could change the lives of both you and your family would make anyone nervous, even more so when aggravated by a medical condition. I could and most often did, guide an applicant through the paperwork. In reply to specific questions, I gave the best possible impartial advice I could but strictly avoided any comment on medical matters. Regardless of my careful explanations about the crucial importance of the result of an examination by the Doctor or Doctors some applicants still thought that the final decision rested with me. And so it was that a couple of times a year an applicant exaggerated her/his minor medical condition in the rather forlorn hope that I would be influenced to grant them the" pot of gold" superannuation payout. Almost without exception the best performers were swindlers.

Superannuation funds pay benefits to disabled people. The benefit may be a lump sum or a pension or part of either and approximately six per cent of applicants for disability benefits are swindlers! It is important that I be absolutely clear in my condemnation that I exclude genuinely ill contributors and their families, from the following comments because genuinely ill people deserve sympathy, support and understanding. This is important so I'll repeat it. My comments relate only to swindlers not to genuinely ill applicants

The dictionary defines a "swindler" inter alia, as a "person representing what he / she is not in order to cheat". They rort the system by falsely assuming the identity of an invalid. So swindlers are thieves who steal using the tactic of misrepresentation rather that a gun or by smash and grab. The swindlers I document here had no disabling physical or mental problems. They were just greedy thieves who tried to obtain disablement benefits by contrived fraudulent means. These swindlers make it tougher for genuinely ill people to obtain benefits as doctors and Trustees are made sceptical. If a swindler obtains cash payment and boasts about it, Doctors are held to ridicule. Small wonder that more intrusive investigations are made to verify claims. The action of swindlers make procedures more difficult for the genuinely ill. If your disability application seems complicated blame the swindlers not the Trustees who must institute procedures to protect the assets of other members.

A basic definition of theft is found in Sec. 72 (1) of the Crimes Act. It is "A person steals if he dishonestly appropriates property belonging to another with the intention of permanently depriving the other of it". There are various subsections of "theft", Sec. 81 "Obtaining property by deception", and Sec. 82 "Obtaining financial advantage by deception" and "Sec. 83 - False Accounting". In an amendment to the Crimes Act, 1st January 2002, the old Common Law offences of "forgery and uttering" were abolished.

Sec. 83A now covers "Falsification of documents" – a more comprehensive modern provision to cover use of photocopy machines, computers, etc, to manufacture sets of false documents that are disquietingly difficult to detect.

Swindlers are thieves make no mistake about it. Some revel in being called "conmen" because they think it makes them appear smarter than other thieves. But thieves they are. Under which particular part or parts of the Crimes Act they are charged is best left to the Police, based on the individual circumstances of each alleged theft and whether it be a sole swindler or as is more often these days, of several swindlers in criminal collusion. A worrying trend is that Australian superannuation funds are coming under increasing threat from well organised, highly technically proficient overseas gangs.

Why take the risk of trying to cheat the system? The answer is money! Lots of it. The first target is a lump sum benefit from a superannuation fund. Defined Benefit superannuation funds are primary targets because they have higher disability payout levels than accumulation funds and they were more likely allow commutation of disability pensions into lump sum payments. Successful swindlers who obtain an unwarranted lump sum payment swiftly hide the money and make their second target a lifetime Centrelink Pension with full fringe benefits based on the fraudulently obtained disability decision of the Trustees of the superannuation fund.

When it works once swindlers try it again and again. It is made easier for former citizens of some Asian and Middle Eastern countries who have names that can be readily juxtaposed. For some groups it's quite a lucrative sport. In a joint effort with the Federal Police one fully employed Railways employee was caught drawing eight Centrelink pensions – typical parasite - reducing resources allocated by the Commonwealth Government from our taxes and designed to assist the genuinely ill. The lenient penalty he got was laughable. Court penalties are supposed to punish and deter. It did neither, rather the opposite in the opinion of many of my colleagues.

People ask how do swindlers do it. The current fashion is what was known in the superannuation industry as the "Archie Bunker" method, that is, keep it "All in the Family". Let's say Dad, at age 60 retires due to a genuine disability and gets a doctor's report and certificate. He has several sons. They alter Dad's Doctor's detailed report. A drop of liquid paper, some artistic work with a ball point pen to change initials and bingo! Dad and sons all get superannuation benefits from their respective superannuation funds with the entire family group possibly getting Centrelink disability benefits as well.

The main problem for men with the Archie Bunker method is that they have all been caught and convicted. They get caught not necessarily because of Centrelink's increasingly efficient cross checking systems, but because of their inability to conceal their prosperity. The apparently unemployed buy expensive new cars, motor bikes, big TV sets, boats, clothes and the like. This arouses jealousy. They are "dobbed-in", usually by female members of the extended family of whom about 90% are sisters-in-law. As I said, it is called the "Archie Bunker" method after a once popular TV show, because it starts and finishes "All in the Family. "

Mothers and daughters can be superannuation and Government pension swindlers too, often switching medical reports between married and single names to try and confuse Centrelink. More often than not, the females are dobbed in by males. Frequently it is the de-facto husband of the daughter who dobs in his partner and her mother. It's his gift to the family when he heads for greener pastures in which to bludge or because he has fastened onto a less emotionally demanding or a more sexually compliant mistress. "Honour among thieves" is a myth as any experienced law enforcement Officer can attest.

Until recently, most reports about suspected frauds against Centrelink were by anonymous letters and telephone calls. The establishment by Centrelink of a website (www.Centrelink.gov.au) "Reportafraud" allows reports of suspicious behaviour to be made via the internet and it is very popular. Centrelink now receives thousands of tip-offs each month. All reports are treated seriously and investigated. Anonymity is preserved. So it is possible to be "dobbed-in" by a family member using the family's own computer.

This one's a beaut. A popular way to make money when you are genuinely sick is to "sell your illness" that is, if it is debilitating enough and well documented – you can't sell tinea or dandruff. Some swindlers participate in their own identity theft. The most popular way is to advertise in "TALKING FRIENDS" in one or more of the suburban weekly newspapers. Have you ever read these adverts? I must say I'm astounded at the number of female sculptors and they all appear to sculpt heads. It seems that every-time I read that section of the local paper there's another female advertising a 48 inch bust. Crooks are chronic copycats and follow fraud fashions assiduously. What is supposed to have started in Melbourne spread to Sydney swindlers almost overnight. Check the "Talking Friends" column in your local suburban newspaper for some version of this:-

A typical "sell your illness" advert could read: -

DISCONSOLATE 29 Y. O. GENT WITH AUTHENTIC WELL DOCUMENTED CARDIAC CONDITION SEEKS GENEROUS PERSON WITH WHOM TO SHARE HIS AFFLICTION. (Contact details)

That's a clear signal to would be superannuation and insurance swindlers. I've seen two similar ads so far this year in "Talking Friends" sections and a colleague told me of a professional criminal who "bought an illness" or at least a Doctor's Certificate to avoid being called to the witness stand in Court to give evidence against another, more dangerous criminal.

When a prospective superannuation or insurance swindler replies to that advert the "disconsolate gent" organises a meeting, usually in a pub or a very public place such as a fast food restaurant. Places with CCTV are avoided. After some questioning of each other to establish bona fides an example of genuine medical documents is shown and if they can be applied to a swindler, financial arrangements are negotiated. A few thousand dollars in cash is often paid up front. The seller and purchaser go to a forger. In late 1970 to mid 1980 there were several acknowledged practitioners of that trade operating in the Melbourne suburbs of Brunswick, Kingsville and Springvale. The disconsolate gent's genuine medical documents have the name and address details professionally altered to suit that of the purchaser. The balance of the fee to the "disconsolate gent" is to be paid, in cash, once the purchaser receives the superannuation or insurance disability payment. By "professionally altered" is meant documents being altered and scanned on a high definition computer scanner. The duplicated records have such a high degree of integrity as to be indistinguishable from the originals to the naked eye.

Now if after reading the foregoing you are tempted to contemplate a similar sort of rort beware. Experience has shown that the unscrupulous sick person sometimes sells so many sets of documents that unfortunate coincidences occur. That's what happened when a "disconsolate gent" marketed genuine records of an illness known as EBSTEINS ANOMALY. It is an extremely rare heart disease that affects one live birth in 200,000. The tricuspid valve is not properly aligned. The symptoms only become evident at a later age in some people. Thousands of Australian doctors never see a case of it in their entire career.

In collusion with his brother a chap afflicted with Ebsteins Anomaly "sold his illness," with the help of a crooked colleague. Both swindlers worked in the health industry and obviously failed to conduct due diligence on the rarity of the disease. These two medical mercenaries sold professionally reproduced copies of the afflicted brother's genuine twelve page medical dossier to nine other potential swindlers in the South of Sydney, whilst assuring each purchaser of the purchaser's exclusive rights to the illness.

Unfortunately for the medical mercenary swindlers, several of the purchasers belonged to the same group of "Defined" superannuation funds and those funds utilised the services of the same panel of Doctors to assess disability applications. Superannuation funds are statistically based on theories attributed to the brilliant English mathematician Sir Edmund Halley, after whom the comet is named. The statistical improbability of so many cases of Ebsteins in such a short time in such geographical proximity triggered a reportable illness medical alarm under the Government Contagious Diseases Reporting Regulations. This resulted in an immediate and intense investigation. The State Medical Officer was notified and was horrified and confused at the prospect of an epidemic of Ebsteins and accelerated the investigation.

Fortunately, at the Doctors' Clinic, the team despatched by the State Medical Officer quickly assembled the medical certificates lodged by each of the swindlers to support disability claims. The team simply compared the documents and found all to be identical in every aspect save for the personal details of each allegedly disabled applicant. The State Medical

Officer has a lot of administrative clout and immediately obtained assistance from senior Police.

Accompanied by Police, several superannuation managers arranged to visit the Cardiac Specialist who had made the original report and issued the disability certificate. Upon hearing of so many incidences of the disease in such close proximity, he was ecstatic, at first. He thought he had discovered the world's first recorded incidence of Contagious Ebsteins Anomaly. Fleetingly he envisaged his photo on the cover of the Australian Medical Journal. Upon being informed of the facts by the Detective, he instantly overcame his disappointment and willingly co-operated with the authorities. He was completely absolved and became highly indignant at the abuse of his reports. Less ecstatic were the swindlers when the Police Fraud Squad called upon them.

The genuinely afflicted man got his superannuation pension and a fairly lenient Community Based Order as punishment. Allowing for his short life expectancy that, to me, seemed just. The two medical mercenary swindlers and all nine buyers of the falsified documents were caught and convicted by Courts on a raft of charges and all received custodial sentences. I heard of the sentences and thought them a lot too lenient, but perhaps I am a bit too protective of my industry and too judgemental. All the purchasers were sacked from their jobs as were the two health industry vendors with only the dismissal superannuation payment. So if you contemplate a swindle on your superannuation fund stay away from rare illnesses.

Australian made anti-dandruff hair soap has a distinctive "smell". The manufacturers would probably prefer I called it a scent. The smell is certainly distinctive and referred to as a coal-tar smell. I rather like it. The soap is still available in some chemist shops despite advances in modern shampoo technology, or should I say advances in advertising shampoo products. I don't know if the ingredients of the soap are the same today as up to the 1980's.

In the mid 1970's some swindlers attempted to get paid a disability lump sum by their respective superannuation funds when there was scant evidence of any real disability. To augment their inconclusive cardiac disability application they listened to a few "bush lawyers" and sought to augment the medical evidence by eating half a cake of this hair soap. The ingestion was timed at 30 minutes before the medical exam by a superannuation fund doctor to determine their eligibility for disability. Anecdotal evidence was that several were successful and as word spread, others sought to follow. As mentioned earlier, conmen are notorious copycats. I'm certain these swindlers did not realise the real danger of a heart attack their action may have caused. When a large amount of soap is taken orally the ingredients in the soap can cause a temporary unnatural heart rate rhythm – a kind of irregular pounding whump and thump in the stethoscope. Actually quite alarming I'm told.

One company with which I was associated as a superannuation manager had an ex-World War Two Army Doctor working part-time as their Chief Medical Officer (CMO). He was approaching retirement but still very competent and claimed that he could spot a malingerer at 100 metres and I never faulted him. It was this CMO who alerted me to the possibility that some of our 16,000 employees were bound to hear of the soap swindle and might be tempted to "give it a go" because our fund was a Defined fund that permitted a disability benefit to be paid as a lump sum. I should add that he was totally opposed to disabled persons being allowed to opt for a lump sum. They should receive pensions he often told me. Notwithstanding our adherence to different views we were good workplace friends. The CMO had a memorable sense of humour and a novel way of dealing with hair soap swallowing swindlers.

It was many months after that warning that the first suspected swindler with a dodgy medical certificate attended for a medical exam for an alleged disabling cardiac condition. The CMO detected the unmistakable smell of hair soap. The Medical Centre nurse later told my secretary that the Doctor was positively ecstatic. He told the swindler to sit on a chair positioned near the male toilet entrance door and on some medical pretext asked the suspected swindler to drink a small 300 ml bottle of soda water. In less than a minute after drinking, the soap previously eaten and soda water mixture reacted and caused the swindler's alimentary canal to convulse and expel all contents, fairly suddenly, via both ends almost simultaneously. The swindler's race to the toilet provided an amusing interlude in an otherwise dull day for the medical centre staff. Enrico, the caretaker, was called to clean up after two unsuccessful races, and was not amused. The CMO bought him a bottle of Chianti to soothe ruffled feathers.

A messy method of uncovering a swindler, but the CMO's pioneering medical prognosis confirmation was very effective and infallible. It worked wonderfully well on another aspiring swindler and became a positive disincentive to others. When word spread through the swindlers "grapevine" of our CMO's humiliating soap test, the incidence of disability claims based on irregular heart function dropped from four a year in mid 1976 to zero in 1981 and we had no recurrence. The CMO unashamedly admitted that the soda water procedure was probably unethical but maintained that no one could sue him or the superannuation fund without first explaining why he had ingested half a cake of heavily scented hair soap. It worked for us. Humiliation sometimes supersedes litigation. I am certain no genuine applicant was deterred by the action of the CMO. All of the CMO's victims resigned without any fuss. If anyone cares to verify my statement, I can recommend the soap, soda water, bucket and a toilet roll.

Another popular way of enhancing a minor medical condition has disappeared today because the product was ordered off the market. In the late 1970's swallowing a dessertspoon full of a certain brand of chlorophyll toothpaste played temporary havoc with blood pressure. If you were healthy with normal blood pressure you could survive. My colleagues, Managers of other sizeable superannuation funds told me of several less fit people, including one woman, who either died or were seriously medically impaired for a long time after attempting a toothpaste fraud.

One would-be swindler, ironically employed by a bus company, heard that a type of brake fluid produced the same heart thumping result as the coal tar scented soap. He made application to the bus company's superannuation fund for total and permanent disability retirement. An hour before he was due to be medically examined he drank 100 mls of brake fluid. Before he got out the door of his apartment he collapsed. He died. A tough way of qualifying his dependants for a superannuation benefit.

Chapter Four

Swindled by a Psycho Manipulator

THIS SUCCESSFUL FRAUD REALLY UPSET me. Try as I might I could never disassociate myself from my job as a superannuation fund Manager. It was no surprise therefore that when the fund was defrauded I took it personally. I felt that I had failed to protect the assets of fund members.

I still can't use the word "hate". My father was a great hater. A soldier, wounded, evacuated, repaired, retrained, and returned to combat. Wounded again he was totally changed by the atrocities perpetrated by the enemy in the heat of a putrid jungle. Prior to the war he was a good cricketer with a cheerful personality, according to our Aunties. On return his body was fixed but the hatred persisted. It caused the break-up of his marriage and his early death. We think it caused the early death of Mum too. My brother, sister and I saw the corrosive effect of hate. Hate distorts the hater. The hatee is mainly unaware or, if aware, doesn't care so what's the point. We three siblings rejected hate. The nearest we permitted was "intense dislike". We could control that emotion and not let it control us.

So it was that Tony, the man who defrauded the fund once using false documents and made another attempt via legal means, became the subject of my most intense dislike. After four years of employment as a mid ranking clerical officer, Tony applied for disability retirement. His application was supported by a detailed two page medical report issued by a Psychiatrist with a certificate of total and permanent disability citing chronic mental impairment. Seldom does any fund receive a fully complying application in a single package. Tony's application surprised his workmates and supervisor. Tony's sick leave record showed only a few one or two day absences due to physical illness. He "fitted-in" well in the work force and appeared a normal healthy 32 year old male. Indeed he had a reputation both as a sportsman and a bit of a Casanova.

The Trustees, justifiably, and in accordance with fund regulations, wanted a second opinion. The Company Doctor opined that the application was a little suspicious because the alleged illness usually manifested itself over a period of time rather as a sudden onset. Not being a specialist in that sphere of human frailty, he provided the name of a psychiatrist qualified academically and by experience to offer a second opinion. Tony was advised of our request for a second opinion. He categorically refused and went to Community Legal Assistance to protest at being unjustly treated. Legal Assistance claimed Tony was being denied natural justice and must be allowed to name his own supporting psychiatrist. How the adviser reached that conclusion without even looking at the Trust Deed was a puzzle. The tone of the legal correspondence was needlessly and disproportionately aggressive and threatening.

A specialist opinion was definitely needed. Under the disability clauses in the Trust Deed an explicit obligation was imposed on the Trustees to be fully and independently appraised of the degree of disability of any illness and its prognosis before making a decision. They thought the demand by Tony a bit rough so in an endeavor to be fair, obtained from the Board of the Psychiatric Association a list of five well qualified doctors and told Community Assistance that Tony may exercise his rights of selection from that list.

More protests were lodged about what Community Assistance referred to as our high handed action in demanding a second opinion, including veiled threats that we may exacerbate Tony's mental illness by our overbearing actions and be sued for a huge sum of money in punitive damages in addition to Tony's superannuation money. Our board of Trustees felt these continuing aggressive responses to be inappropriate and bordering on intimidation. The collective experience of members of the board of Trustees was that aggression often masked improper activity, so extra caution was warranted. The Trustees were acting with the prudence of a "reasonable person", as the Trust Deed and Common Law required. Trustees are stewards of OPM, Other People's Money. They have a legal responsibility to ensure OPM is properly deployed.

The Trustees stood firm on their direction that a second, qualified, opinion be obtained, despite further threats. Eventually Tony had a 40 minute consultation with one of the Psychiatrists on the list. The Company Doctor received a brief report from that Psychiatrist the next day. It simply stated that he agreed with Tony's treating Psychiatrist, and included a bill for $350 for us to pay. Who said Ned Kelly is dead!

Faced with that independent supporting opinion and perhaps somewhat daunted by the belligerent attitude of Tony's legal advisors, the Trustees felt they had no option but to consent to Tony's retirement on medical (psychiatric) grounds. Community Assistance was informed of the prompt decision of the Trustees in favor of their client and the date of implementation for calculation of his pension benefits. This created another great upheaval – Community Assistance protested vehemently by heated phone calls and a strongly worded letter. Tony, they said, insisted upon a lump sum settlement and they demanded that he must have it. This was the first we had heard of it. To this day I am unable to understand the rude and aggressive attitude of that suburban community group. They treated our board of respectable Trustees like dirt! I was affronted because I held the Trustees in high esteem.

The Trustees resisted commutation of the pension to a lump sum payment on the grounds that if Tony was so mentally disabled as to be incapable of handling relatively simple clerical work in the employ of our parent company, then he was surely unable to handle the investment of the sizeable lump sum. A veritable deluge of verbal and written threats of legal action emanated both from Community Assistance and, surprisingly, Tony's treating Psychiatrist.

To resolve the matter it was reluctantly agreed to commute the pension to a lump sum. However on the advice of our lawyers, conditions were imposed. These included that the treating Psychiatrist and the supporting Psychiatrist both certified in writing that Tony would be capable of competently managing the money. And also that Community Assistance certified to us in writing that they would properly supervise Tony's disbursement of the money. The opposition parties, as we now thought of them, claimed to be insulted at our unreasonable demands. We were by now becoming immune to their aggression and refused to budge. Eventually Community Assistance relented and produced some draft paperwork. We assumed that they were near to or had exceeded the amount they could claim as fees from the municipality. As their client claimed to have no money, their only prospect of being paid was from the settlement of a lump sum.

Several amendments were made and when those documents were deemed satisfactory by our lawyers, the superannuation fund paid Tony's commuted benefit of $59,800 to Community Assistance on his behalf. We could not dispel the feeling that we were being manipulated. The claims by Tony's treating Psychiatrist that our actions may endanger Tony's mental health left us with no viable option. Candidly we were cleft in our feelings. Partly we cared that Tony's condition not go downhill and partly to preclude more legal complications.

Exactly 14 days after delivery of Tony's cheque we received a letter from a previously unknown city based firm of solicitors acting on behalf of Tony. The letter advised us that Tony had been on a shopping spree and spent almost all the money received from our superannuation fund as a disability benefit. He had only several hundred dollars left, the solicitors said. He needed compensation and he needed it now. The Trustees were stunned. Me too.

The solicitor's hurry-up, follow-up letter accused the superannuation Trustees and the Manager of gross negligence, willful abandonment of our duties as Trustees and Manager and demanded that the pension to which Tony had originally been entitled be re-instated immediately, together with a 50% augmentation as a penalty for our outrageously negligent conduct. Bloody hell! Just what we needed. Another lawyer who thought his law degree was a licence to intimidate. I can't record here what I said as I read that letter because I was enormously angry. I intensely disliked it.

Our Company's lawyers were more sanguine and carefully built our defence against that claim. Upon being informed of Tony's spendthrift actions, both Psychiatrists attempted to withdraw, reclaim or to tone down their certificates as to Tony's competence to manage the money. But Community Assistance got tough with the two Psychiatrists because Community Assistance had based their indemnity to our superannuation fund on those certificates. Now the boot was on the other foot. Should our fund be taken to court, we would claim Community Assistance be joined with us and any damages and costs would most likely fall on them. They were now faced with responsibility for their own actions.

Our lawyers tore into them, in a dignified legal fashion, with a similar degree of aggression that they had unnecessarily flung at us. Community Assistance refused to explain to us how Tony got the money, but they constantly pleaded that we allow to them the very same legal concessions they rudely denied to us. After six months the matter just died. I think the city solicitor became exasperated with Tony and, as you may assume, the solicitor did not get paid. The city solicitors were reasonable to deal with and probably appreciated that Tony was manipulative and unreasonable.

In the light of that fund's widely publicized adverse experience within the industry, I guess readers can understand why many Trustees are extremely wary about retirement claims based on mental illness. An allegedly mentally disturbed person can get away with just about anything. They have the perfect defence should illegality be discovered. Their mental condition prevented them from understanding their illegal act. The Trustees and I were of the opinion that Tony was a fraud and that our fund was swindled.

As a postscript, I mention that many years later one retired Trustee found out by accident that Tony and his female Psychiatrist were living together at the time of his departure from our fund. It explains her complete dossier and the source of his high quality coaching that fooled the independent Psychiatrist in his short and expensive interview. There is evidence that Tony obtained payment from at least one other fund in another State using similar tactics to those used against our fund.

By the time we were apprised of those facts it was too late. The Limitation of Actions Act applied. Any action was debarred by elapse of time. Also by that time all of the Trustees who were involved had retired or moved to other employment. The current Trustees felt there was no point in a pursuit of Tony.

A few years later Tony's female Psychiatrist was charged by the Police with irregularities over prescriptions for drugs. Rather than face her

Professional Association she resigned, gave up psychiatry and when last heard of was breeding sheep or goats or something similar in central NSW. Tony was no longer her partner, he had a new, younger, girlfriend and was a salesman selling "natural" health products. Tony beat me and I didn't like being beaten. I vowed to be even more cautious in future. Possibly one or two people who later applied for total and permanent disability on psychiatric grounds experienced a degree of antipathy on my part. As explained, I do not hate. I don't hate Tony but likewise I don't forgive or forget.

Chapter Five

Two Departures, Plaintive and Painful

BY FAR THE MOST PREVALENT motivation to defraud a superannuation fund via a false disablement claim is money. Revenge can also be a full or part motive. One unsuccessful swindler confessed that he "tried it on" as he put it, "out of sheer bastardry". Words of wisdom from Arthur, reputably the biggest work-dodging bludger in an organisation with 18,000 employees. Arthur was obviously an Irishman. He had the look of a leprechaun. His parents left county Cork when he was only six years old but he must have sneaked away to Blarney Castle and kissed the stone because, begorrah, he had the gift of the gab still tinged with an attractive Irish brogue despite his long years in Australia.

His leprechaun look and gift of the gab were his only two attractive attributes. Arthur's parents, brothers and sisters indulgently excused his expulsions from schools, minor teenage crimes and extended unemployment periods on his inability to settle in the "New Land". On his twentieth birthday he married his heavily pregnant girlfriend. It was a quiet wedding in a Civil Registry Office. Her parents attended but his parents and some siblings refused to be there because the marriage was not in a Catholic church. Unfortunately the child was born physically deformed and mentally retarded. Arthur vehemently denied paternity, accused his newly-wed wife of infidelity and tossed in his job because men on Government unemployment benefits do not have to pay child support.

Arthur drifted away alone from the family home in Newcastle. He found a job in the street maintenance section of a North Sydney council for nearly a year before the Child Support Agency located him, whereupon he again tossed in his job and relied on unemployment benefits for the next year during which time he met another much younger girl. The teenager" proved her love" for him by having unprotected sex. The inevitable pregnancy occurred. This child too was born with serious birth defects. Arthur deserted her the same day on the pretext that she must have been unfaithful to him because the child was born distinctly deformed. Arthur had now fathered two children who would be maintained financially by the Government. He was oblivious to any sense of responsibility for the children. His sympathy was entirely reserved for his "poorly betrayed" self.

No doubt I have depicted Arthur in a bad light and, as I write, I wonder whether I have done so to mitigate my later shameful and semi-legal actions of allowing him to remain in pain for such a long time that he was nearly rendered impotent. Was I that vindictive? Probably. Meetings were held monthly between company management and each of the three unions. One "White Collar" Union, one "Skilled Blue Collar" Union and one "Unskilled Blue Collar" Union (UBC). The agenda was wide and included anything to do with employment. Superannuation reports were made by a ten page brochure to members half yearly, but any questions about the fund in the meantime were promptly given a response at the monthly meetings. For several years the meetings progressed smoothly, opinions were forcefully expressed and some meetings were heated but all parties had respect for each other and neither Unions or Management were exploitive.

One large company suburban division had its own employee recruitment section. Arthur's gift of the gab scored him a job there as a General Duties "Laborer and Traffic Control Lollypop Sign Man." Most readers will have seen the type. Hard hat, fluorescent jacket and a circular sign with "Stop" and "Go" affixed to a two metre pole. After several lessons with the Foreman he learnt to turn the sign the right way at the right time. Regrettably a vacancy occurred as a Union Representative for the "Unskilled Blue Collar" (UBC) Workers. Due to apathy of the other members, Arthur was nominated. He was not over endowed with brain power but appeared to any new acquaintance to be an amiable type of rogue with a cheerful Irish brogue. Arthur was elected. That was how I got to meet him at monthly meetings.

I reached the conclusion that only an Irishman could cope with the seething cauldron of contradictions that oozed through his brain. Never a meeting passed without Arthur enlightening us with a homily on how to improve the world. He wore a crucifix on a thick gold chain around his neck yet professed to be an ardent Communist. He refused to join the superannuation fund claiming it was a clever Capitalistic control tool. Like religion it was the opiate of the worker, he claimed. He chastised fellow members for wasting their money by contributing to the company's excellent defined benefit fund. He told them loudly and frequently that they should treat superannuation as religion. Sin all you like during your lifetime, repent when near death, get absolution from a priest and live happily ever after in heaven. "Do the same with Super" he told members at a Union meeting. "Keep your money and enjoy it now. Join the bloody superannuation fund only when you get really sick, make only one payment then clear-out with a big super cash payment "he said, often adding" That way we will bankrupt the Capitalist System and hasten the Dictatorship of the Proletariat". Of which, of course, he expected to be one the dictators.

He shouted down those fellow workers who tried to tell him that superannuation was a trust, the ownership of which was vested in the members. It was not owned by the boss or the company. The action he advocated would rob his fellow workers and their dependents, they said. Quite a few monthly meetings were adjourned as a result of verbal stouches between the union delegates with management often forced to be the mediator.

Ballarat was the meeting I recall with a shudder. Arthur needed a ride back to Melbourne and I was persuaded to take him in my company car. How I allowed that to happen I am at a loss to explain. Arthur professed to despise me as part of the capitalist class system that oppressed the working class. Yet from the moment he clicked on the seatbelt, he began to talk. He told me of his childhood, his parents, his siblings, of bosses he worked for over the years who failed to appreciate his superior skills. He was in actual tears when he blubbered about the two women who sexually betrayed him. He droned on and on and on and I felt as if I were his confessor priest.

The night sky in its immense beauty has ever aroused a question in my mind. Why does the cosmos exist? Arthur supplied the answer on that tedious drive to Melbourne. The cosmos exists to persecute him! In my adult life I have tried to preserve or enhance the dignity of my fellow man but this blubbering piece of self obsessed humanity was beyond my meager skills. He exhausted my reservoir of sympathy. As we got closer to the city he must have tired a little because I managed to slip in a reply to one of his repeated rhetorical questions about deformed babies. My reply went something along the lines of "You know, statistically two babies with the same deformity for two different women could mean a fault in the genes of the father." True. Maybe I was cruel. He never said another word for the short trip to the car park. On arrival he got out, slammed the car door and walked away. Had I put into words his unspoken fear?

Two weeks before graduating from Business College, Gloria applied for the job as Secretary to the newly appointed Manager of a superannuation fund recently formed by the amalgamation of a group of utility service companies. She was the best qualified academically, even if inexperienced, and I decided to give her the job. The day she started, all nervous and eager, was her nineteen birthday. I was 12 years her senior and felt more like her father than an elder brother. Gloria was welcomed as the youngest member into an unofficial, elite, exclusive and influential Group. What that Group didn't know wasn't worth knowing. They were the Executives' Secretaries Group. This Group of variously aged ladies all knew of Arthur. They knew the dates of his work visits to Head Office and they knew to avoid the canteen and the elevators when "Awful Arthur" with wandering hands was around. As the superannuation fund grew due to more mergers so too did Gloria and me grow in competence and confidence. Gloria told me that she only saw Arthur once. It was in the foyer of our building. He was waiting for an elevator. She thought she recognised him from his description. Identity was confirmed when she heard his Irish accent. Gloria walked the stairs to our sixth floor office.

When the weather was really bitter the "Street Division" where Arthur was employed moved into a large shed and worked undercover cleaning tools and equipment. Arthur was given a job but when the Foreman came to inspect the work it had not been started. A well lubricated Arthur staggered back to work two hours later and told the Foreman where he could stick his job. The Foreman reported Arthur.

About the same time in the late afternoon as Arthur was staggering back to work a small farewell party was taking place in my office. Six years had passed since the young girl joined our team. In that time love developed and she married an Engineer when she was 23 years old. Now at 25 Gloria was leaving to become a full time mother. I felt as though my heart was being pulled out. In a very proper way I know we had a kind of love for each other. I was her first and only boss and she was my first and only Secretary. Of the nine applicants for her old job she said that Carol would suit me best. Carol was the oldest of the panel, at 35 she was only two years younger than me. Gloria was right. Carol stayed with me for the next 14 harmonious years

Next day was a freezing cold Melbourne morning. The Chief Medical Officer (CMO) phoned me in my superannuation office and asked me to come to the Medical Centre. "Have a look at the chap in the waiting room as you come in" he said. Curiously, I walked through the waiting room and instantly recognised Arthur, one of the company's problem people. His record showed him to be often absent without excuse, persistently late and lightfingered. Arthur was the type that did not so much "sign on" for work; it was more like he signed the "visitors" book. He was let off a few times to placate the Union but took advantage of it and finally was warned in writing (twice) that one more transgression and he would be sacked. In retrospect it seemed that he predicted an inevitable sacking. Arthur realized that after his absence from the work shed and his drunken tirade to the Foreman, dismissal was certain. Three strikes you're out. He knew that the paperwork procedure would take a few days and decided to exploit that time. Arthur planned to swindle the superannuation fund with a pre-emptive grab for cash with what turned out to be a false disability application.

Despite the cold morning I could see that Arthur was sweating, twisted, bent over and looking horribly uncomfortable. He gave me a dirty look as I went past because I was definitely not one of his favorite people. It was mutual. I was surprised when I learnt that he elected to join the fund after some 14 month's service and constant denigration. I must have missed seeing his name on the monthly entry/exit schedule. Surprised and also wary. I phoned my 2i/c to double check his enrolment and details. After one month of superannuation contributionship, Arthur had submitted his disability application, supported by a five page medical report containing a doctor's certificate that verified the patient was totally and permanently disabled due to a spinal injury. Arthur was seated awkwardly in the waiting room awaiting another meeting with CMO. If the CMO certified Arthur was disabled, he would walk away with around $80,000 from our superannuation fund. A much better outcome for him than a $1900 dismissal payment. His total contributions were $48.

The CMO greeted me warmly, and offered me a brewed coffee. He only served his special brew to celebrate some unusual event. Drinking the CMO's excellent coffee was not an unalloyed pleasure however, because he served it in a glass beaker, the side of which was marked with measuring graduations. A mental effort was required to suppress my imagination because the beaker looked awfully like a specimen jar used for collecting urine samples. As we sipped our coffee the CMO told me that only seven weeks ago he examined Arthur and found him fit to join the superannuation fund.

Arthur had now applied for total and permanent disability retirement benefits for a spinal condition that he claimed was so debilitating as to preclude him engaging in remunerative employment for the rest of his life. He was rendered incapable of standing and couldn't turn around the "Stop" and "Go" lollypop sign. Paradoxically the condition described in the medical report was so devastatingly chronic that the CMO knew that anyone so afflicted could never get out of bed to attend the company Medical Centre for an examination. The CMO said that he recognised the medical certificate Arthur had submitted earlier. It belonged to a totally immobilised patient at the Repatriation General Hospital in the Melbourne suburb of Heidelberg. The genuine patient had a serious back condition caused by Japanese mortar shrapnel sustained during fighting in New Guinea in 1944 during WWII and Arthur wasn't born until 1956.

In the follow-up investigation it was discovered that Arthur had to act quickly and so grabbed the first authentic looking set of documents that some of his crooked mates were able to arrange. The medical records were bought for cash from a hospital office employee. The stolen medical records were of a man born in 1923.

Arthur never could leave well enough alone. A surgical appliance-manufacturing firm in Swanston Street Melbourne was re-locating and had a sale of uncollected tailor- made appliances at very cheap prices. Arthur walked past the shop window. He was impressed by the appliances made of stainless steel rods, pads, leather straps and metal buckles. On impulse he brought a cheap metal & leather lower spine and pelvic brace to embellish his disability application. He went into the gent's toilet next to the Melbourne Town Hall in Collins Street and put on the brace beneath his trousers with some assistance from the attendant. He staggered bow-legged to his appointment with the Company's CMO in a Flinders Street building some 300 metres distant

Arthur really was in great pain as he sat in the Medical Centre waiting room because, unfortunately for him, the brace he purchased was made to correct a problem in a female pelvis. I doubt if I need explain here that the pelvis of a male and female differ. The pads in the brace to which he was tightly strapped were severely restricting the flow of blood to vital parts of the male's lower body. The CMO had quickly examined Arthur on his way through the waiting area to his office. That quick look was all he needed to recognise a female brace. Something needed to be done swiftly to alleviate poor Arthur's increasing agony.

The CMO knew with absolute certainly he was on a winner in picking Arthur as a fraud because he was a consultant to the treating Doctor for the real patient. In fact, a large amount of the medical records submitted by Arthur to support his disability application had notations in the hand-writing of our CMO. The only bogus information in the medical records was Arthur's name, date of birth and physical description, all of which had been altered.

What should be done? The CMO told me about the wrong brace. He and I contemplated a solution to Arthur's problem as we slowly sipped our coffee. The CMO liked medical literature and told me of a book he was avidly reading about the sexual practices of the Scottish Highlanders. " It puts a whole new interpretation on the title of the song, The Campbells are Coming ", he said. The CMO had to leave for another appointment and asked me to get Arthur out of the brace. I promised to do so and the CMO left through a side door. The nurse looked out into the waiting room every few minutes to tell Arthur that the CMO was delayed. I phoned my office and my new Secretary Carol had a standard letter of resignation typed in Arthur's name and brought to the Medical Centre. That took some time. I phoned the Police.

I wasn't bound by the Hippocratic Oath so why should I rush my coffee for a crook? My brother would have applauded.

I was well into my second coffee, when the nurse said she thought Arthur was near collapse. I went out and told him that if he signed the letter of resignation now the nurse and I would immediately help him out of the brace and relieve his agony. If he did not sign the resignation he could sit bloating in the brace until the Police arrived. It was blatant coercion. I admit that, but I really enjoyed it which is why I should be ashamed. Not every day did I have to opportunity to be so sadistic with such little effort in protecting the finances of our superannuation contributors. We heard later that if Arthur had remained in the brace much longer, his ability to father more deformed children would have vanished. When I heard that I felt sorry for letting him out too soon. It's highly likely that today I would be convicted of something.

Arthur signed the resignation, the Victoria Police arrived – exit a bandy legged Arthur. The Fraud Squad said there was not much point in putting him up before a Magistrate given that his application was detected before any real damage was done, so he got off with a stern warning. Later the hospital office employee, who sold the confidential records of a truly disabled war veteran, was sacked. I never heard of Arthur again.

Gloria had a boy. In fun I suggested she call him Arthur. She said that Murgatroyd would be preferable to Arthur. They named the boy Eric, after her grandfather.

Chapter Six

Dangerous Dependents

BELIEF IN THE EXISTENCE OF a supernatural being, a god, erodes each day. The concept of god was an invention by primitive mankind to try to explain the inexplicable, such as the wonders of the universe, life and death, earthquakes, volcanoes and the like. What I see today is the perpetuation of the god myth in the interests of cultural cohesion of ethnic sections of the community. Some of these cultural groups are beneficial to the world. Others are medievally malevolent. I experienced the malevolence of a warped religious sect and was lucky to survive with only cuts and bruises.

When I was appointed Manager of a sizeable superannuation fund I was prepared to work for it but I never expected I would have to physically fight and bleed for it. Then again I could never, in my wildest dreams, expect that I would meet an allegedly deeply religious family who were collectively prepared to inflict injuries in pursuit of coercing undeserved benefits, attempt to falsely imprison, lie under oath, endorse and facilitate under-age sex, and commit arson. Obviously they chose to ignore the words in the Bible, First Timothy, Chapter One, "for the love of money is the root of all evil". Almost as remarkable was that the male patriarch who had died, and whose death was the reason for my visit to this favourite suburb of Dame Edna Everage, Moonee Ponds, was described by his fellow workers, when I asked them prior to my visit, as "Unassuming, insignificant and almost invisible".

The male patriarch was named Henry for short by his fellow workers at the Essendon depot because he had a rather long and resoundingly aristocratic real name. His employment record showed his place of birth as Goa. As part of my pre-visit preparation, I relieved my ignorance a bit by consulting an encyclopedia and learned that Goa is a State in Western India once a trading port of the Portuguese. The Portuguese influence accounted for Henry's noble sounding name. I also learned that Goa is the burial place of St Francis Xavier and that prompted me to ask the fellow workers of the Henry about the religious affiliation of the deceased. It was helpful to know about the religion when visiting the family of a recently deceased member of the superannuation fund to try to be more sensitive in the family's time of grief.

You will have noticed my use of the words "fellow workers" when I made enquires about the late Henry, rather than "work mates". Everyone from the supervisor of the appliance installations section to the office boy in clerical records said that they knew of Henry but never knew him. He was a loner. Henry came to work on time, diligently maintained appliance and meter connection vouchers then departed at day's end. He never shared a meal with anyone in the canteen at lunch time preferring to eat his brought-to-work lunch in solitary at his desk in winter or in a sunny spot in the outer depot in more pleasant weather. One section leader told me that Henry's religion forbade him to eat or drink in the company of non-believers.

Several said that he wore an ornamental gold Catholic-style Christian cross on a chain around his neck. He would sidle into any conversation remotely connected with religion and quote extracts from the Bible. But football, cricket, sex, pay rises, cars and fishing dominated the verbal agenda of the appliance connection and maintenance depot. Henry was offered scant opportunity to regale his fellow travelers in this journey of life with his repertoire of selective recitals from the Book of Revelation. When they told me that Henry quoted from Revelation it caused my first feeling of unease because when I was much younger I was allocated the task of reading that last book of the New Testament as punishment for something or other. It's pretty scary. I formed the opinion that King James the First of England and Scotland was conned when he allowed the 22 chapter book to be incorporated into the Authorized Version of the Bible.

Apparently other workers in the depot held views similar to mine, at least about people who quoted Revelation at the drop of a hat, because Henry had no true work mates. He sought none unless he became hopeful he could convert them to his religious philosophy. Evidently he was not a good salesman for his sect. In the twenty four years he had worked in virtually the same job at the depot he had no converts. I had to ask a lot of questions to try to form some picture of the late Henry because I had no recollection of him at all.

Each year I visited every branch and depot of the Victoria-wide parent company at least once, so I had a good knowledge of the faces of the members whose names appeared in the superannuation register. Yet I had absolutely no recollection of Henry. I learned that he stood around 163 cm (5 foot 4 inches) tall, had intensely black hair now graying around the ears, large dark eyes, and an olive complexion and very thin build. His English was good but a little accented and he moved and spoke slowly.

The demise of Henry was relatively swift. The 55 year old developed pains in the stomach. Months of collective prayer by sect members could not alleviate his pain. Give him credit; he must have come to work for some time despite the pain. He took sick leave and the family reluctantly called a doctor. The doctor arranged some tests and on getting the results, promptly had Henry carted to the Peter McCallum Hospital for cancer patients. Henry died eleven days after admission.

Before becoming totally incapable Henry had requested from the superannuation fund a statement of his entitlements. That was prepared and duly delivered to his home together with one of the first copies of the newly printed updated version of a twenty page booklet containing extracts and examples that the Trustees regarded most apt, from the rather voluminous Trust Deed. Notwithstanding that prompt response a further letter was received requesting a copy of the entire Trust Deed. A copy of that one hundred and forty pages book was also promptly delivered to the home of Henry only a few days before the superannuation fund received notification of his death. His widow delivered the Death Certificate to the depot Manager.

The usual condolences were sent to the family by the superannuation fund's parent company. An offer of a visit by the company's social worker was declined. The family's response to the superannuation fund statement of benefits and commiserations was a rather formally worded request for a "person of authority" to visit the widow at her home in Moonee Ponds. Carol made the arrangements by telephone and my visit to the family of Henry was agreed for 5 pm on the Tuesday evening some six days after Henry's funeral.

I told my wife I would be home a bit late that night. " Make a meal for yourself and the kids don't worry about me. " I said. "The meeting with Henry's family should last about an hour and I'll pop into a McDonalds for a burger and chips on the way home. I expect to be home about 8 o'clock. "I added. I drove my company provided Datsun Bluebird Sedan to Moonee Ponds and located the address. It had a cream painted picket fence with a dark green wire mesh front gate. The house was a fairly typical suburban double fronted Victorian villa with a verandah roof across the front covering a tiled verandah floor. In the centre was a patterned heavy door adorned by a large cast iron door knocker. On each side of the door were large windows with the lower sills almost level with the ornate ceramic green, tan, and white tiles of the verandah.

Beautiful thick green rose bushes grew as borders to the verandah with abundant blossoms of full blown yellow, pink and red flowers. The green lawn was nicely mown with trimmed edges. All in all an attractive residence. At the appointed time I parked directly outside the entrance gate, collected my briefcase and opened the car door. As I got out I noticed the white lacey curtains over the window at one side of the verandah twitched. I guessed that someone was watching for my arrival.

My guess was confirmed because the front door opened before I had the opportunity to use the fancy door knocker. The woman who opened the door was petite with black hair drawn back tightly into a plaited bun. Attractive in face and figure she was surprisingly dressed not in somber black, as somehow I had expected, but in a bright "mother-hubbard" with a sunflower motive of yellow and green with splashes of reddish brown. Around her neck was a heavy gold chain suspending an equally heavy ornate crucifix that hung down almost to her waist. Several fingers of each hand had numbers of gold rings and each wrist was covered with eight or nine gold bracelets. The adornments and her golden skin made it a bit difficult to equate this attractive self assured forty something year old woman as the widow of an unassuming, mid-fifties, barely noticeable clerical worker.

She asked me to come in and indicated the first door to the right down the carpeted corridor. My condolences were acknowledged with a fleeting smile and an inclination of her head. I was still half looking at Henry's widow when I walked into the room to find six people arrayed in straight backed chairs around two walls of the long room. One wall was mostly the large window overlooking the verandah. At the opposite end were frosted double glass doors. Along the centre was a large bare polished blackwood table with a carver chair at each end. On one wall were framed pictures of forest scenes and on the other an unusual circular brass studded shield. Protruding from the top of the decorative shield was two curved blade decorative daggers of the type called a Kris in Malaya.

The widow quietly moved and sat on the chair at the end of the table near the double glass doors gesturing to me to take the carver chair that backed to the window overlooking the verandah. The widow gestured towards three teenage girls. All very attractive, petite, black haired, dark eyes, golden skinned replicas of the widow. They sat stiffed backed but with no sign of strain. The widow told me the girls were the daughters of herself and her late husband, Henry, but did not introduce each by name. Their dresses were similar to that of their mother, voluminous and brightly coloured. The voluminous nature of the dresses hid from me for some time the fact that each young girl was heavily pregnant.

On the opposite side of the room from the girls sat three men. I guessed each to be in their early twenties and from their skin tone, small stature, delicate features and hands, they seemed of the same ethnic origins as the widow and her family. One wore a light blue suit with a light blue shirt and a maroon tie; the other two wore white shirts and dark grey trousers. Two wore several gold neck chains with crucifixes and all three wore several gold rings and bracelets. No introductions were offered.

I said a general "Hello" then opened my briefcase and took out the file in which I had placed details of the superannuation benefits payable upon the death of Henry. As soon as the file hit the table the widow told me that the man in the light blue suit was the lawyer assisting her in relation to Henry's estate. She asked that I explain to him and all present the options available. I rose and offered my hand to him in a friendly gesture but it was not accepted. He rudely waved away my hand. I told him my name and offered him my business card which was taken. He did not offer his name or card in reply. Tingles of unease rippled my skin. I reminded myself that this mob believed in Revelation.

As politely as I could but with an edge in my voice I asked the lawyer his name, his legal firm and phone number. He responded only with his first name and phone number. As I wrote that into my file the widow rudely asked me to start doing my job. No evidence of grief here. It was all strictly business. I explained simply and clearly that the fund offered the choice of a pension, a lump sum in full commutation of the pension or a partial pension and a reduced lump sum. The widow produced a sheet of paper from somewhere and reading from it began asking detailed questions about the calculation of the pension. From my records I answered each question fully and frankly.

A couple of times I intercepted signals from the lawyer to the widow and each time she asked me to repeat the answer to the question. Reading from her list she now turned to the commutation factor to be used for commutation of the pension. How the factor was compiled and what were the key elements in determining the factor? As a result of consultation with the fund's actuaries over many years I was reasonably conversant with the actuarial calculation elements however I sought to cover myself a bit because I am not a qualified member of the Australian Institute of Actuaries. So I popped in a few provisos when explaining the composition of the factor.

The lawyer produced some papers from beneath his chair and began an argument that the superannuation fund was reprehensible and cheating its members in adopting a commutation factor that was manifestly too low. I welcomed the word "reprehensible". It means that the lawyer who uses it is bereft of any facts. It's a subjective derogatory frightener. From the experience I had over the years it did not intimidate me-just the opposite. I denied his allegation about cheating and pointed out that the actuaries to the fund who set the factor are independent and that he might care to discuss his theory with them. I offered to make an appointment for him. He shook his head" No".

One of the young men got up and left the room. I looked at my watch and was a trifle surprised to see the time was just past 6pm. Shortly afterwards the widow also left. The lawyer now proposed that the appointment of the firm of actuaries was improper because they were sycophants who colluded with the Trustees of the fund to deprive members of their due entitlements. The unwarranted attack annoyed me. I countered that he should be careful about statements like that or he might find himself being sued for defamation. He gave me a five minute opinion on the defamation laws of Australia. The young man and widow returned to the room and the other casually dressed young man departed with two of the young girls.

The lawyer haughtily told me that truth is a defense against defamation. A fact with which I was already familiar. He launched into further allegations of misconduct of the Trustees for artificially and improperly, even grossly illegally depressing the fund pay outs. In his view the superannuation fund benefits could be or should be about 40% higher. He spoke at length about the possibility of an evil collusive pact between the Trustees and actuaries and the auditors to deprive fund members of their proper entitlements. He told me that he considered the investment policy of the fund was seriously flawed, in a lengthy diatribe riddled with factual errors about accounting and investments. Thanks to his legal training and vigilance he said, he could ensure that Henry's widow would not fall victim to my fund's evil scheme. The young man and two young, pregnant girls returned. One girl was wiping her lips with a paper serviette.

The other girl left the room. The lawyer abruptly stopped talking and followed her out through the frosted glass door which he did not fully close. I could hear the clinking of cutlery and crockery and realised that the staged exits were to allow the widow, her daughters and the young men to have something to eat. I remember that I had been told about Henry not eating with unbelievers. Thinking of food made me realise that I was hungry. I saw from my watch that the time was near 7 pm, I had been there two hours. I asked for a glass of water. The widow said "Soon" but did not move.

Both of the young men started to talk, in a language I could not identify, becoming more agitated as they worked themselves into a lather of indignation. In the absence of the restraint of the lawyer the two young men berated me in English for mentioning only the miserly lump sum benefit to be paid to the widow and asked how much commission I would get for cheating her. I was now getting really angry. I have learnt not to act when angry and so made no reply to their taunts. I decided to get up and go. They alternatively demanded to know what lump sum benefit, not a pension, would the superannuation fund be paying to each of the three daughters of the deceased.

I told them again that the fund paid a commuted lump sum benefit only to a widow. It was up to the widow to provide for children from that benefit. The widow swiftly asked to me to repeat that and I did. The lawyer was called back in and he entered still chewing. The line they then put was that the late Henry was the husband of the widow but under their religion he was considered to be the "husband" of his three pregnant daughters until each was married to the man who had impregnated her. It seems they adhered to a "try before you buy" tenet in their beliefs. I guess that this practice is sanctioned in the bible, but I don't know where.

The lawyer produced a copy of the Trust Deed of the fund liberally jutting with coloured blows, each of which he claimed marked a clause that denied natural justice to the members to an extent that the Trust Deed was unlawful and unconstitutional. As rightful compensation on behalf of all wronged fund members the lawyer demanded recognition of each of the three pregnant daughters as "widows" equally with their mother. In short, the family demanded four identical lump sum payments as a consequence of the death of the late Henry. By now it was 8 pm. Again I requested a glass water. My request was ignored. I began packing up as I could see no point in re-hashing the unwarranted demands. I mentioned that the Australian Trust Deeds Act did not include provisions for specific religions. My comment seemed to upset them. The lawyer produced more paper and pulled his chair closer to the table. Before sitting he held up his hands, closed his eyes and mumbled something which the others evidently recognised as a short prayer for they too extended their hands and closed their eyes. It lasted about fifteen seconds and seemed to give them second wind. I used that time to complete packing my briefcase.

The intensity of their allegations of illegality and demands for payment of four identical lump sums increased. Three men and the widow were shouting at me. My recollection is that I remained outwardly calm but I cannot guarantee that my composure did not become frayed. Inside my head I was swearing. I do recall that I repeated to them that the late Henry made one contribution to the fund to entitle his family to one benefit and that they would get every cent to which they were entitled but no more. In different ways I said the same thing but to no avail because they always swung the conversation back to their religion's dogma that the pregnant girls were additional beneficiaries and must be paid at a widow's rate.

The lawyer began writing on a paper and a lull occurred in the conversation. In a moment of silence I stood and said I would leave as there appeared no point in me covering the same ground over and over again. I suggested that they put their allegations in writing, addressed to the superannuation fund lawyers. With a glare and in a growl the lawyer ordered me to sit down. I remained standing. He told me that he was writing up a deed of payment by which the superannuation fund would irrevocably guarantee to make four payments of a sum equal to the commuted pension capital sum, one to the widow of Henry, one each to the two fifteen year old twins and one to the thirteen year old youngest daughter. He claimed the deed would be beyond challenge. Apparently he put in the deed the names and dates of birth of the four females to ensure that the document was unchallengeable. . I was amazed at the young ages of the girls.

I knew now beyond doubt that the so-called lawyer was a ratbag because no legal document conjured by man is immune to challenge. Almost lesson one of the Commercial Law I studied as part of the Commerce Degree at Melbourne University teaches that anything can be challenged because the whole basis of commercial law rests on the premise of a challenge. So I picked up my briefcase and with a dry throat and unkind feelings towards the rude and inhospitable widow, the bossy, barmy lawyer and the two loud mouthed but ignorant, white shirted young men, made to leave.

In a split second the situation turned really nasty. The lawyer told me that I, as a person of authority, would be compelled to sign the paper he was drafting, irrevocably committing the superannuation fund; otherwise I would not be permitted to leave the room. He waved at one of the young men who stood and turned the key in the lock of the sturdy wooden door through which I had entered. The thought shot through my mind that any contract entered into under duress was invalid and also that the Trust Deed of the fund contained a clause to the effect that any contract was only valid if the Common Seal of the fund was affixed and attested by the autographic signatures of two Trustees or one Trustee and the Manager. My appreciation of the situation at the time ruled out my trying to educate an ignorant lawyer in favour of me trying to get out of the house. By now

I was both angry and fighting mad. I confess that an element of racial prejudice crept in and made my anger more intense.

Weeks afterwards a senior lawyer acting for the family claimed that I instigated the violence of the night by not simply complying with the demand of the lawyer and signing the form with the name of a Walt Disney character. That way I could have simply walked away without provoking an affray. It's easy for a defense lawyer to formulate a theory to shift the blame from his clients in the solitude of a comfortable office sometime after the event. There may have been a speck of truth in his contention. However in the circumstances when I was being denied my liberty, could there have been any guarantee of me being freed after I signed the useless contract, no matter what name I signed on it?

Even in retrospect the senior lawyer's effort to shift the blame from his clients to me did not hold water. I never make the first aggressive move either verbal or physical. I did not throw the first punch. After the wooden door was locked the widow and her daughters stood and moved in front of the double frosted glass doors. I considered that their move ruled out an exit through the double glass doors even if I knew what lay beyond. There was no conceivable (pardon the pun) way I could punch my way past three petite, heavily pregnant, teenage girls.

The blue suited lawyer grabbed my left wrist, put a hand to grip my throat and tried, I guess, to push me back into the chair behind me. I resisted and the young religiously inspired idiot next to him reached out to try to punch me. The punch missed its mark because I saw it coming and ducked sideways. His fist hit the back of the lawyer's hand that was trying to grip my throat. With my chin tucked into my chest and my shoulders up I caught a glimpse of the lawyers chin and swung the heel of my right hand towards it in an upper cut.

I will never be Mohammed Ali, let me make that absolutely clear, however my British paternal and Polish maternal biological heritage conferred upon me a sturdy bone structure. Normal Aussie sports of football, cricket and swimming plus some teenage boxing at Ambrose Palmer's Gym at Footscray plus many years of various activities in the Army Reserve made my 175 cm (5 foot 9 inch) Aussie body fairly formidable. Compounding on that was the fright and fury of a 36 year old who does not like to be pushed around by religious ratbags and you have a fair assessment of me as I swung the heel of my right hand at the lawyers chin.

It missed the target. But not by much. Had it fully connected he would have been down and out for a while. It caught his neck and spun him sideways. He fell into and impeded my other assailant before slipping again and cracking the side of his face on the edge of a chair. As was revealed later, he suffered a depressed fracture of the cheek bone and two broken teeth from the contact with the chair. He took some time to get up again. Up to then, luck was with me. Meanwhile the third man climbed on to the table and aimed a kick at my head. It hit my shoulder and it hurt. He tried again and missed. I grabbed his trouser leg and in an unscientific manoevre simply pulled like hell. He dived forward with some momentum and surprise, put out his hands to save himself and landed on the chair I had recently vacated. The chair tipped backward and smashed the window overlooking the front verandah.

The widow and the pregnant parade began high pitched shrieking. The widow threw knick-knacks from a small table in my direction and the lawyer on the floor grabbed my ankle. The second man had disentangled himself from the lawyer and started throwing punches. Three hit me and each hurt but he was too light to cause serious damage with punches to my upper arms and shoulder. With both feet firmly planted I managed to hit him with a hard straight right beneath his left armpit and toppled him backwards.

The lawyer's hands were climbing up my leg. It was a weird sensation. With hindsight it may be that he was only trying to use my leg to help him stand up. He later claimed that he tried to stop the violence. From my fighting position I had one man behind me and another on the floor with hands rising up my leg towards the family jewels. In a reflex protective move I chopped the edge of my hand down on the only part of him I could see I could clearly hit. Desperation gave me strength. I felt his collar bone break. His screaming joined that of the females.

The guy who had taken the unforeseen dive from the table did not attack me from the rear as I feared while disentangling myself from the prostrate, loudly yelling lawyer. Instead he had retreated to the centre of the room. What looked like decorative daggers on a wall mounted shield display turned out to be fully functional blades. He pushed one across the table towards his look-a-like friend and headed towards me holding the other. So far my heavier frame had survived a kick and half a dozen punches without any discernable disadvantage. The lawyer was definitely out of action and I had two light weight but nimble opponents between me and some form of exit from this nut house.

Daggers in the hands of lightweight faster opponents altered the balance of power. Fists cause damage. Daggers are designed for death. It was time to go and I now knew the way. I picked up a chair and used the legs to smash away the shards of broken glass sticking out from the window frame. Then I threw the chair at the closer of the two armed men. It copped him full in the chest because he had not much room to dodge between the table and the wall and some other tipped over chairs. He went down heavily. The other man had advanced less confidently, a bit bent over perhaps in pain from my punch beneath his armpit. At that moment he realised he was the last one standing. He started to turn away and to encourage him I picked up another chair and threw that at him. It hit him in the back and obviously hurt. He dropped the dagger and fled toward the females. I bent down and threw myself through the frame of the broken window onto the tiled front verandah.

In the movies when James Bond jumps through a window he does it with such athletic grace that it is almost a ballet movement. My exit looked more like the movement of an arthritic elephant. Bits of glass I couldn't see through the shadow of the lace curtain made minor cuts in my head, shoulder and hands and a large cut in my left leg that required stitches later. And those beautiful roses. I rolled across the verandah and right through those bloody awful bushes that concealed the world's sharpest, most prolific thorns. I had to get over 30 thorns removed and most punctures turned septic. Once through the roses I stood up on the lawn and felt that I needed a weapon. Near the gate I kicked a picket off the front fence, went through the gate and it collected from the footpath. Holding it as if it were a rifle and bayonet at high port rather than holding it as a baseball bat. I shakily ran backwards towards the railway station.

White blobs over fences gradually focused into faces. About twenty neighbours were gazing over their fences in the last of the late summertime light attracted, as I later found out, by the noise of shattering glass and shrieking women. The testimony of those neighbours made my life easier when the Police became involved. I recall shouting at several of them to" Call the Police please. " I reached the cross street near the railway station before seeing the two young, white shirted men run onto the road still carrying the twisted blade daggers. They were shouting and waving the daggers. The neighbours saw them too.

About this time two events had occurred that changed the face of Melbourne. One was late night shopping and the other was that Police officers were armed. I ran into the bright lights of the Puckle Street Moonee Ponds shopping strip and almost into two Policemen, a 35 year old senior constable and a younger constable. Like showdown time in a Western movie, the hand of each man went for his revolver. I could not understand it. I was one of the good guys not a Wild West baddie. I saw a reflection of myself in a shop window. The relatively small cut in my forehead near the front hair line had bled in two lines down my face. My shirt was torn and bloody at the shoulder, my left trouser had a triangular rent at the knee, both hands were bloody and I was holding the wooden picket, a weapon.

The situation seemed so ridiculous to me that I laughed. Not a good idea. The Police assumed I was demented and drew their revolvers, pointing them at my feet. I dropped the fence picket and sat, collapsed more like it, onto the footpath in front of a shop and told the Police my story for what would be the first of a dozen or more repetitions before midnight. Thoughts were buzzing through my brain. Foremost was that I was safe under the protection of the Police pistols. Another that I must phone my wife to let her know I was alright and somewhere on the fringe of thought the phrase "the love of money is the root of all evil" hovered.

The senior constable kept his pistol pointing more or less in my direction while he waited for the junior to return from a reconnaissance of Hall Street. The junior returned to say that there were half a dozen people in the street trying to put out a fire in a white Datsun Bluebird sedan parked half way down the street, but there was no one matching my description of two twenty year olds carrying curved bladed daggers.

A train must have pulled into the station for I recollect about twenty people standing on the slanted elevated walk way to the platform all looking down at me with unfeigned curiosity. Again I felt a bit mixed up and had to suppress an urge to laugh. I almost felt that I too was a spectator. Maybe it was because I was hungry and terribly thirsty. Only the pain from the glass sliced wound in my leg and the bruise of the kick near my shoulder confirmed the reality. Probably in response to phone calls from the householders in Hall Street three Police vehicles arrived. Two pulled up near my burning company car and used their fire extinguishers to put out the flames.

A tall thin, authoritative, fifty year old plain clothes detective appeared from somewhere and took control. I gave him my company ID laminated card with photo, which he kept and he ordered that I be taken under guard to Casualty at the Essendon and District Memorial Hospital in a Police sedan. The constable spread a newspaper on the seat so my blood would not soil the upholstery and drove me the less than one kilometre distance to the Casualty entrance. A young male Doctor and a more mature female nurse examined me, cleaned me up, and gave me some pills. A doctor put seventeen stitches in my left leg, a couple in my left shoulder, arm and palm of the right hand. The nurse used tweezers to extract a lot of rose thorns. The constable stood guard. We were each given a cup of coffee. Beaut!

The plain clothes detective and another uniformed constable arrived just after I had completed the phone call to my wife to explain the delay and let her know I was OK. The time was near 10. 30 pm. I told them my version of the events of the evening and the detective and uniformed Policeman took notes. As I concluded they looked at other notes on their clipboards and began questioning me in a manner that caused me to form the opinion that the other notes were the stories told by the people at the house of the late Henry.

Taking it in turns, a bit like "good cop, bad cop" questioning technique, they suggested that I instigated the violence by making demands for sexual intercourse with the widow and each of the teenagers before agreeing to hand over to the grieving family their just entitlements following the recent death of the breadwinner of the family. I was shocked and strenuously denied any such suggestion but the two Policemen maintained a concerted line of questioning on that subject for a long time. At times they switched to other questions relating to finance but always returned to the question of my alleged inappropriate demands for sexual favours. I partly heard them discussing my statement with a senior detective and his common sense must have prevailed because the Police attitude changed. They started addressing me more as a victim rather than a sexual pervert. It was well after midnight before they finished questioning. Someone had typed up a statement of what I told the Police and I was asked to read and sign it. I did read it and made seven or eight handwritten adjustments each of which I initialled. They gave me a carbon copy and the doctor returned to say I should stay the night at the hospital. I felt so rotten I agreed. I slept an uninterrupted six hours and awoke with some surprise wearing one of those embarrassingly open-backed hospital gowns.

After a quick partial shower to keep my left leg dry, I put back on my dirty blood stained shirt and trousers, made a brief reassuring phone call to my wife, wolfed down a hospital breakfast of scrambled eggs, toast and coffee and at precisely 8 am. phoned the Supervisor at the company's nearby Essendon depot.

Explaining only the barest details I requested that he send me any clothes he could spare plus a company car and a driver to take me to my office. The Supervisor was obviously consumed with curiosity for he drove up in a Toyota Hi Ace van and from the hurriedly assembled pile of clothes I chose a large grey dust coat of the type used by the technicians in the meter calibrating section. It covered all of the damage and almost made me appear respectable. On the trip to my office in Flinders Street in the city I told him the full story. The tale spread throughout the company like a bush fire before a north wind. I guess he spent most of his morning on the phone telling it to his fellow Supervisors at the other metropolitan depots.

At the office my staff were most supporting. Carol fended off phone calls from friends who were dying to hear the gossip and made her own call to my wife to reassure her. I made an appointment with the senior in-house company lawyer then made a quick shopping trip to Woolies Big W and bought a pair of trousers, a shirt, socks and shaving gear. At 10 am I presented myself at the company's legal office with my carbon copy of the statement I had made to the Police. Four lawyers gathered around and photocopies of my statement were distributed. Questions were directed at me from all angles. At times the tenor of the questions seemed aimed at protection of the company against the unwise action of one of its servants; me. Other questions seemed more on my side; others seemed to be testing the Trust Deed, others seemed to be slanted towards criminal assault – but either by me or against me I could not immediately ascertain because the questions were many and rapid. It was quite an interrogation. Mid way through, the Chairman of the company came in to ask about my injuries and reassure me. He categorically instructed the four lawyers that the entire resources of the company would be at my command for support. A great man my Chairman.

Not long after noon the interrogation was completed, so I quickly reallocated office tasks, indented a temporary replacement car from the motor pool and went home. After plenty of hugs and lunch with my wife and three children I went to bed and slept for ten hours after which I got up and filled 14 pages of a lined writing pad with further recollections of that evening. Those additional notes, legally called contemporary notes, proved invaluable over the sixteen months it took to wrap up the superannuation aspects of this case. In fact this chapter is largely based on those notes.

"Auntie Jean phoned from New Zealand while you were asleep. She told us about your stitches" said my eldest daughter as she kissed me and left for school. I thought I had misheard, but phoned my sister Jean, Matron of the Christchurch General Hospital. I learned that a Matron's Mafia existed. Jean and the Matron of the Essendon Hospital trained together as young nurses. She recognised my name and phoned Jean with all the clinical details of my stitches and the events that caused them. I was sitting with my staff in the general office when Carol held up a phone handset and said" Its Ray". I took the call. Sister and brother checking on me. No matter how old or big I got I would remain their "little brother". Ray and I chatted for five minutes and he said he was glad to hear that I was toughening up. I did not think of it that way, after all I was the one who scrambled away. But if it pleased Ray then I was happy.

A summary of the events may serve better than an exhaustive recital so here goes. After I escaped from the house the two young men took some time to locate the key to the door after apparently declining to exit the way I chose. They ran into the street and were dissuaded from following my retreating figure along the lamp lit street by the number of curious neighbours looking over fences. One young man picked up the heavy bell shaped metal cover off the water meter located near the front gate. Using that cover he smashed in the window of the company's Datsun car.

A short time later one young man threw my picked through briefcase and abandoned suit coat into the car through the smashed window. One of the two men splashed the contents of a one litre plastic bottle of methylated spirits into the car and put a lighted match to it. Quick work by a neighbour with a hose contained the fire until it was fully extinguished by the Police. Charges of criminal damage and arson were laid but withdrawn by the Police, because of lack of positive identification. The two young men so closely resembled each other in body size, hair style and clothing on the night that witnesses could not agree on whether one man caused all the damage or two. Given the darkness between street lamps, conviction by uncertain identification was ruled unsafe. The men received the benefit of the doubt and walked free convinced of the intervention of "the power to save" by their twisted version of the Almighty, rather than the scrupulous fairness of the laws of evidence of the State of Victoria.

As to the charges, countercharges, allegations and denials about the occurrence inside the house that night, the legal notes on our side alone came to about a thousand pages. In the early stages things looked dark for me. As the Police said, "The story told by your opposition sounds absurd but seven well rehearsed people are accusing you and you are alone". In law, as Napoleon is supposed to have said about the Army, "God is the on side of the big battalions". But the voices of the big battalions that initially condemned me for improper sexual advances to minors, violence and fraud, once started, were not to be stopped.

Their lawyer in the light blue suit proved inadequate to stop the Police learning from the under aged, pregnant girls, that both Mother and Father had arranged and virtually stage managed their impregnations. Perhaps Henry had a premonition of his death and sought to secure the continuance of his DNA because the impregnation of the youngest daughter took place when she was twelve years and eight months old. The girl had only become physically capable of conception two months before. The two young men and the religious ratbag lawyer were disturbed to hear of the probability of charges of Statuary Rape and a top Melbourne criminal lawyer was engaged to represent the trio. This more experienced, expensive, legal eagle managed to have a lot of the admissions made to the Police on the night by the girls declared as inadmissible evidence. But no matter what clever legal machinations he implemented, the pregnancy of the three under aged females was indisputable. His initial attempts to save the young men by trying to depict the girls as wanton, sexually depraved jezebels floundered on the rocks of religious beliefs. He shifted the emphasis of the defense to one of religious beliefs imposed by the departed Henry on an unwilling group of three twenty two year old men. It sounded thin to me when I heard it but at least it was consistent with the legal axiom of "always blame the dead because they can't defend themselves".

Ironically all three girls gave birth to healthy children at the Essendon hospital, the same hospital at which I had received treatment. The high priced legal eagle persuaded them to drop all charges against me to avoid disadvantageous complications if I was called to give evidence of what had been told to me by the widow, the lawyer and the young men about the pregnancy of the girls in their attempt to claim superannuation. The legal eagle had the accounts of the superannuation fund examined by independent accountants and actuaries and categorically advised the widow to drop any dispute about the superannuation benefit levels and elect to take the cash. It seemed to me that their lawyer wanted to make more secure the payment of his own substantial fee. However, I admit to a degree of prejudice against lawyers described as "criminal lawyers" so impute your own motives to the advice given to the widow.

The lawyers for the superannuation fund made it plain that once the documentary evidence of marriage certificate and Henry's certificate of death were observed and noted then no barrier existed to the payment by the fund of the death benefit. It could not be retained as a surety in any way against payment of claims for damages against the fund or me. So I insisted that a caveat be placed on the house. I was sick of being maligned and decided to strike back. Evidently a bit of luck descended on me because the recording of the caveat occurred at the time the family home was to be advertised for sale. The caveat caused an element of upset greater than expected on a family that was, by now, under considerable legal and Police pressure. Our lawyers were invited to parlay a settlement and in a short space of time the company was paid around $4000 being the estimated cost of the loss of the Datsun Bluebird sedan, adjusted for the existing distance travelled and insurance compensation. I received, without their admission of culpability, the sum of $2045, comprised of $100 for each of the seventeen stitches inserted in my leg at the Essendon hospital plus $280 towards a new suit and $65 towards a new briefcase. My caveat was lifted on receipt of their bank cheque in payment.

The house was sold, the parties concerned plus another four families who adhered to the same deranged excuse for a religion moved to the Northern Adelaide suburb of Salisbury. Under the more permissive rules of the State of South Australia, the girls married their impregnators and charges under Victorian State criminal law were not proceeded with. Eventually the charges lapsed.

I'm not religious. That is not a loud boast nor an admission of an anti-social misdemeanor, simply a quiet assertion of my right not to be self-delusional. I mention it in all honesty so my bias may be assessed when I tell of my irritation at the undeserved forbearance extended to religious organisations particularly in the 1980's and early 1990's. Police and lawyers alike extended leniency to the "religious" family far beyond that which a non-religious group would have obtained, otherwise more serious charges would definitely have been laid. Even those fewer and lesser charges that were laid were not pressed with any vigour. Consequently most lapsed and those that were pursued resulted in suspended sentences. I remain totally opposed to religious groups being granted Income Tax exemption, except for their community activities.

A few years later when I was in Adelaide with my company's cricket team a local friend told me that the twin girls had left the sect and there had been some publicity in the print media because the sect sought legal aid to retain the children within the sect. I don't know any more than that.

The immediate ramification of the Moonee Ponds Incident was that visits to widows were curtailed by the Trustees. Only in extreme cases would a superannuation fund representative visit a home and then always with prior Trustee approval and accompanied by another person. Via the company's regularly issued magazine and the superannuation quarterly reports, the Trustees gradually sold the story to contributors that it was in the interests of bereaved family members to visit the office of the fund where business matters could be more expeditiously dealt with in a neutral, less stressful environment.

Only on two occasions in later years did I respond to a request for a visit. One was to a young widow at Bell Post Hill near Geelong. A medical problem and young children made it difficult for her to even visit our Geelong regional office, so I went to her. As my accompanying adult I had big Mick. Mick was a street gang foreman from our Fitzroy depot. At 196 cm (6 foot 5 inches) he was a solid Aussie / Irish block of muscle with fists as big and hard as ten pin bowling balls. At the kitchen table the widow and her mother were intelligent and easily understood the superannuation benefits and relationships to Government widow's pension benefits, fringe benefits and income tax. Mick spent most of the time flat out on the floor of the adjoining room playing with the two children.

Two years later Mick and I went to visit another widow in North Williamstown and Mick spent two hours kicking a football around the park with two teenage boys. Mick told everyone that superannuation was beaut, it was real fun. He did not share my opinion that superannuation can be murder. I remain grateful that I can write the foregoing sentence and not have someone else write a book, featuring me, with the title "Superannuation **is** Murder".

Chapter Seven

Successful Superannuation Thief

INDISPUTABLY I AM A DEVOTEE to the power of positive procrastination. My dedication entitles me to categorically assert that this story about Alan is total fiction; at least I think it may be, perhaps, possibly. But then again there could be, probably, an element of truth in it. Possibly Australia's most successful superannuation thief was named – let's say – Alan. I liked him enormously. The following narrative tells a cohesive story about thefts of identities and millions of dollars. I learned bits and pieces from various sources over a period of several years and put them together.

Alan was born in a tiny village on the North Yorkshire Moors of England not far from the port of Whitby. He told me that the reputed discoverer of Australia, Captain James Cook, lived nearby and that Cook departed from Whitby to discover Australia. Alan deplored the mean streak in the British Admiralty and amongst British Royalty for refusing to posthumously promote Cook from the rank of Captain to Admiral for his amazing achievements. He said that many others received promotion for contributing far less to the British Empire and that refusal of recognition resulted from the modest social status of the parents of Jimmy Cook. In an offended tone Alan called it a "bloody example of Tory discrimination". I agree with Alan. If there is a "Promote Captain Cook Society", I'll take out a subscription.

Alan spoke "Aussie" English almost all of the time having arrived here at the age of eleven. Only with a few infrequently used words was his Yorkshire heritage apparent, words such as knuckle and buckle he pronounced "knookle" and "boockle". Alan was said to look like an elongated version of the Welshman, Harry Secombe. Alan was a popular man, a good raconteur, liked a drink had plenty of jokes and was a cheerful and competent clerical person in a very big organisation with a matching big superannuation fund. As the Union representative in a State Head Office Branch, he was regarded as a political moderate who achieved Union aims by good natured, well prepared negotiation and a pleasant personality. When the organisation introduced employee elected Trustees to its superannuation fund, Alan was one of three members to be elected by contributors to the board of the fund. The large number of member votes cast for him showed clearly that he was very popular with the superannuation fund members.

Not long after taking up his position as a Trustee, Alan had a serious accident aboard a yacht whilst on holidays He was hospitalised for ten days and was off work on sick leave for 3 months. Alan was not a sick leave shirker and diligently obeyed the exercises set by the physiotherapist in an endeavour to get back to work. During Alan's absence another person did his office job. Also during Alan's absence, the organisation expanded by a take-over of another company. In the integration, his old job changed in character. The replacement employee was considered to be better at Alan's re-organised job, partly because of superior keyboard skills as more computers were rapidly introduced.

The superannuation fund staff was hard put to keep up with the influx of new employees who were transferred as contributors into the fund. The fund manager asked for another clerical officer to assist, especially with member communication matters. So on Alan's return to work it was decided that as he was already a Trustee, he would be offered the job to assist in the superannuation fund secretariat temporarily, before another job could be found. His remuneration package remained unaltered. Being a Trustee, Alan could countersign cheques, jointly with the superannuation fund secretary and so save time chasing other busy Trustees for signatures. Fund rules at that time specified autographical signatures. He worked less than a full week for a while to help ease him back into the work environment. If he nurtured any resentment at his displacement from his previous job, he concealed it splendidly.

Alan, as I mentioned, was a cheerful type and proved to be a good communicator. Often he went around the Head Office departments and to other suburban and country work sites to talk about the superannuation fund provisions and answer questions from contributors. Feed back to Company management was good. Alan's visits were beneficial. So far as employee relations were concerned he was a distinct asset. Being both Union Representative and superannuation fund Trustee suited his talents and personality. No conflicts of interest were perceived. He created industrial relations harmony. Management decided to offer him a full time job as a superannuation fund staff member with a rise in rank and salary. He accepted their offer without the slightest hesitation. He voluntarily resigned as at next election date as a Trustee, to prevent a conflict of interest situation arising but remained a co-signatory of documents.

Alan proved easy to work with. In his mid-forties he was a bit slow to learn new computer things but once he grasped the concept or procedure, that knowledge stuck with him. He would willingly help out any other staff member who was overloaded. Alan was a general clerk rather than having a rigidly specific job, so he had a degree of independent movement within the organisation. Filing was one of his more mundane jobs and filing of share certificates and other securities often fell to him. Superannuation Trustees and management felt more comfortable having Alan handling important share certificates rather than other general clerks, so after a while it became his exclusive job by custom rather than specific job specification. The certificates were kept in a vault and Alan was trusted with the combination of the massive metal door. Alan told his fellow Trustees that being a superannuation clerical officer could be construed as a conflict of interest. When his three year term as a Trustee drew near, he declined to nominate for re-election, as promised.

In the nine years 1972-1981 he made the recording and filing of share certificates of a very large, active portfolio his specialty. The fund was a busy investor and he had plenty of work in that area as well as duties in member communication. He saw that the superannuation fund had holdings of shares in companies that were recorded on several different State registers

– in those days big companies had a register in each State, partly because of State stamp duty variations. Prevalent in that period many companies favoured issuing bonus shares to reward shareholders rather than increasing their dividends. Largely this was encouraged by the difference between taxation on dividends and the lack of tax on capital gains. Capital Gains Tax (CGT) was implemented during September 1985.

Exactly how Alan realized that the audit system was faulty he never explained but it was faulty in relation to recording details of bonus issue share certificates. The auditors checked bonus issue share certificates directly against the original share certificates filed in lever arch files kept in the vault. It was a procedure written into the Audit Verification Schedule. The inherent fault escaped the notice of a generation of auditors. What could be more authentic than an actual check of the newly received bonus share certificate against the existing total of share certificates in the file?

Regrettably, the Auditors did not cross reference the total in the superannuation fund's main asset list – rather they verified by reference to a list or a "cover sheet" in the file – and that cover sheet had green ink initials and dates of inspection of the junior auditor – so it must be right. Each newly recruited junior auditor scrupulously followed the laid down procedure and always found that, if say, there was a one for ten bonus issue and there were 100,000 old shares and 10,000 new bonus shares then entries were correct. He certified those with his initials in green ink, and all was well. The audit procedure error lay in missing the fact that the superannuation fund may have held 120,000 shares prior to the bonus issue. Say 50,000 on the Melbourne Register of a Company, 50,000 on the Sydney Register and 20,000 on the Adelaide Register.

If Alan simply removed the Adelaide Register original share certificate and "cover sheet" from the file – a temporary misplaced filing – then the auditor would not know of it. Alan could expropriate the bonus issue of 2,000 shares applicable to the 20,000 shares on the Adelaide Register without anyone being the wiser. After the auditor left, Alan would replace the Adelaide Register share certificate and cover sheet back into its correct place in the share certificate file. The Main Asset List would show the correct shareholding but the certificates would always be short, even though audited as being "correct".

As he was trusted with the combination to the vault, Alan had access to the superannuation fund common seal, letter heads and blank share transfer forms. Other Trustees, who regarded him as an expert because he was a former Trustee, signed whatever he put in front of them. There was no seal register. Alan found it easy to transfer the 2,000 bonus shares mentioned above as an example, into another name. Once the formalities of registration in the other name were completed and a small amount of stamp duty paid, Alan sold the bonus shares and invested the proceeds.

He told me that in almost 7 years he pocketed $480,000, well over $2.6 Million in 2014 value. He invested the entire amount in Gold Coast properties. His investment choice was not motivated by a belief in extraordinary Gold Coast asset appreciations but rather because it was near the sea which he loved and it was a long way from Melbourne. He owned, freehold, 7 houses originally all tenanted by holiday makers. About 1980 he demolished 2 adjoining houses owned by his wholly owned property company and built a block of 20 flats on the site at the popular holiday spot of Broadbeach, Queensland.

On a Friday in 1982 Alan's tight knit plan began to unravel. The superannuation fund manual system was replaced by a new computer system. Surprisingly the system transfer was running ahead of time. Alan was away on holidays. His work mates thought he was fishing at the Victorian resort town of Lakes Entrance but actually he was at the Gold Coast. The computer programmers had problems writing a program with a selective application in the accounting for previously issued bonus shares. On past long standing historical records it appeared that bonuses did not consistently apply at times to certain company shares on certain registers. The programmers were perplexed because they could not find any consistency. The internal auditors were at a loss to explain it. The programmers and internal auditors asked the superannuation fund Manager for clarification. He thought they were confused in drawing that conclusion about inconsistency and had the records brought to his office first thing next morning to show the auditors and computer programmers the error of their assertions.

As it happened, I knew the Manager of that fund as well as I knew Alan. The Manager told me some years later that he spent from 9 am that Thursday morning until 11pm that night examining the share certificate files and his Main Asset List. With dread he drafted a discrepancy report. He felt so sick he could not eat all that day and he did not sleep that night. The magnitude of the discrepancy became obvious but he still didn't twig that Alan was the culprit at the time.   The external auditors were called in next day, a Friday, as a matter of urgency. Despite the urgent nature of the request the audit firm sent a junior at 10.30am. The junior who arrived called his office at 11.30am. By 12.30pm two senior auditors arrived. By 1.30pm two of the firm's partners – annoyed at having their lunch at the Athenaeum Club interrupted by a panic stricken phone call, arrived. They worked until late Friday night and returned again on Saturday.   All plans to attend the cricket test match vanished. All that week-end selected superannuation fund staff and the internal and external auditors worked on the crucial report.

By noon on Monday, after direct checking with the registries of the 30 or so companies that issued the missing bonus shares, it became clear that a massive long term fraud had occurred. The draft discrepancy report figures were confirmed. The auditors, bound by the Trust Deed, must report to the Trustees who were in turn, bound by the Trust Deed to report to the Board of the parent company upon discovery of a defalcation.

Alan returned from holidays on the Monday morning. A junior staff member, who was unaware of the suspicions that were now aroused about Alan in the minds of the auditors, was operating the new photocopy machine. Thinking she was doing the right thing and knowing that Alan was "Mr Superannuation", she handed Alan a copy of the crucial report as he walked past. Luck often seems to favour the felon. Over his mid morning cup of tea Alan skimmed through the report then abruptly left to go home, allegedly due to illness. Alan did not go home to rest in fact. His neighbours later responded to questions, saying Alan had a big burn-up on his large brick BBQ. He burnt papers for nearly 2-hours. He was very thorough about burning every scrap of paper, churning up the ashes and raking the ashes into the lawn. Nothing of any value was ever recovered.

Next day two members of the Victoria Police called at Alan's home. He declined their invitation to attend the Police station on the grounds of illness and supported that contention with a recently obtained Doctor's certificate. The Police questioned Alan for about 3-hours but got nothing of any significance about the alleged investment discrepancies.   Only an oft repeated denial of any wrong doing and that his memory deteriorated after his serious accident. Circumstantial evidence pointed strongly in his direction but without a confession or time to trace the deployment of the stolen securities, they could proceed no further.

Meanwhile the Chairman of the Board of the parent company, who was also Chairman of Trustees of the superannuation fund, was seething with embarrassment. He had a well-earned knighthood and a defalcation from an organisation which he headed would do his reputation and prestige much harm. He felt personally affronted. To minimize publicity the Chairman used his substantial political influence. He wanted a low key, iron clad case mounted against Alan so it would be quick, clean and attract the least possible attention. He brought in the Company's Legal Advisors, one of Australia's oldest and most prestigious law firms.

Over the next ten days Alan remained at home on sick leave. His house was searched by the Police under a warrant, a warrant that some say would not have been issued with so little evidence unless a considerable amount of political pressure was applied. The piles of ashes now spread as garden mulch, were sifted through but yielded nothing. Police told the Chairman that they had insufficient evidence to make a charge against anyone, least of all Alan. Many of the early records in particular had been removed from the superannuation fund and reconstruction would take a lot of time if it was possible at all. Even then the evidence against Alan could be entirely circumstantial. Regrettably, when certain records were recorded into computer files, management had ordered destruction of some original files in an overzealous attempt to remove office clutter. A lot of paper records were pulped. Thus the company itself contributed to the destruction of many years of "audit trail" evidence.

The clearest records still on file were audit certificates certifying that nothing was amiss during Alan's tenure as "Investments Officer" and the Police advised that, in law, Alan could dependably rely on those audit certificates as a defense if the Police were to lay charges. The old established firm of Legal Advisors to the Company moved more ponderously, used polysyllabic words but basically gave the same advice as the Police.

Either someone leaked this advice to Alan or he sensed it. He now returned to work. On discovery of Alan sitting at his desk and working as if nothing had happened an irate but imprudent superannuation fund

Manager loudly told Alan that he was sacked, but not why he was sacked. Without his permission Alan's briefcase was snatched, opened and searched. It only held his lunch and a yachting magazine. Security guards locked Alan in a storeroom for 20 minutes while the Manager thought what to do. Alan was then grasped by both arms and escorted from the premises by security guards in the conspicuous view of many of the staff.

Alan headed straight to the Union's Lawyers to claim improper dismissal, false imprisonment and damages to his reputation. He was innocent until proven guilty but the State Manager had already condemned him publicly without a shred of evidence, and publicly humiliated him, so went his complaint. The Union's lawyers accepted his case with relish.

Alan's lawyers served an appropriate wrongful dismissal writ and in discussion with the company's lawyers mentioned that their innocent client broached the subject of a rumour circulating within the company (with no mention of the confidential report that Alan had been given by the photocopy operator). The rumour they said, centred upon the superannuation fund being defrauded of substantial sums over a long period. The Union lawyer opined that if the rumour proved to have any credence, then it seemed to indicate incompetence by the superannuation fund auditors, who also audited the books of the parent company. The rumour, so the Union lawyer said, included hints of incompetence by the Chairman of the company and the superannuation fund Manager and some people, in circulating the rumour, made suggestions that an innocent scapegoat had been found.

The Union lawyers also opined that if a Union representative were to be made a scapegoat, then monumental industrial trouble may follow, unless incontrovertible evidence of guilt could be produced very soon. Then the actions of the State Manger were raised. He exacerbated the crimes against their client by false imprisonment, manhandling that constituted assault and denial of natural justice in refusing to allow Alan to say a word in his defence. Shocking, absolutely shocking behaviour from a company that espouses customer consideration. No doubt their recently returned from illness client was now mentally traumatised, a trauma that would require substantial compensation to remedy.

After an agonizing reappraisal of events and on advice from their top shelf lawyers, the company and superannuation fund Trustees reinstated

Alan on full pay but accorded to him an unspecified period of paid leave. Extraordinary efforts were made by the Police, the auditors and other investigators to locate any assets owned by Alan that were of a magnitude beyond Alan's standard of living. Given the influence exerted by the high profile Chairman, several State Police forces were involved and at least four Private Inquiry Agents. Likewise, the embarrassed auditors undertook their own investigation utilizing every friendly firm of accountants. Not one item detrimental to Alan was ever uncovered. He lived modestly within his means.

Four months after the discovery of the fraud, Alan was offered a deal. In exchange for a very generous redundancy package Alan would drop his wrongful dismissal claim against the company and guarantee to remain silent about the rumour of a fraud on the company's superannuation fund. In return both the company and its fund would withdraw their complaint to the Police about Alan. All of Alan's legal costs were to be paid by the company. Alan's lawyers negotiated a 15 % increase in the already generous one-off package to Alan and recommended acceptance. After he received details about the period of time before any Police charges became statute barred, Alan signed the documents. It was his 53rd birthday. The generous redundancy payment Alan received was invested in an 11% p. a, eight year non-residual annuity, i. e. it was used up both as to principal and interest after eight years, when Alan would be aged 61. Because a large component of the monthly payments was of a capital nature, little was paid by Alan in the way of tax for eight years. After eight years, any matters relating to any missing items from the superannuation fund would be statute barred. Charges against him could never be reinstated. Alan's lifestyle was thus well above average with net disposable income almost twice the average male weekly earnings for eight years. Alan and his wife had overseas holidays each year. The wealthy Australians visited Yorkshire a couple of times.

In 1990, Alan was aged 61. He sold the family home in Thornbury, Victoria. He moved with his wife to the Gold Coast. They moved into a spacious ground floor unit of a three storey apartment block. Alan worked for the Property Owning Company that owned the apartments, as the live-in salaried manager / caretaker/ maintenance man of the 20 residential units.

Despite the Statute of Limitations Act deadline on any offence now having passed making Alan reasonably immune from prosecution, the former Chairman, now retired, had a continuing discreet check on Alan each year by a firm of Private Inquiry Agents. He was undoubtedly moved by personal pique and justifiable revenge. The Agents were paid from the pocket of the former Chairman. Shortly after Alan re-located to Queensland and accepted new employment, the Private Agent employed reported that Alan's new employer, the Property Owing Company, had been in existence for nearly 10-years and was owned by a person with an address in Brighton, Victoria. The Private Agent checked ASIC records and consulted the firm of Accountants who attended to the affairs of the Property Owning Company. It was concluded that no connection existed between the beneficial owners of the Gold Coast property and Alan. The 1990 enquiry was the last undertaken because the vengeance seeking Chairman became seriously ill with an age-related complaint. He deteriorated slowly and died a couple of years later, as did the last enquiry about Alan.

In the early 1990's I attended a conference of the Association of Superannuation Funds of Australia (ASFA) as had been my practice for over 20-years. On a lovely spring evening I went for a walk along the Southport, Queensland waterfront. A 35-foot cabin cruiser pulled into the dock in the estuary. Admiring the beautiful craft, I did not see the "Captain" of the cruiser until he called out my name. It was Alan. Until he left his employer, we had shared many ASFA conferences together. Although some details about Alan's departure from the industry, under a cloud, had filtered around I had no reason to refuse to return his greeting. I helped him tie up and he invited me to step aboard his opulent cruiser for a drink. One drink led to about five or six more for him plus a packet or two of potato chips and some peanuts.

As I mentioned before, Alan was a good raconteur and loved an audience. Partly it was the alcohol, a desire to unburden, or maybe it was boasting or maybe just the comfort of being re-acquainted with an old friend, but the story I have recounted is that told to me by Alan with a few bits that I learned from other people. He avoided all discoveries and lived a wonderful life financially. His wife never knew anything of his activities nor did his children or, now, loving grandchildren.

To preclude discovery, Alan had found the identity documents of a deceased person in the superannuation fund files. The person died without dependents so the file was small. The dead man was roughly the same age as Alan. As Alan began stealing the bonus issue shares he set up a sole director Propriety Limited Company and a series of bank accounts using the identity of this passed away person. The bonus shares were transferred into the name of the "dead" man's Pty Ltd Company and then the bank account was the repository of the sale proceeds from the bonus share sales. Cash was withdrawn from that company. The cash was paid to another company registered in the name of another dead person whose details Alan also found in the superannuation fund files.

The Property Owning Company was established using the name of yet another deceased person again, culled from the superannuation fund files. Cash sums were paid into it as "loans". Alan stressed that he ensured that proper taxation was promptly paid by the Property Owning Company on all its income. Alan prefaced much of the story he told to me with the words "theoretically speaking". That being the case I was not bound to take the matter further. I put much of it down to imagination stirred by red wine. I thought it had a lot of the elements of a great yarn but decided not to tell anyone in case it got Alan into trouble.

Alan died in Queensland in 1996 aged 67 i. e. four years after he told me of his "theoretic". I did not hear of his death until a couple of weeks later when his wife, now a widow, phoned me. She wanted my help as an old and trusted friend of her late husband. In his Will he bequeathed to her one hundred percent of the shares in a company that she never knew existed. She was staggered to discover that the Property Owning Company that employed Alan was actually owned by him via a Trust and a Power of Attorney that she didn't understand. And what flabbergasted her was that the Property Owning Company owned $8.3M in Gold Coast properties. Did I know anything about it? I offered her my condolences and said I knew nothing. What would you have done?

Chapter Eight

Contributor's Rorts

PHILOSOPHY IS A DISCIPLINE WITH which I have only a passing acquaintance as the reader will have ascertained. A world renowned Melbourne-born philosopher espouses the tenet that to live a life of compassion and consideration for others is both morally correct and personally enriching. As a naive unsophisticated boy it's probably pretentious of me to suggest a reservation to that tenet. I would exclude from his unqualified definition of" others" those in jail and those who should be in jail who cause death or reputation destruction in pursuit of unwarranted enrichment. Each of the following three attempted frauds against a superannuation fund involved an attempt to damage another person. Each occurred in a different Provincial City in Victoria.

The "Organgrinder" was the intended derogatory nick name given to a man by his fellow workers. He attempted a disability fraud on a superannuation fund. He was aged 50 when he applied for a laborer's job in a mid- Victorian Provincial city. That age is usually considered a bit old for a manual job with a pick and shovel, digging trenches in laneways where machinery could not be operated safely. On the other hand all 183 cm (6 foot 3 inches) of his solid frame was straight, he had wide shoulders, muscled arms, a full head of dark blonde hair and moved like an athlete. During the pre-employment interview he impressed the Personnel Officer because his voice and phraseology marked him as a man of some education.

The references given on his employment application proved difficult to check. He explained that he was once the joint proprietor of an earthmoving equipment company that was placed into liquidation after his partner "ripped-off" money then disappeared. He was as much a victim, if not more, than the creditors who were left lamenting for the money they were owed. Unjustifiably, but understandably, creditors who suffered severe losses when the partnership was bankrupted, renounced their former friendship with him and were loath to speak in his favor, hence no written references he said. Later, the Regional Personnel Officer said he did not pursue checking the references because the job did not involve entry to private premises, did not provide access to any tools of value and so, with some sympathy for a guy down on his luck, he was offered the job, subject to a successful pre-employment medical. The Organgrinder attended the nominated clinic, completed the questionnaire about past medical history and after a physical check by the doctor, was found to be fit for work. Paperwork was processed, a birth certificate submitted as proof of age and within a few days he was admitted as a contributor to the company's superannuation fund.

One part of my job I enjoyed immensely was visiting company depots. The superannuation fund Trustees encouraged communication with members on updates in benefits due to good investment returns and at many depots I assisted members who might be considering retirement or early retirement. Regrettably as well there was sorrow and widows and families to counsel when their husband / parent – our superannuation contributor died, or retired due to disability. This counselling aspect of the superannuation fund was taken very seriously and the company's relations with its employees was extraordinarily good because of the two way respect, built over a long time, in which regular visits by superannuation fund officers played a part. Of all the country work centres I called into, this particular Provincial City was a delight to visit. The Manager was as well known for his community work as he was for the excellent way he ran the depot. All up the chain of command his beneficial influence was apparent – he ran a tight ship but it was a happy one. His business and community success was particularly commendable in view of tragedies that had earlier occurred to members of his family.

I found that some of the "Street crews" played a card game of Five Hundred in the lunch room next to the pump house during their lunch break. A minor accident prevented one of the eight players attending (two tables of four players each – with a rotation system) I was invited to join in. Over a decade, I became a "regular" whenever I visited, usually twice but sometimes up to four times a year. One player would stand down for several "hands" to allow me to play through. I remain privileged to have shared the friendship of that group. At one of these games the name "Organgrinder" was raised for the first time in relation to a recently employed manual labourer.

So far as his work was concerned, I learned the Organgrinder did what was asked, but that was all. In a six man team, he considered himself a class above the rest. He did not join in conversations on any subject not even on sex, football and cricket. Apart from his name, the address of the boarding house he lived in and the fact that he drove a five year old Chrysler Valiant P76 sedan car, little else was known. He kept very much to himself and discouraged any attempt to strike up a friendship. Every depot of over 100 employees had at least one misfit. One thing in his favor was that he was not a religious nut.

He rarely ate lunch with others in the lunch room and often sat under the canopy of the truck to eat. There was one peculiarity –and it was the subject of a lot of speculation. Each day as he arrived at work, he took from the voluminous boot of his car an ex-army steel ammunition box. Welded to the box was a heavy metal hasp and staple secured by a sizable brass padlock. Wrapped around the box was a length of heavy gauge galvanised chain. The Organgrinder carried the box to the "Street crew", "rocket launcher" truck (i.e. 3 tonne vehicle with containers for 6 metre lengths of metal pipes along each side of the tray extending over the driving cabin). Here the box was chained to the solid cabin protector roll bar with another massive padlock.

My fellow card players told me that a driver inadvertently put a hand on the metal ammunition box when the crew was working on a roadside pipe repair. The Organgrinder leaped up from a trench with a shovel raised and told the driver to keep his hands off the box. The driver was told that if he touched the box again, he would get his hair parted by the Organgrinder's shovel.

As the driver was bald as a billiard ball that brought a few laughs but they were strained laughs. Crews needed to work as teams to safely do their jobs that often involved moving heavy objects. Team work implied cooperation and mutual respect. The threat of violence was a grave breach of team protocol. The crew kept their distance from both the strongly built Organgrinder and his strongly chained box. They were not intimidated but did not want to unnecessarily provoke a fight.

Speculation about the contents raged throughout the depot, but not within earshot of the Organgrinder. Inevitably the box was given the name of "monkey".

When I visited that Provincial City depot a few months later it was not a happy event as my duty was to counsel the widow and family of a highly respected employee who died. The usual lunch time shenanigans game was distinctly subdued.

Someone said something about the funeral music and another remark led to another comment about music that helped me understand how the eccentric labourer obtained the nickname "Organgrinder". In the centre of the city was a popular music store. The owner was an attractive forty year old widow with great musical talent who taught students to play the electric organ. Frequently an electric organ would be wheeled on the footpath at the front of the music store and the widow would serenade passers-by. According to my card playing colleagues, the Organgrinder often assisted the music store proprietor to move heavy items such as organs and pianos. After a little while he was helping the widow in a more intimate manner, with a different organ, hence he acquired the nickname "Organgrinder".

That's the background to what turned out to be a short, sharp vicious contest. Does the end justify the means? Do you fight fire with fire? Should you descend from your lofty principles and adopt the low tactics of your opposition purely to win a case? Some philosophically inclined people debate issues of principle. I do not have the intellectual ability or the appreciation of the virtues of maintaining lofty principles to allow them to stand in my way when a dirty opponent launches an attack. Instead I draw upon my background as a boy in the Yarraville Docks when weakness to fight dirty meant you lost. Fight dirty only when your opponent or his legal eagle initiates the descent from decency- but fight and fight to win.

The Organgrinder opened his campaign to defraud the superannuation fund after eight months in employment when he failed to arrive for work one Monday morning. Next day his lawyer lodged an application for total and permanent disability on the ground of soft tissue injuries to his arm, shoulder and neck occasioned, his lawyer claimed, entirely by gross negligence on the part of the employer, especially the incompetence of the Regional Manager. The Organgrinder's incapacity was attested by a medical certificate allegedly issued by a prominent Melbourne orthopedic specialist. Such early involvement of a lawyer and a specialist was highly unusual. No certificate from a local GP, usually the initiator of an application. When I heard of the speed of legal involvement I smelled a rat.

Apart from a sizable superannuation settlement, the Organgrinder sought substantial damages for negligence – not only employer negligence but, and here the emphasis of his claim shifted, negligence and neglect by me He cited what he insisted was a fact. That when I visited the Provincial City where he worked, I was too busy playing cards to seek him out to enquire as to his health and how he was being treated by his work colleagues. The way that the claim was eventually written, an unbiased reader could assume that I was the Organgrinder's personal social worker not a superannuation manager. He felt neglected. He wanted compensation for that neglect. The lawyer's letter made it appear that the Manager and I were derelict in our duties and we deserved to be dismissed to appease his client's feelings of rejection. The letter also threatened that any delay in making payment would exacerbate his client's condition and thereby cause an increase in the size of the, yet to be negotiated, compensation claim.

Card playing in the lunch break was absolutely and totally legitimate. No gambling was involved and a good time was had by all except the Organgrinder who seldom entered the lunchroom. I sought to engage him in friendly conversation on more than one occasion but was ignored. I guess he was too busy watching his chained ammunition box. After a couple of rebuffs I took the hint and ignored him. Obviously his absurd claim was an ambit attempt by his feral lawyer to coerce the superannuation Trustees into viewing his disability claim more favourably by making an accusation against both the Regional Manager and the superannuation fund Manager. The claim had an inherent contradiction because while it asserted that, on one hand I was the life of the lunchroom party, on the other hand it claimed I was aloof and unapproachable to superannuation members. Some thought his claim contained an element of pre-emptive threat so that if his disability claim were refused he would try to challenge on the grounds of pre-existing bias.

As usual, I was suspended on pay pending resolution of a member's complaint by an independent arbitrator. During that two day suspension period my card playing colleagues telephoned me. They said that the Organgrinder indicated that he would be turning up at his appointed place of work but, on legal advice, refused to undertake any labor on the grounds that his injuries precluded him from lifting anything as heavy as a shovel. Evidently his chained, ammunition box was excluded because he still carried it despite it being obviously heavier than a shovel.

Over the phone another one of the card players, I forget who, offered to arrange an accident whereby the Organgrinder would fortuitously fall into a trench half full of water due the recent heavy rains and the 1 ½ tonne air compressor would fall on top of him due to an "Act of God" i. e. subsidence of the side of the trench caused by the recent inundation. I cannot recall ever receiving such a wonderful compliment. I accepted it on behalf of the Manager too. I felt churlish at having to strenuously decline the offer and forbid implementation of any action. I told the caller that the fund did not want to be up for a death benefit payment. That clinched my argument. The offer prodded my memory about the Organgrinder's chain girded; padlocked steel ammunition box and several telephone calls took place over the next hour to start a plan in motion.

Right on time next morning the Organgrinder arrived at the depot. Although being allocated no heavy work he was ordered to accompany his crew "mates" to a site near a prominent war memorial gate where a trench was to be dug to install a regulator valve. He was given the light duty job of tea boy. After some grumbling he acquiesced and, miraculously, his soft tissue injuries recovered sufficiently for him to carry his heavy chain and ammunition box from his Valiant car to the crew truck – a distance of over 120 metres. The effort apparently caused some muscle relapse as he required assistance to climb into the truck. Probably he only got the lift up he demanded because the rest of the crew knew what was coming.

Arriving on site, the crew established the exact start point to excavate a trench and started to unload a "ditch-witch" petrol driven trench digging machine brought on a tandem trailer attached to the rear of truck. A burner fueled by a Liquid Petroleum Gas (LPG) cylinder was set up by a crew member in a sheltered spot and the Organgrinder was asked to boil water for hot drinks whilst other crew members unloaded the ditch-witch from the trailer. Unfortunately this usually efficient and experienced crew realised that one of their number had drained the fresh water drum on the truck and forgotten to refill it. This meant the Organgrinder had to use the only available container, a one litre plastic bottle, to get water from a tap about 80 metres distant from the truck. With a degree of reluctance and outnumbered five to one he set off in his Wellington boots over the waterlogged paddock to the water tap. As he turned on the water tap, the truck with his ammunition box chained to it drove off down the road, the tandem trailer having been unhitched.

I have heard several different eye witness versions of what the Organgrinder's reactions were but have to treat each with some reservation. His speed in returning to the road and volume of his voice appear anatomically impossible compared to, say a Cheetah and the fog horn on a huge tourist ship. As it transpired, the truck pulled up in front of the Police Station and the driver reported that an unusual object was chained to a company vehicle without company permission. The driver said he was concerned for the safety of himself and his crew in case it was a bomb. The Police constable he reported to called his sergeant who decided that he should look into the unidentified box in the hope of finding the owner's identity. Happily, the driver had an enormous pair of bolt cutters in the truck and under Police supervision he cut free the box then cut the padlock off.

Inside was not a bomb but a lot of money – in excess of $80,000 plus newspaper cuttings from a NSW newspaper, a legal paper referring to a bankruptcy, two passports and what appeared to be a an original genuine medical certificate issued by a prominent Melbourne specialist to a person with a name that was not the name of the Organgrinder but described the same medical problems that were supposed to afflict the Organgrinder. The Police were complimentary to the driver. Two constables were dispatched to invite the Organgrinder to assist them in their enquiries. The fact that the truck driver and the Police constable both played in the same local football team is completely irrelevant to this narrative.

Briefly, to conclude, the police found that the Organgrinder had indeed been a partner in a heavy earthmoving equipment business that was placed into liquidation. One of the business partners absconded with a lot of cash when the business showed signs of serious cash flow difficulties. Rather than being the betrayed partner however, the Organgrinder was the betrayer. A warrant for his arrest was current in New South Wales. In part, the charges related to $90,000 of missing money. The Organgrinder had stolen the identity and passport of the innocent former partner. He was employed by our company under his partner's name.

The Organgrinder aspired to build up his personal treasury with a false disability claim supported by a falsified medical certificate; the veracity of which he hoped would be concealed by his lawyer's belligerent attack on the company's Manager and me. The false medical certificate submitted to support his disability application was a copy of a genuine certificate, stolen from a neighbor. Given the amount of cash and the incriminating documents, it is understandable why the Organgrinder kept a vigilant eye on his ammunition box. The consensus opinion of the Trustees at a formal meeting convened to comply with Trust Law advised by the fund's lawyers, recorded that his accusation against me was totally mendacious and designed as a distraction to apply pressure.

The Organgrinder counted on creating the threat of an expensive legal case with the company being cast in the role of Goliath and him as David. He reckoned the company / superannuation fund would back-off from a defence that may incur bad publicity. If the claim looked like faltering, he thought to negotiate a lower, but still substantial sum, and then depart. He had read reports of the administrator of his failed earthmoving company negotiating with creditors to reduce claims from a full payment demand to only 35 cents in the dollar. He thought to use a similar negotiating process against the company / superannuation fund aided by the contrived overlay of belligerence and threat of bad publicity.

Organgrinder never had his disability claim assessed. It lapsed because his efforts to oppose extradition to NSW precluded his attendance for a medical exam. When that failed his focus shifted towards minimizing his New South Wales custodial sentence of two years and eight months. We never tried to fight the Organgrinder on his chosen battlefield. Instead we attacked from an unexpected direction. We hit him in his weak spot, his box. There was an element of risk. Events proved the risk was worth taking. Does the end justify the means? I believe the answer depends entirely on the circumstances. Categorically I say "yes" in this case and equally I categorically congratulate a team of wonderful men dedicated to justice, digging trenches and playing cards at lunch time. Thank you friends. You are all on my list to receive a complimentary copy of this book.

"Heaven has no rage like love to hatred turned, nor hell a fury like a woman scorned" – it's a quotation often erroneously attributed to Shakespeare, whereas it was actually penned by the English playwright and poet, William Congreve (1670-1729). He also wrote "You must not kiss and tell". Both quotations sit well in the case of Nicole, the girlfriend of 25-year-old manual worker Jerry. He apparently took ill shortly after joining the company. Jerry was good looking, well built, played water polo and was supremely self confident especially in the company of ladies. He was employed at a branch of the company in a North Victorian Provincial city and joined the company's superannuation fund. For the first month he worked well and his foreman seemed satisfied. Then over a three week period medical certificates from three different Doctors were submitted in support of his absence from work on sick leave.

The Personnel Department at the Melbourne Head Office of the employer company conducted regular checks of the records of employees on sick leave. One of these routine examinations of medical certificates indicated that poor young Jerry was suffering from a variety of illnesses. His sick leave would shortly expire and the company was genuinely concerned for his welfare. But neither Head Office staff nor Provincial branch staff could contact Jerry at the address recorded as his home. Inquiries were instituted – perhaps he was in hospital? A check of hospitals was made with no result. A wider inquiry was implemented headed by a company security officer who was a retired Victoria Police Officer. After a busy week his investigations revealed that not only was Jerry on sick leave from our company but also on sick leave from at least three other companies simultaneously, some as far as 200 kilometres distant. He was suspected of receiving Centrelink sickness benefits as well. All up, 5 pay-cheques per-week. Jerry's domicile was still unknown but he had been seen at pubs with women.

If the company ceased making payments of the last bit of sick leave to Jerry's bank account without asking him for an explanation it stood liable to be sued unless a lengthy and complicated process to ensure "justice to the worker" was implemented. It was essential that the company be able to incontrovertibly prove fraud before stopping payment and sacking him. The company was excessively cautious because of a perception that in litigation, sympathies of the Circuit Court tended to be slanted toward the employee. Also the local Member of Parliament in that Provincial city was rabidly anti-commerce, pro the "worker", to an almost obsessive degree.

The company's local Medical Officer (MO) carefully reviewed Jerry's medical records. The MO opined that Jerry's medical certificates could not possibly be correct, because with so many illnesses he would be permanently bed-ridden. After obtaining legal advice to clarify its responsibilities, the company put together a small team to resolve the problem and the team focused upon the fact that most medical certificates issued from different Doctors but all Doctors practiced at the same city centre Clinic. .

Further investigation led to a local sports club where the investigator learned that Jerry could not be incapacitated because he consistently shared his favours with several women. More checking revealed that one of the ladies was Nicole, a, receptionist at the Clinic from which the suspect medical certificates were issued. Nicole stood above average height for a woman, her head topped with short-cut brown hair parted in the middle and a square cut fringe across her forehead. Her deep set black eyes imparted a vaguely reptilian but still attractive appearance.

The investigation team consisting of the former Policeman, the local personnel manager and Jerry's crew foreman visited the Clinic. When questioned at the reception desk; Nicole denied any knowledge of Jerry. In a pre-discussed tactic the team told the Clinic Administrator about Jerry and his other live-in lovers in her presence. The investigator showed evidence of Jerry's prodigious spending on those young women at night clubs and pubs. Nicole realised that she was taking risks for Jerry to spend lavishly on several other, younger, women, some she recognised as teenagers.

She relented a trifle but was reluctant to incriminate Jerry. Tearfully she provided details about the multiple medical certificates even though she was advised her admissions would lead to Police charges. At the Police Station she confessed to typing copies of genuine medical certificates on Clinic letterhead, issued to other patients and substituting Jerry's name on the second copy. Doctors at the Clinic would sign maybe 20 certificates at a time at the end of the day. They were unaware that occasionally their trusted receptionist slipped in certificates in the name of her boyfriend, Jerry.

The receptionist believed that Jerry was trying to save money so that they could be married and buy a house. Nicole's marriage had broken up and after a divorce she had several relationships, none of which lasted very long. When she met Jerry she fell deeply in love. It was the motivation to help him swindle his numerous employers with fake sick leave certificates. In spite of her partial confession Nicole still refused to directly give evidence that would lead to Jerry being charged over crimes against the company and Centrelink.

The local Policeman took a punt," You say you have saved money in an account at the local Credit Union, how much?"

Nicole: "About $30,000"

Policeman:" Are you the only signature to that account?'

Nicole: "Yes, I mean no. Jerry can sign too. "

Policeman:" Why don't you phone the Credit Union now and ask for a balance of account. You can remember your PIN can't you?"

Nicole: "Yeah, I've got the PIN. "

Nicole called the Credit Union and made the request. The anguish in her eyes answered the question about the "saved" cash before she said in a croaky voice "They say there's only $21 left in the account. "

Jerry "blew" over $30,000 on "wine, women and song" but barely a cent did he spend on her, despite the fact that she was taking risks for him. Nicole provided details of Jerry's motor car and motor cycle, each registered in the name of another person. She revealed the location of a suitcase containing Jerry's numerous bank books, false driving licences and various records that assisted him to get multiple jobs and unemployment benefits. Jerry was adept at stealing identity documents. In many instances he stole documents from relatives of his current mistress.

Nicole was charged and released on her own recognizance. In over 15 years as a Junior and Senior Netballer, Nicole was never known to be violent. The company team confirmed that multiple Police charges would be laid and following a phone conference with lawyers and on legal advice about evidence, Jerry's services with the company were summarily terminated.

When the unsuspecting Jerry visited her that evening for a sexual session, she struck him with an empty heavy green champagne bottle. Fury added speed and force to her attack, the first blow was a clean hit on his head. Screaming she swung a second time. Instinct made Jerry raise his hand that partly deflected the second strike that laid him on the floor. Nicole kicked the prostrate Jerry until she was breathless. Bleeding, Jerry crawled on to the footpath where neighbours saw him and called an ambulance. He was taken by ambulance to hospital. Consequently he received his first genuine medical certificate for two years. It reported a fractured skull, concussion, two broken fingers and traumatic lower abdominal bruising. The Police arrested and charged both Jerry and Nicole.

I'm a dummy at understanding the law. Despite her cooperation and guilty plea, Nicole got a ten month custodial prison term in the County Court for assault causing bodily harm and for obtaining financial advantage by deception for duplicating the medical certificates. Deceived in love, robbed of her savings and without benefiting from any of the thousands of dollars of unlawfully obtained money, she had to pay her own legal costs and lost her job. The same Magistrates' Court gave Jerry a concurrent suspended 18 month prison sentence on charges of defrauding his eight employers and Centrelink plus a120-hour community based order and ordered restitution of the $5900 he fraudulently took from Centrelink. Restitution by easy instalments. In fact he received more Centrelink benefits while in Medicare -paid hospital care.

Community Aid paid his legal fees. Due to one of those quirks in the law that favour perpetrators, Jerry did not have to repay the $3400 he received from the company in sick leave. Similar amounts swindled from other companies with falsely obtained sick leave certificates were not subject to court repayment orders. Evidently the Magistrate accorded Jerry a degree of leniency for the damage inflicted by the "Hell has no fury" Nicole. Some months after release from hospital, Jerry was awarded a five figure cash sum under the Victims of Crime Compensation Program. That might be the law but it did not seem like justice.

My friends and I are intensely irritated when we see criminals who exhibit contempt for society so swiftly exploit State-funded free legal assistance to obtain cash compensation. Far too often it seems that their injuries result from their own abuses or ego-driven provocation of accomplices. We are sure that many criminals view the Victims of Crime Compensation scheme as part of their own private Workcare.

At least the superannuation fund was not up for a disability claim.

The highly regarded Southern Region Sales Manager for the company retired at age 65 and his retirement triggered the misbehavior of Megan, his Personal Assistant. Prior to his retirement her record in all aspects was admirable. Quite naturally, the company appointed an up and coming young man eager to make good as the new Sales Manager. Megan bitterly resented the change.

The formidable, well respected, well groomed, well spoken 56 old Megan began a series of one and two day absences each week. This became a regular pattern over a three month period. Company personnel policy allowed up to two days of absence without the employee being required to submit a certificate of illness from a doctor. Megan never exceeded the two days at a time so no certificate from a doctor was needed. People around her became concerned that she no longer joined in conversation at morning and afternoon tea. Work colleagues tried to cheer her up but felt, constrained to question her too much because they thought she was being treated for depression by a doctor.

After three months of toleration the new Sales Manager concluded the Megan must be shifted because her work standard had deteriorated. Her constant two day absences and morose attitude were affecting the efficiency of the entire Sales Department. Megan frequently forgot to record and pass on telephone messages. New sales opportunities were missed or made more difficult. And successful sales were jeopardized as Megan overlooked processing information that caused delivery delays. The new Sales Manager was most unhappy. His tolerance eroded.

The Company's Personnel Manager was sympathetic to Megan. He took into account that she was a widow (with adult children) well known for her voluntary work at her church and at the local Elderly Citizens' Club and had over 12 years of excellent service with the company. He felt obliged to extend more consideration to her than he may have to an employee with less meritorious service. The Personnel Manager understood the frustration of his Sales Manager and appreciated that the work load in the sales area in a competitive market could not be impeded. He arranged for Megan to speak with a professional Counselor.

The Counselor's advice was disappointing because it seemed that Megan resented the newer, younger Sales Manager. She yearned for restoration of the workplace environment in which she had been so respected and so happy for so long working with her old boss. There was never any suggestion of any romantic association between Megan and her former boss, just the warmth of mutual respect between two people who work closely together for a long time. Obviously Megan's yearnings were unreasonable and could not be fulfilled, but in the opinion of the Counselor, Megan was not affected with clinical depression.

Out of consideration for Megan, a special position of Sales Administration Supervisor was created in the department, at the same salary, and Megan was persuaded to accept the new position. The requirements of the position were judged to be well within her skill capacity. Both the Personnel Manager and the Sales Manager rightly felt that they had exercised constraint and demonstrated above average concern for an employee who responded grudgingly to everything and showed no gratitude. Head Office wanted a resolution; they let it be known that the Regional Manager was extending too much leniency. An Executive friend contacted the Regional Manager and suggested he look at the" Quote of the Day" on his calendar. It read," Tolerance ceases to be a virtue beyond a point. Thereafter it becomes a weakness". He took the hint. As the Sales Manager commented, much later, when he was accused of "roughshod tactics" – "Who did she think she was? She expected the entire Regional branch of 300 employees to be rearranged to suit her exalted perceptions of herself. The company had to stretch budgets to accommodate her salary;

she knew that but gave no credit. Had it been left entirely to me I'd have sacked her within a week because a truculent person is the last thing I needed when trying to motivate my sales staff". That sums the situation up. Everyone has problems. Sulking never solves them.

Megan only half performed her new job during the first week which greatly disappointed those trying to help. Her friends had hoped that a new position may demonstrate to Megan the esteem in which she was held. A well qualified young married lady was selected from a dozen or so applicants for Megan's old job. The formidably sized Megan stood very close to her successor and heaped abuse on the smaller, younger woman for several minutes. If anyone could be accused of "roughshod tactics" it was Megan. Her confrontations and surprisingly unlady-like language constituted intimidation. The Personnel Manager heard of this and decided that the company could not allow bullying of its employees. His patience with Megan ended. First thing next morning he went to see Megan and quietly asked her to please come to his office. He could have simply telephoned Megan but he made a personal and respectful approach out of final consideration for her.

Instead of going to his office, Megan picked up her bag and coat and stomped out of the building without a word to anyone. Next day a typed letter was received from Megan advising that she was ill, had an appointment with a Doctor, and would make contact after being advised by her Doctor. The Personnel Manager decided to extend last latitude to Megan as it was possible that Megan's abrasive attitude was the symptom of a deeper medical problem. He noted in his diary that he would make more enquiries next week if a Doctor's Certificate did not arrive by then.

A Certificate did arrive. Her Doctor, a young man who had recently set up practice in the area, claimed that Megan was suffering from severe Repetitive Strain Injury (RSI) in both hands. His patient would be unable to perform any duties given her age and the company work demand that kept her typing up to eight hours a day without a proper rest. The Doctor advised he intended to report the reprehensible conduct of the company to higher authority. The Personnel Manager was flabbergasted.

A few days later another letter arrived from a lawyer demanding Megan be paid a total and permanent disability benefit from the superannuation find on the grounds of her "crippled hands". Additionally, Megan was claiming six figure dollar damages from the Company whose irresponsible work practices and unreasonable demands were the total and sole cause of Megan's painful and crippling RSI problem.

The Company's senior management was outraged. They had extended to Megan a degree of compassionate treatment above and beyond that required of employers. They were terribly disappointed at Megan's ingratitude. In accordance with standard company practice, they picked a team of three plus the company lawyer and determined to fight the untrue and unwarranted allegations. The team began an analysis of Megan's claims over a sandwich lunch. They focused on the assertion by Megan's Doctor, after only one consultation, that she was totally unable to use her fingers in any useful manner thus blighting forever her enjoyment of life.

To the team it seemed impossible that the company could be responsible for such a degree of disability and that it came about so suddenly. Evidence from Megan's previous boss, the recently retired former Sales Manager, put her typing activity at no more than a couple of hours per day at the maximum. That maximum typing time was confirmed by other employees who were circumspectfully asked for comments during the afternoon. The retired Sales Manager declined a request to "Have a talk" with Megan.

As knock off time drew near, the company's local MO called in. He listened to a briefing on the medical claim and opined that such a sudden onset of debilitating hand and finger enfeeblement was impossible physiologically without sudden severe trauma. However he did caution that some forms of psychosomatic illness could cause sudden physical disability. He said he would give the matter some thought and recommend a suitable specialist from whom to get an independent physical report but cautioned that psychiatric advice may need to be sought. The Doctor rose to leave and almost as an afterthought, he asked the name of the female person involved. When told it was Megan he stared in disbelief. He astounded the team by saying that earlier that day he called at the Elderly Citizens Club and Megan was playing the piano at the lunch time community singing. The doctor said that Megan's allegedly crippled metacarpals and phalanges appeared to be coping easily with Cole Porter, Franz Lehar, Lerner and Loewe. The MO suggested the team advance the Megan matter no further until he communicated with us again, and it was so agreed.

The following morning the MO telephoned to say that he understood that Megan would soon drop her damages claim and settle for a routine early retirement. Beyond that, the MO would say nothing. He knew that Megan was scheduled to be playing piano at a local church function next evening. He persuaded Megan's young Doctor to attend. Together they saw Megan playing piano with hands and fingers that were supposedly crippled by RSI. Our MO's motivation was primarily to preclude embarrassment to a professional colleague. After Megan had been applauded for her expertise in accompanying several young vocalists, her Doctor emerged from the foyer and told her that the performance he had seen contradicted the statements Megan made to him in his surgery. He intended to rescind his diagnosis of RSI, or words to that effect. The company MO mentioned something about criminal implications and advised her to re-consider. Megan withdrew all her claims and formally applied for early retirement from the company. She was paid only the entitlements to which her service made her eligible.

Comfort zone is the term used to describe the lifestyle rut that most of us fall into at some time. Within her comfort zone Megan was productive and respected. When forced from it by the retirement of her boss, Megan felt unable to re-adjust. She felt deeply hurt at being removed from her comfort zone and determined to make everyone associated with her hurt also feel hurt. Megan sought misplaced revenge upon a company run by decent human beings. So decent were those people that when Megan withdrew her claims against the company and superannuation fund, most of those people embraced the "forgive and forget" philosophy. They even invited her to the office Christmas party.

I wrote "most of them" when mentioning "forgive and forget", but I exclude myself from among the "most". I regarded Megan as a thief. A thief who got caught and escaped the penalty due primarily to the good sense of the company's MO. To argue that she was good person because she played piano for her church and the Elderly Citizens Club is no exoneration. The ethics of her church were absent. Almost every convict in prison has some redeeming feature. Had Megan's claim succeeded she could have got a minimum of $100,000 from the company's insurers and $18,700 more from the super fund that she was entitled to (ie the difference between early retirement based on actual years of contributorship that did not include prospective years to age 65). Her reward for mendacious representation of her illness could have been $118,700. Try and rob a bank of that sum and see what the law does to you should you be caught.

And Megan was a thief not only of money but of reputations. For Megan's claim to succeed she would have needed to blacken the reputation of the people who had tried the most to help her. Irresponsible and reckless abandonment of their duty to protect the health of an employee are the words in the claim drawn up by her lawyers. Such a claim would have rendered the company and the senior staff liable for penalties under the Occupational Health and Safety Act. When I expressed that view at the Board meeting a couple of senior company officers dismissed it by saying that Megan probably "didn't think it would go that far" but I remain unconvinced. From what I saw of Megan she was out to punish someone and neither truth, religious morality nor compassion for others was obstructions. She sailed onwards propelled by the arrogance of ignorance.

Evidently her fury was deflected from the company towards her Doctor who "betrayed" her after he saw a demonstration of her manual dexterity. How lucky was he to have had a compassionate colleague. If Megan's case had proceeded to court, a specialist Doctor and competent lawyers would have demolished his diagnosis and with it a large chunk of his reputation. I bet that the next matronly lady who denigrates her employers to him will get scant sympathy. If Megan had continued and won her case, she would have wrecked her own life. She would have been forced to give up playing piano. At time of writing, almost nine years after the event, Megan was still playing the piano for her church, the Elderly Citizens and most recently, a dancing class. People in her social group think she is wonderful.

Additional comment on this case is that RSI was one of several short term "fashionable" illnesses that conscienceless contributors used to try to obtain benefits to which there were not properly entitled. There were/are genuine cases but they remain few. Ergonomic furniture, equipment designed to lessen physical stress and education have reduced employee injury to a minimum. When RSI was first diagnosed, quite a few suffered a form of mass self-hypnosis of imaginary pain from which a sizeable payment of cash would bring instant relief.

I predict the next spate of illness with be "Navel Pneumonia" and it will be a peculiarly female disorder. My prediction is based on observations of female attire in wintry Melbourne. Young ladies seen in the streets wear woollen beanies, long thick scarves, gloves, leg warmers and coats that are short and jeans so low that a mid-riff gap of about 28cm leaves their navels exposed to the worst of the weather. Navel Pneumonia the next epidemic – remember, I predicted it first.

Comments on USA Rort

At a superannuation fund conference on disability retirement rorts, working party groups were informed of the action of a swindler in Ohio, USA. A forty something year old female jewellery store manager tripped, knocked over a display case and was rendered unable to work due to injuries such as neck and back sprains, headaches and blurred vision. Shortly thereafter her condition further deteriorated until she became both blind and unable to walk, or so it seemed from the documents submitted by her lawyer to support her compensation claim.

In fact her injuries did not truly worsen, as claimed. She was barely bruised in the staged accident. In less than three months she was working full time in the office with an expert firm of medical claims lawyers, one of whom had represented her in her action against the liability insurer that covered the jewellery store.

All up, the attractive female jewellery store manager received a disability pension for 10 years for her alleged serious incapacity. When caught, she and her lawyer were sentenced to 18 months and 21 months jail respectively. In my view they got off very lightly. Particularly so the lawyer who betrayed his oath of Fidelity to the Department of Justice. Between them they were ordered to pay over US$309,000 in restitution to the insurer. But I bet they won't; instead I expect they will file for bankruptcy. All of the medical certificates submitted to the insurer were altered copies of genuine certificates sent by mail to the lawyer in relation to other genuine claims he was handling. The trusted lawyer easily stole the medical identities of his clients.

What should be of interest to superannuation fund fraudulent claim investigators in Australia, and the reason for including this report, is that the manger and her lawyer were charged with mail fraud, in addition to worker's compensation fraud. When it comes to the law, I confess I'm a dill. I think even a dill learns that most swindlers who seek to defraud superannuation funds get off lightly, so lightly that many Trustees feel it's a joke and are dissuaded from lodging criminal complaints on the grounds that the bad publicity is not worth it.

Perhaps we can take the USA action as a template and persuade the Australian Federal Police to prosecute swindlers who use Australia Post to convey fraudulent medical information and similar false documents. That will help protect the assets of members. We do not always have to tackle swindlers in a head-on fight on their chosen territory as demonstrated by the defeat of the Organgrinder. Legal fights cost a lot of money and the outcome is always uncertain. The loser is often required to pay the legal costs of the winner. Crooks who lose frequently contrive to go bankrupt with monotonous regularity and so incur no financial burden. Honorable Trustees cannot avoid payment to their lawyers so the funds financially lose even if they morally win.

Like a lot of others I want that changed, let's hit the thieves so hard with Commonwealth Mail Fraud that other thieving bastards are dissuaded from attacking the retirement money of superannuation contributors. An unexpected approach, from a mail fraud angle may be the disincentive that prospective swindlers heed. The Yanks can be versatile. They got Al Capone for tax evasion not criminal activity. Are we any less innovative?

Chapter Nine

Diplomatic Complications

A BLOOD SPLATTERED KITCHEN SURROUNDED Ivan's dead body. So badly chopped up was the body that both Police constables summoned to the scene vomited. Fortunately their training about not contaminating a crime scene prevailed and they held on long enough to throw up in the back garden. Ivan, a big, gap- toothed storeman had arrived home late that night. Drunk, he loudly he demanded his meal. When his terrified, prematurely aged wife took the stir fried chicken and rice from the microwave and put the plate on the table; he slammed it onto the floor.

Ivan screamed more abuse, punched his wife, tried to slap his 16 year old daughter who was attempting to protect her Mum and nearly busted a kitchen chair as he slumped onto it. Without warning he belched loudly then threw up a belly full of stinking beer on the kitchen floor tiles. He collapsed forward into a pool of his own vomit. By no means was this the first time he had been violent. His wife, daughter and son all carried mental and physical scars from his years of abhorrent behaviour. Having endured his violence for over a decade, the wife's mental balance became unstable. She went to the tool shed blank- eyed and zombie-like, according to the children and returned with an axe. She hit her unconscious husband 17 times.

The unusual superannuation aspect of this was not so much the murder – the wife freely confessed, was convicted in the Supreme Court and sentenced to prison. Rather it was the surprise appearance of a nasty relative, a younger brother of the dead husband, who arrived from the family's original European homeland, behind the "Iron Curtain". A Security Official from the Consulate in Australia acted as his interpreter and his keeper. Through his English-speaking interpreter the brother claimed , or was put up to claiming , that his country's superior and infallible legal advisors assert that he was entitled to claim the entire superannuation payment of his dead brother. His claim to be a beneficiary was based upon the fact that Ivan regularly sent money to him. Because of the duration and regularity of the payments, he claimed to be entitled to a "beneficiaries" interest. Furthermore, he contended that, as the children, his niece and nephew sided and sympathized with their murderous mother, they should be disinherited.

There could have been an element of justification in his claim to be a beneficiary, if he was dependant for financial support on his brother. The Trust Deed placed no domicile restrictions on a claimant. However his claim that the Trustees must abandon any consideration of the children as beneficiaries could not be accepted by the Trustees. Upon being told that proof of the alleged payments would be required, the Consular Official who acted as an interpreter became belligerent. He claimed to be offended because the fund wanted proof. As a representative of his nation he claimed that his nation's veracity was impugned by demanding proof. The word of a Consular Official alone should be taken as absolute, was the constant claim.

The more he waved his arms about the deeper became the shade of red over his face. It spread right over his Nikita Khrushchev look -alike bald head. The brother was yabbering is his own language and gesticulating with closed fists. However the fund Manager was obdurate. Polite despite broken English denigration of Australia; he was unrelenting in insisting upon compliance with Trust Deed requirements for solid proof of any claim. He told the Consular Official and the brother that they either provide proof or the children alone would be judged to be beneficiaries. Eventually this loathsome couple left and a week later submitted over thirty international transfer records to prove that Ivan had sent regular sums of money to the brother.

After examining the records of the money sent overseas over several years it became apparent to the fund Manager that the money dispatched far exceeded the salary that the company was paying to the now deceased employee. Victoria Police reported that several stashes of cash were found hidden in the bloody kitchen. Fearing that the parent company of the superannuation fund may have been defrauded, the Manager had an audit made (the auditors served the company better than those of ENRON, WORLDCOM, and HIH) of the relevant department, which showed no significant deficit of money, equipment or appliances.

Where did all this money come from? The Manager became suspicious. He phoned an old Army mate who was in the Police Fraud Squad. The Fraud Squad Sergeant agreed to look at the records as a matter of urgency. The Fraud Squad examined the records and passed them over to the Drug Squad. Disregarding chronology in the interests of keeping the focus on the superannuation aspect and avoiding deviations about complex criminal aspects, a brief comment is that the brother was arrested and tried on drug charges – he got two years jail and was then deported. The diplomatic protestations and lamentations about the unjust capitalist system appeared half-hearted.

Victoria Police Fraud squad proved that the records that the brother submitted to claim the superannuation benefits were those of a jointly run drug operation between the two brothers, without the knowledge of the wife and children in Australia. The Police uncovered some highly persuasive but inconclusive evidence to the effect that the cocaine may have entered Australia in the diplomatic bag of the Consulate.

Certainly the belligerent intervention of the Consular official seemed to corroborate the hypothesis. The superannuation claim was a distraction. The brother was a scapegoat. Had the Police asked the Australian Government for sanctions the Consulate would have accused the Trustees of denying a benefit to the brother to cloud the drug importation charges. With the brother's claim revealed as bogus, the "children" (the daughter was now 18 years old) were determined as dual beneficiaries. If you remember the media reports of this murder case you may also recall that the wife was later pardoned when details of the incredible brutality of the dead husband were confirmed. Upon the wife's early release, both children handed over all of the superannuation money they received to their Mum.

Throughout the thirteen-month period of time required to resolve the superannuation matters, the Consular officials adopted bullying tactics, demanding the fund hand over the superannuation money to the brother. They were so used to intimidating their own people in their own country that when they showed their badges and made demands, they expected to be instantly obeyed. One Consular Security Officer was forever pushing his badge in the face of the fund staff as an intimidating tactic. He was shocked when one of the new receptionists in the superannuation fund office asked if he was a tram driver.

On international issues the Manager confessed to Consular Officials that his education appeared deficient. He asked questions like "Why was the brother so desperate to get a relatively small amount of superannuation when, according to their country's English language booklets (with which they inundated the superannuation fund reception area) the brother lived in a golden utopian, socialist workers' paradise where people lacked for nothing". They never gave an answer, just dirty looks and a raised, clenched fist. Their unrelenting harassment disrupted the office schedule. The Manager eventually told them to "buzz off. " In truth, he used stronger words than "buzz off"

The Consular Security Officer reported the Manager to what was then the Australian External Affairs Department. The Consulate wanted him dismissed for showing a lack of respect of such magnitude as to be an insult to their country. When the Manager told the Security Officer to "buzz off" his exhortation lasted about three seconds. The complaint lodged with the External Affairs Department covered seven typed pages. The superannuation Manager apparently insulted everyone in the overseas nation starting with the General Secretary, the Steamtrain Drivers Union, the Kindergarten Teachers, the Potato Farmers and the Journalists Union members. Not bad for three seconds.

As the Manager was employed by a Victorian authority, the Federal External Affairs Department referred the matter of a possible dismissal to the Department of the Premier of the State of Victoria for resolution. The Premier himself took an interest and studied the facts of the case. A former Australian Army Lieut. Colonel he convened a meeting between himself, the Manager and the Consular Official. The Official arrived with another interpreter and a lawyer. The Official dispensed with the formalities of introductions and began a harangue about the faults of the Australian justice system. During a pause, the Premier intervened to ask about the alleged insults. That provoked another five minute propaganda diatribe but no facts. The Aussie lawyer had the good grace to look embarrassed. The Premier stood and declared the meeting to be at an end and asked the Consular delegation to leave. The Consular Official refused. The Premier pushed a button beneath the edge of his desk, two large security men entered. The Premier glanced briefly at his notes then told the delegation to "buzz off" using identical words to those spoken by the Manager. The delegation left. The Premier complimented the Manager on resisting the illegal harassment of what he privately referred to as "Commie bastards". A relieved Manager walked back to his office. Did you ever consider that the murder of a contributor could lead a superannuation fund into a diplomatic incident? That's why I claim that Superannuation can be exhilarating.

Deadly Deception

Most complications caused by irresponsible contributors make me irritable. This one made me cry.

Maria the young mail-order bride looked very innocent, an attribute accentuated by her long shiny black hair and big, sad, dark eyes. Maria was born in a small rural village in Europe. Relatives told her she was 17 but she wasn't sure of her true date of birth. Her parents had died whilst she was very young. Slightly built, she lived with ageing relatives who considered females a burden. So when the relatives had the opportunity to send her to Australia they wasted no time in getting the village headman to complete the paperwork. Maria did not have much experience of the love and support of a family. Her single solace was her devotion to God. She was intensely religious. Maria was married by proxy in her home country to a man who had migrated to Australia from her region some ten-years earlier.

She was deceived from the outset by the marriage arrangers. If the husband had been an item covered by the Trade Practices Act, say had he been a piece of furniture, little Maria could have gone to the Victorian Civil and Administrative Tribunal (VCAT) and got a refund on the grounds of misrepresentation of goods. Her misrepresentation case would have stood on five main points. Firstly she was given a photo of her "husband". She was told it was recent. It wasn't. It was about 12 years old. He was 34, almost double her age, but she didn't know that until the day she arrived in Australia.

Maria was told he owned a big house. In fact he was paying off a small run down weather-board dump of a house in Coburg, a Melbourne suburb, jointly with three mates. Only after arrival did Maria find out she was expected to keep house for all four ill-mannered men. To urge her acceptance of the proxy proposal, the young woman was shown a photo of her prospective husband's shiny new car. In fact the only car he partly owned was a ten-year-old, 2-door Fiat. The photo she was shown was a page copied from the Women's Weekly magazine - it was Elvis Presley's pink Cadillac. Maria was told her future husband was a social drinker, but he drank anything alcoholic. He drank much more heavily than "social". His employer had warned him several times about appearing at work "under the weather" and his wage had been cut because he was not permitted to operate certain earth digging machines as a penalty for being caught drunk on the job.

By far the most important deception perpetuated on this naive young girl was that he was depicted as a paragon of Christian piety. In fact he seldom went to church whereas she was extremely devout. That point cannot be stressed enough. She was totally absorbed in her religious faith; so absorbed that the distinction between religion and superstition was unclear. She arrived in Australia, already married and her religion, the religion that dominated her life, regarded divorce as a mortal sin.

At Port Melbourne, Maria walked down the migrant ship's exit ramp wearing a hand-me-down black overcoat several sizes too big, a patched hat of a type abandoned by fashion 25 years ago, carrying two small tattered, fibre suitcases each tied with string. In cash she had the local equivalent of $3. It was all she owned in the world. At the bottom of the ramp Maria set foot in her new country. She knew barely ten words of English.

Within an hour of getting off the ship and meeting her far heavier and far older than expected new husband for the first time, he raced her to his grubby home. Barely had he got her through the front door when he roughly insisted upon his conjugal rights. When I heard of that many years later the word "rape" sprang into my mind.

Five years later, after four children and a miscarriage, broken teeth, numerous broken bones, denied all contact with her church, never allowed out of the house without her husband keeping a watch on her, constant abuse and violent sexual demands of her husband and his drunken "friends", not all of which she was able to fight off, Maria saw a bottle of weed killer in the garage. The skull and crossed bones symbol is the universal warning of poison. Words are not needed. Maria put the entire contents of the bottle in her husband's evening meal of spaghetti marinara. He wolfed down the meal and within minutes collapsed in agony. One of his mates called an ambulance. He died in 36-hours. Some say he got off easier than Maria.

Police arrested her on a report from the Hospital. The Court-appointed interpreter still harboured his homeland prejudices against women, so Maria was not well served by him. Through that interpreter Maria freely confessed. Her religious devotion acted against her. She was horrified at herself for having committed murder. She was catatonic, sitting motionless for hours, barely eating. Maria was unable to understand that an essential part of her religion involved forgiveness, or if she did, she did not believe she deserved forgiveness for such a horrific crime. She would not defend herself, only reiterating through the defense interpreter "I killed him". The Court case was brief because she pleaded guilty. Forensic evidence from the Government Pathologist was conclusive.

The Melbourne Supreme Court where capital charges are heard is a beautiful building. Deep blue carpets, gleaming mahogany timber, polished for 100-years, glistening brass chandeliers with bright tulip-shaped lamp shades. The judge wears a white wig, crimson gown trimmed with light grey and a wide black cummerbund. Above the judge's bench is an elaborately carved wooden canopy bearing the Australian Coat of Arms and on each side are highly polished panels flanked by Doric columns. The impression is of gleaming, brilliant splendour. And power.

On the day that Maria was sentenced to prison everything gleamed in the Courtroom except Maria. This tiny little person stood askew in the dock, shoulders and hands twisted from untreated broken bones. Just turned twenty-one years of age, according to her immigration certificate. Her shiny, long black hair had lost all lustre; dark eyes downcast, black dress, deformed hands clutching amber rosary beads. From the visitor's gallery looking down into the Court she looked like a frail velvety black butterfly – that was slowly being crushed.

Maria died in prison less than a year later. On her death certificate in the section for "Cause of death", the prison doctor wrote "unknown". She died because she could not bear to live. Maria felt that murdering her husband denied her the love of God. Her crime was so terrible in her eyes as to be unpardonable. I guess that a young vulnerable girl did not find prison life easy. In reality a double death occurred for when she poisoned her husband she spiritually poisoned herself. He died in 36-hours; she suffered for a year and a half.

The superannuation benefit of the deceased – which frankly wasn't much – became the focal point of a vitriolic battle between "his" side of the family and" hers". You have probably heard that saying, "Where's there's a Will...there's a relative". Neither side of the family had lifted a finger to help the wife of this cruel man prior to his death, but each side fought furiously to get "his" money. Some relatives mistook superannuation for compensation. They had the idea that the more meritorious the reputation of the deceased could be depicted then the greater the magnitude of the cash payout. Many strove to convince the Manager that the deceased was a modern male version of Mother Theresa. Finally it seeped through to all concerned that benefits were for the four children. Each side of the family demanded that the superannuation fund hand over to them the children and, of course the children's money. Threats and writs came from both sides. The fund viewed them as the epitome of stupidity. The fund had no authority over the children. The Victorian Government Human Services Department obtained an order from a Magistrate and placed the children temporarily in care of a church.

In all conscience, the superannuation fund Trustees could not see the children with either side of the family and so the fund conferred with the church and sought several Court Determinations that resulted in all four children being placed in custody of their church. The surprise came when the judge separately ordered that the superannuation fund be appointed Trustee for the money of the children. The "parent" company of the superannuation fund generously made a sizeable ex-gratia payment to increase the pension payments for the children after the Court determination. The Manager of the fund met the children five or six times a year over a period of up to fifteen years and could not but admire them.

The church did a wonderful job with the children. The church arranged foster homes for the children and the foster families were wonderful. The eldest boy turned out to be an athlete and was enrolled on a Church scholarship at a boys' College not far from Melbourne. On his sixteenth birthday he voluntarily chose to adopt the surname of his foster parents. The College had a reputation for turning out excellent football players. The boy's football skills elevated him to championship status as a forward in the Australian Football League. That caused the superannuation Manager to have divided loyalties as he watched this young chap whom he had come to admire over the years, crashing through the defences of his beloved Bulldogs.

This story had a most inauspicious beginning but as near to a happy ending as could be expected. All four children have grown to be commendable Aussie citizens.

From a superannuation fund viewpoint the accounts about the foregoing deaths have one virtue. **There was an identifiable corpse in each case.** What happens when superannuation fund Trustees get a death benefit claim from a "widow" but there is no corpse? How can Trustees verify that their fund contributor is really dead? This attempted fraud occurred just before the Superannuation Industry (Supervision) Act 1993 became law.

Nick was a 27 year-old tradesman who pre-empted the unshaven fashion for men by many years. Employed during the day by a Government Transport Department, he was a contributor to its superannuation fund. He "moonlighted" in a second job most nights as a taxi driver. Nothing wrong with that. Many people have more than one job. The Ford Falcon sedan allocated to him by the Taxi Company was found very early one Saturday morning in the bushes near the Kananook Creek not far from the Mile Bridge between Frankston and Seaford, two Melbourne beach-side suburbs. The driver's door was open. A few dried drops of blood were found on the sheepskin seat cover. Faint marks on the hard ground and deeper, clearer marks in the mud nearer the creek indicated that a body had been dragged to the creek-bank and dumped into the green algae slime of the slow streaming creek. One of Nick's shoes was found twenty metres downstream in the reeds. The scene had all the characteristics of robbery – a type of crime prevalent then against taxi drivers – that had escalated to murder.

Yet there was no corpse - only a grieving "widow" who lodged a claim for a death benefit commuted to a lump sum. The promptness of the lodgement raised some suspicion. Suspicion because 99% of the time it was the superannuation fund that initiated, or at least assisted beneficiaries in lodging a claim. Occasionally a solicitor lodged a claim but it was seldom indeed that a beneficiary claimed and even more rare for the claim to specify immediate commutation. By far the most frequent experience was that the fund learned of a death via the Personnel Department of the parent company or by a direct notification from a work mate of the deceased. Condolences were extended and an offer of assistance made.

It was easily established by Marriage Certificate, etc that the claimant was legally the sole beneficiary, but in this claim there was no confirmation of a death, by way of a Death Certificate. Only the word of the putative widow. During the next month she called frequently in person at the superannuation fund office asking for payment of the superannuation death benefit. My Secretary, Carol, remained professionally polite to the "widow", Glenys, but told me privately not to get carried away by the generous mammary display.

Without an identifiable corpse, can superannuation Trustees make a payment? Generally in these circumstances, Trustees can make payments free of challenge only for presumed deaths in two circumstances. The first involves a military person MIA, (Missing in Action) on the battlefield of a Government authorised conflict. The second is loss at sea certified by a ship's Captain. But the Kananook Creek is hardly comparable to the Pacific Ocean and no war was declared in that area.

Petitions to have a person declared dead are frequently referred to as Random Harvest Petitions. Many of the older generation may remember the scene from that great black and white movie "RANDOM HARVEST"© when the star Greer Garson as "Paula", gets a death certificate from the Court, for her co-star Ronald Coleman as "Smithy". Many may also recall how long "Paula" had to wait before the petition seeking confirmation of presumed death was granted. It was seven years, and that Law still prevailed at the time of Nick's presumed death as it has since 1746. The benchmark today is the Crimes Act 1958, Section 64, - Bigamy, has the words "Nothing in this section contained shall extend to any person going through the form or ceremony of marriage as aforesaid whose husband or wife has been continuously absent from such person for the space of seven years then last past and has not been known by such person to be living within that time".

But should a widow have to wait seven years to receive benefits? Could a pension be paid prior to the issue of a Death Certificate? If a pension was paid and something went wrong the Trustees would be liable to reimburse the fund from their own wallets. The indemnity given by the fund to Trustees was considered inadequate to cover them in such a situation. The Trustees were struggling with the ethical and legal aspects of this problem when the Police called and let the Trustees and Manager in on a secret. Late on the day of the alleged incident with Nick, the Fisheries & Wildlife Department, as it was then named, had put a net across the mouth of the Kananook Creek downstream at Frankston. The Department was conducting some kind of marine life survey.

Given that timing, if Nick had met foul play and his body dumped in the Kananook Creek, it could not have been washed into Port Phillip Bay, nor could it have gone upstream against the pressure of the downward flow of the creek. Something smelled and it wasn't just the Kananook Creek. The Police asked the Manager if he could slow down proceedings. Now ask yourself – can Government Departments slow things down? Does a fish know how to swim? If "slowing down" was an Olympic event this Government superannuation fund would have earned more gold medals than the Aussie swimming team.

The Manager stalled on every aspect, eg Statutory Declarations found inadequate in lieu of a Death Certificate; documents needed certification, etc. After six weeks of these delaying tactics, and tearful visits to the office, Glenys, the wife, considered all staff connected with the fund to be heartless swine. Her Solicitor made all kinds of legal threats. The staff of her Member of Parliament threatened action to have the Manager sacked. The Member of State Parliament quickly backed off when visited by Police and told that his complaining constituent was a "person of interest" in a murder enquiry.

Although the Police did not reveal any improper information, it seemed clear that they suspected the presumptive 'widow" of some form of a plot to dispose of her husband to benefit financially from his superannuation and from a substantial life insurance policy. On each visit to my office the alleged widow , Glenys, jiggled in wearing high heeled shoes, skin tight jeans and a tight tee shirt that struggled to contain a prominent but unsupported veranda. Very high -heels on a hard lino tiled floor produced eye-catching undulations. From the neck down Glenys could make men drool. Upwards was a bit rough. The Police nick-name for her was "doorknob" – everyone had a turn.

Thirteen weeks after Nick's alleged demise, in the middle of the night, Glenys vanished from Melbourne. She journeyed for 22 days via coach, train & airplane through Adelaide, Mildura, Sydney, Wagga and Toowoomba. She doubled back twice. She used credit cards obtained months before. The cards were in different names. Obviously a well pre-planned trip designed to foil followers. Glenys changed her appearance constantly with wigs, glasses and clothing. At all times she looked haunted and unhappy. Finally the un-merry widow arrived in Cloncurry, Queensland. Victoria Police surveillance was maintained throughout. They did a great job.

Gentlemen, readers, promise you won't tell anyone else and I'll give you a piece of confidential advice. If you want to defraud a superannuation fund and disappear, don't take lodgings in a boarding house located next door to a Police station. Nick the moonlighting taxi driver made that mistake. Of course he was not using his own name. As it transpired Nick was alive. He and Glenys conspired to fake his death. They expected (naively) that she would collect his superannuation death benefit payout together with the proceeds of a large insurance policy.

They planned to meet in Cloncurry Queensland, after six-months, the time they estimated it would take to collect the payments and convert large cheques into cash (notes). But Glenys was unable to stand the strain of being refused the anticipated payments, the persistent Police questions and in the absence of her husband's moral support she panicked. She implemented the pre-planned "escape route" devised by Nick and arrived three months early. Nick was terribly surprised when she arrived early because he was entertaining a "lady", when she came rushing into his boarding house room at 9.30 at night.

Her brain snapped when she saw his naked betrayal. Glenys dashed next door into the Police station before Nick could get his pants on. Virtually she ran into the arms of the Victoria Police surveillance team who had been following her. They called at the local Police Station to establish their credentials and to ask for cooperation. Glenys released the tension caused by guilt that had implacably built up over thirteen weeks. She told how Nick crashed the taxi deliberately then cut his hand to draw blood and how she was waiting in another car to drive him away. That's a brief summary of events.

Back now, to the superannuation aspect. Nick's employer sacked him for being absent from his workplace without permission. Rather than $160,000 in superannuation and insurance benefits that the couple conspired to obtain, the dismissal benefit from the fund of less than $2,000 was paid. (Being a refund of his own contributions plus interest). Nick tried a half-hearted legal attempt to overturn the dismissal payment, claiming he was physiologically ill or else he would never had tried to obtain a financial advantage by deception. Therefore he claimed to be entitled to the much higher disability benefit, but the concocted claim just fizzled out.

A Judge in the Victorian Supreme Court put Nick away for four-years, but he was released in two-and-a-half-years. Glenys got eighteen months, reduced to ten months on appeal. She divorced Nick. I thought they got off lightly. The important thing from the superannuation viewpoint is that their elaborate scheme did not allow them to get away with any of the contributors' superannuation money. The superannuation fund was protected from fraud, not because of its actions, but because, on Police advice, it actively did nothing.

Chapter Ten

Soliloquy of a Superannuation Sleuth

IN MY YOUNGER, GREENER, DAYS I searched for a way to protect the assets of superannuation contributors. Spurred by altruism I wanted to discover what caused crime. If I found that out then I could weave into superannuation administration a protective net. With the enthusiasm of ignorance I plunged into Criminology, the disciplined examination of the nature and causes of crime. In order to understand Criminology I needed to know what constituted a crime. Was it just a matter of good versus evil or right against wrong? The first important fact I learned as I started my search was that over seven thousand years ago other searchers undertook the same quest and legions have followed since. What is a crime? No answer can be dogmatic, no one really knows.

The majority of Philosophers and Criminologists agree that the definition of a crime should relate to a notion of right and wrong. But even those concepts can vary between times, cultures and geography. Three hundred years ago the punishment for witchcraft was death. Today most people think followers of witchcraft are more or less harmless ratbags. In primitive societies where all is communal, the cultural concept of theft does not exist whereas in our society theft as a crime is rife. Abortion, with or without preconditions, is legal, even mandatory and State- imposed in some societies, but classed as murder in others. Voluntary euthanasia, including medically assisted, is encouraged in some States whilst in others it is classed as suicide, a crime. Persons who assist are fortunate to be charged with manslaughter not murder. All sorts of problems with regard to inheritances are arising.

A nation may have laws that make it lawful to carry out some acts but are they moral? Should immorality be a crime? Nazi Germany approved legal actions against sections of its population, Jews, Gypsies and others that Democracies abhorred as immoral. Under Taliban rule in Afghanistan it was a crime for females to expose their faces in public or to acquire an education. These few examples demonstrate that crime has an elastic definition.

In ancient Babylonia, King Hammurabi devised and imposed a workable code of laws. Most religions pillaged his laws and incorporated versions of them into their own dogmas. They claimed divine inspiration for those dogmas and thereby defined crime as an offense against their Gods or God. Crimes were sins. It was claimed that these sins were initiated by the Devil. Expiation of those sins was cruel execution. It is a tribute to human delusional ingenuity that these non-existent demons were named, described in precise details, some being scaly or batwinged. Further ingenuity was necessitated to explain how, if God was the omnipotent epitome of goodness, from whence came evil? The answer that emerged in the major monotheistic beliefs was that Eve introduced evil when she ate of the forbidden fruit. Some answer: blame the woman. Blame for bringing sin into the world has blighted females ever since.

Crime was attributed to demonic possession much earlier than the formulation of established religions; as early as 5000 B.C.E. Crime was attributed to Zodiac and planetary influences. Mistreatment of idols was a crime according to a 3500 B.C.E. text. About 400 B.C.E., Hippocrates postulated that too much blood caused a diminution of inhibitions so some people had a greater propensity for crime. Absolution by haemoglobin diet- caused crime said an adroit Attorney at a murder trial in San Francisco. He convinced a Jury to convict his client of manslaughter not murder for gunning down two innocent men. Soluble carbohydrate dissolved personal responsibility and instigated a double homicide. Too much sugar in a tea cake allowed the killer to walk free from prison in less than six years.

In retrospect I should not have been surprised to learn that there is no universally accepted definition of crime, although most societies proscribe what the average person would call murder. But whatever crime is, I wanted to know what caused people to commit criminal acts. Criminology in its modern format owes much to an Italian Marchese, Cesare Bonesana whose book published in 1764 "On Crimes and Punishment" was a pioneer in an attempt to define crime and describe its causes. In essence, Cesare rejected the notion of crime being a sin; rather crime was an offense against society. His theory developed into today's recognition of a "social contract" under which a rational relationship exists between individuals and the State, entailing an exchange of rights and obligations for the greatest good for the greatest number with a minimum imposition on the natural freedom of individuals. In simple terms, crime is a violation of the rules of that social contract. The rules are laws. Punishment for prescribed violations is designed to outweigh the benefits that a violator hopes to obtain. It should deter others. It must be proportional to the extent of the violation and must be just and inescapable. Like humanity itself, the law is not without flaws or implicit internal contradictions.

Even the character of murder has changed. In the fragmented Europe of Charlemagne (771-814AD), murder was a crime against the clan or the tribe. It obligated a clansman to kill the killer and was deemed a form of clan protection. Vengeance perpetuated social fragmentation. "Blood Money", "Wergeld" was gradually introduced as an alternate penalty to curtail endless vendettas as Princes strove to consolidate clans into kingdoms. Over centuries, murder permuted from a crime against a clan to a violation of the Monarch's law.

For years I tried to define what a crime was so I could learn how to stop it. During those years the attitudes of societies worldwide changed. Some crimes were de-criminalized, (personal use of marihuana), others were viewed as being of a lesser degree of community violation (horse theft) and punishments abolished or diminished. New crimes related to technology were declared criminal.

Crime causations variously were or are attributed by "experts" to Phrenology (assessing criminal propensity from cranial topography) Osteopathy (musculoskeletal disturbances) poor juvenile academic performance (including Winston Spencer Churchill?) environment, peer pressure, heredity, society, psychiatric imbalance, toilet training maladjustment, genes, social status (does not explain crime of high-brow criminals) law and "strain theory" wherein the perpetrator is really the victim because of an imperfect society (should we offer prizes to the man who beats his female partner with greater brutality?), effects of War on ex-combatants (are all ex-servicemen and women automatically criminals?)

Karl Marx's convoluted claim that crime results from class warfare caused by Capitalism fails to explain crime within Communist societies such as Russia, China, Cuba, etc and dismisses non-economic crimes such as rape. Feminist representatives, with justification, claim that the male-dominated Police / Judicial system under-penalizes rapes and violence against women. A gender double standard exists. Terminology; social ecology, strain theory, objective phenomenon, social labelling, New Right Criminology, Left Realism, Communal Evil, male domination issues etc. Frankly, I became confused. I was an uncomplicated Accountant simply looking for ways to prevent the members of my "Defined" superannuation fund from being ripped off.

The definition of crime and its causes was beyond my comprehension. The ardour of my unattainable quest attenuated. Frustrated, I retreated and accepted that the laws of my country, based on a thousand or more years of the laws of Great Britain, are a reasonable compilation notwithstanding their complexity, susceptibility to minor manipulation and flaws. My less ambitious acceptance of Australian Law sounds simultaneously egotistical and patronizing but I was young and no self interest was involved. Criminology, the discipline of discovering the causes of crime, how crime and law relate to society and how Courts deal with crime would be relegated to second place in my agenda. First place would be Criminal Investigations, the practice of investigation, and incitement of the apprehension of the perpetrator of a crime within the superannuation industry, and presentation of evidence to a Court leading to conviction and justifiable punishment.

The Federal Magistrates Court in Melbourne was the venue for my transfiguration. It occurred as I listened from the public gallery to a trusted senior clerk of a metal manufacturing company's superannuation fund being tried for obtaining property by deception. She corrupted the fund's computer. That resulted in monthly retirement pension cheques in "phantom" names being credited to her bank accounts. Her defense lawyer was claiming the role of the victim for the thief. In essence; the case he put sounded more like mitigation in advance. If the wealthy superannuation fund did not exist and had not put irresistible temptation before his poor, recently divorced, client, she would never have stolen from it. He attempted to sell the notion that the temptation warranted abandonment of personal responsibility. It was bullshit but very well articulated bullshit. The appearance of the Magistrate during that discourse indicated to me that the lawyer had no hope of dismissal of the charge.

During the lawyer's diatribe my mind wandered and questions about the direction of my future coalesced with clarity in my mind to only a few points. I assessed those points and opted for Criminal Investigation. The discipline of Criminology slid to the back burner. Maybe investigation will reveal aspects of criminal behavior that I could use to solve future crimes and prevent others. Indeed my attendance at the trial of this senior clerk in my holiday time was to learn how she did the embezzlement and to devise ways to prevent my fund being exposed to a similar theft. I was also curious to learn about Court procedure. Curiosity led me to attend several "Crime Forums". Criminologists addressed these forums and most remained true to the principles of their discipline. A few deviated in pursuit of a personal agenda by deliberately claiming their pet theories as proven facts. One rationalist claimed that organized religion, not money, was the root of all evil. Up to a point he was convincing but his "facts" left unexplained the 5000 year old punishments for crime in primitive pre-religious societies. A couple of speakers blamed modern politics for crime; one with a Right-wing slant the other with a Left.

The Right stressed inadequate public punishment that failed to deter criminals (public executions, branding, the stocks?) whilst the Left was unconvincing with his variant of Marxist / Leninist practice. He was immune to embarrassment when unable to answer the question as to why the Communist Soviet Union had over double the number of their citizens incarcerated, per head of population, than any Capitalist country. Another speaker was needlessly offensively racist (shades of Nazism?). It seemed to me that "Crime Forums" were the only venues available for Academics with warped theories to try to gain credibility by sharing a microphone with more celebrated Criminologists.

The only consistency in their talks was their emphasis on the scientific aspect of their theories. I had difficulty in acceptance of that contention without reservation. Science is constantly developing. Some Criminologists seemed ossified. I was comforted when a very senior Criminologist conceded that consensus existed that only a low percentage of the vast dimension of their avocation was known for certain. He compared his investigation into the causes of criminality to that of an astronomer. New technology revealed new dimensions in space. So too it was with Criminology. New techniques opened new fields, eg DNA. That admission confirmed my resolve to concentrate totally on investigation of crime, specifically crime in the superannuation industry. It offered the higher degree of certainty that somehow I felt I needed.

An inept trio of conmen tried to permanently borrow $10M from the superannuation fund of which I was General Manager. I uncovered the amateurish attempt. Victoria Police were informed and the trio were "warned off". A month after the incompetent conmen fled the State of Victoria I attended a regular meeting of Trustees. At the conclusion of the morning's agenda we had our customary sandwiches and orange juice lunch and talked about a wide range of subjects. One of the independent Trustees commented that our society was becoming increasingly litigious. Another remarked that the company and superannuation fund were well protected because both were comprehensively covered by insurance.

Another Trustee challenged the contention of comprehensive insurance cover. She asked whether I, as an Accountant, was covered by insurance when I undertook investigative work to assist the Police. Nobody knew the answer so later the question was put to our insurance Broker. He did not know and referred the question to the insurance company's lawyers who replied in the negative. They opined that investigative work was beyond the cover in the Directors' and Officers' insurance contract. Furthermore my action may be outside of the indemnity provided in the Trust Deed. Even the insurance company's QC was unable to give a conclusive, comforting positive answer. Another question was asked as to how to obtain insurance cover whilst assisting the Police in an activity that could, without too much of a stretch, be called protecting the fund.

After several months and a lot of rigmarole the answer returned. It recommended that my job description be amplified to cover investigations, as formally approved by the Trustees, beyond the scope of normal accounting duties. Such duties to be limited to those specifically requested by a Law Enforcement entity of competent jurisdiction. The insurance policy would be adjusted to cover the new, expanded, job description. The surprise came at the end of the report. To ensure that I complied with the job description it was suggested that I obtain some formal qualification in investigation procedures. In so doing no viable loophole would be left for a "feral" lawyer to initiate a claim of some type not covered by insurance. The insurance company lawyer commented that a formal qualification would make it difficult for evidence I might give in Court to be rendered inadmissible.

So I enrolled in an Inquiry Agent's qualification course and graduated. I thoroughly recommend it to anyone in the industry. With qualifications in both Accountancy and as a licensed agent under the Private Agents Act 1966, I could properly refer to myself as a Forensic Accountant, but I seldom do. Instead, when the occasion warrants, I call myself (incorrectly) a Private Investigator. For some reason it carries more impact.

Ray drove down from the Gold Coast to stay at our place for a week. The family physical fitness fanatic, hard as Murray River Red Gum, Ray metamorphed into a cuddly kitten when around our three children. The youngest daughter had just started learning at school but she needed no lessons in how to twist uncle Ray around her little finger. Some nights Ray and I talked until midnight drifted past. Ray was intrigued by, as he put it, "my administrative endurance" and my investigator's license. Likewise I was fascinated to hear of his strength, skill and application of techniques to train both horses and new riders. At the end of the week Ray departed leaving me with his parting advice," You'll need to toughen up if you want to be an investigator. You're a bit too soft".

At times I thought Ray was right. My attitude to the court illustrates this. A colleague was subpoenaed to give evidence against a dishonest member of his own staff. I went out of curiosity and sat in the Public Gallery of the old courtroom. I guess I was so soft that the cathedral-like architecture awed me. Naively I assumed that everyone in such august surroundings, having sworn an oath on a Bible, Koran or Affirmation, would speak the truth. I felt deeply offended when the accused superannuation clerk answered questions with blatant lies. Lies that pressed to the precipice of perjury. My awe of the "Hallowed Precincts" dissipated after a few appearances. I was seldom in the witness box for more than a few minutes each time. Mainly my evidence referred to disputed payments to beneficiaries. The Superannuation (Resolution of Complaints) Act 1993 curtailed 99.9% of similar appearances. I felt that most of my appearances were a waste of time. Occasionally it seemed that the defense lawyer was posturing for relatives of the accused in the Public Gallery, who were to pay his bill.

Sometimes the court provided entertainment, viz:-

Defence Lawyer (DL): My client has a University Degree. Do you have a Degree? Me: Yes

DL: What Degree is that?

Me: Bachelor of Commerce.

DL: I see, and did you get your degree from full time study?

Me: No.

DL: So you got your Degree as a part timer?

Me: Yes.

DL: Would you agree that a full time Degree is superior to a part time Degree?

Me: No.

DL: Oh come now; look at this realistically, a full time student obtains a more prestigious Degree than a part timer. You must agree with that.

Me: No.

Judge: Where is this leading?

DL: Simply to point out that my client's qualifications are superior to those of the witness. More evidential weight should therefore be given to the testimony of my client.

Judge: I got my Law Degree part time.

DL: Oh! (Turning back to me) Now as to the alleged false medical records.......

Digressing and contorting chronology, for which I crave reader indulgence, advance 16 years. That defense lawyer is now a judge. I responded to a subpoena to give evidence about an accused, adept at identity theft. I'm in the witness box, after taking the oath on Affirmation. The judge seemed not to recognise me. An extract of proceedings is this:-

DL: My client graduated with a Degree from the University last year. I see you have a Degree, what year did you get it?

Me: 1965

DL: 1965 you said. You would have to agree that your Degree is almost ancient, would you not?

Me: No.

DL: Oh come now, your Degree is 1965, that's over 20 years ago; surely you must concede that it's out of date?

Me: No.

Judge: Where is this leading?

DL: I am obliged to inform the jury that my client's University Degree is modern, up to date and is thus superior to the ancient Degree of this witness.

Judge: I can't see that being relevant. A degree signifies competence and the witness has been applying that competence for years otherwise he would not be holding the position he does.

DL: With respect, it should be clear that the more recently obtained Degree of my client is superior to that of the witness and should be accorded more credibility.

Judge: I will direct the jury to disregard it.

DL: But can't you see that a 1965 Degree is obsolete?

Judge: I got my Degree in 1963.

DL (Turning back to me) Please tell the jury about this alleged electronic funds transfer......

Judge: (To me, with a brief smile, before I could answer the DL) I think you and I have trod a similar path before.

Me: Yes, your Honor.

Chapter Eleven

Saints and Conmen

WITH CHRISTMAS FAST APPROACHING AND it is only briefly that it never is, let's lighten up the mood with a little pre-Christmas quiz. In the Christian lexicon of Saints,

St Nicholas is the patron saint of who? Children, yes, he's Santa Claus.

St George – the dragon slayer, of? England.

St Andrew – the Scots, and also the Russian Navy.

St Patrick – the Irish and;

St Christopher is the patron saint of? Travellers.

And now, St Dismas? He's the patron saint of who?

St Dismas is the patron saint of thieves and conmen – true or as near to true as is anything connected to religion. His commemorative day is 25th March in the Gregorian Christian calendar. You may confirm that by reference to the Oxford Dictionary of Saints, there's probably a copy in the Reference section of your local library. St Dismas, remember that name, the patron saint of thieves and conmen. If I were the worrying kind I would worry about the work load imposed upon this fellow. Is Dismas to suffer for eternity? Did he not suffer enough being crucified beside Christ at Calvary? What heartless Pope inflicted additional perpetual punishment upon him by allocating to his ministrations the likes of Laurie Connell, Christopher Skase and Peter Foster? Obviously double jeopardy does not apply in the realm behind the gates of St Peter.

Two future potential candidates for Dismas tried a fraud upon a superannuation fund of which I was General Manager and, sadly for St Dismas, I hope he sees both conmen very soon. Both despicable characters failed miserably because they were well out of their gutter level league when they took on the superannuation industry. In describing those two that way I do not attribute any superiority to myself. They really were just incompetent. But not seen through the eyes of their massive egos.

The conman who did the most talking introduced himself as Gordon Rylance. From later newspaper articles I read that he had been known by a dozen or more names and may currently use the name de King.

He cheated scores of people out of several millions of dollars, including a champion woman golfer, a winner of $1 million in Lotto and a 70-year old invalid just out of hospital, to name but a few. Note that each person he cheated was vulnerable due to physical illness or emotional trauma. Other business ventures he undertook to fleece decent but trusting individuals included pet care products, restaurants and suspect properties.

Rylance, I use that name because it's as good, or bad, as any he has assumed, introduced his accomplice to me as the "Honourable Phillip". I did not catch his surname at the time but later learned it to be Wickham. The immaculately dressed "Hon Phillip" completed the introduction with a one hand over the other sincere handshake as if meeting me was the highpoint of his life. In an awful Oxford English accent that sounded as if it came out of Springvale Primary School the "Hon Phillip" reassured me that I had no need to be excessively deferential to him because he was only "minor Royalty, heir of the Duke of Gloucester you know". Rather than royalty, Wickham was gutter spawn and probably mentally warped. A criminal with numerous convictions of obtaining financial advantage by deception. Always, of course, from the vulnerable members of our community.

The meeting with these conmen took place because a day earlier, a man telephoned me at my superannuation fund office for an appointment. He said his name was Rylance and he was following up the letter he had earlier sent to me. He claimed that his company, Aldersyde Investments, had a Secured Trading Program and that the company was authorized to represent the Collateral Bank of the World. As the Pacific Region representative of that Bank he told me he was visiting selected superannuation funds in

Melbourne and offering a completely safe investment product returning 4% per month – in simple interest terms, 48% per annum.

To me, 48% per annum seemed too good to be true so I stalled him. Then I telephoned the Reserve Bank of Australia who advised that no such Bank as the Collateral Bank of the World existed. An officer of the Reserve Bank advised me that the Victoria Police Fraud Squad were keen to hear about conmen claiming to be Bankers. I telephoned the Victoria Police Fraud Squad and spoke with detectives who expressed great interest. So keen were they that two detectives visited me within the hour. They asked for my help to obtain information about Rylance. "Mr Rylance" and his associates were rumoured to be extremely wary about the people with whom they spoke. I sought and received approval from the Trustees of my superannuation fund to help the Police.

For any superannuation fund Trustee or Manager it is prudent to establish good contact with the various law enforcement services. These authorities include the local Police, The Australian Federal Police, the Australian Securities and Investment Commissions (ASIC) and, although not law enforcers, the Australian Bureau of Criminal Intelligence and the Australian Institute of Criminology. Information is power and the information freely promulgated by most of these authorities is excellent. The information provides the power to protect your superannuation fund from fraud.

Before I could phone him, a very keen Rylance telephoned again and proposed that we meet not at my office but rather at his office, where he said he would fully explain his marvellous but secret investment proposal in total security. I called the detectives and told them of the meeting and certain arrangements were made. I went to the meeting – as the Cliff Richard song goes – "Wired for Sound" – that is, with a battery operated recorder supplied courtesy of the Victorian Police Fraud Squad. I was comforted by having another small device with a panic button to push should I feel threatened. One push of the button and armed Policemen would rush to my rescue, so I was told. But no physical threats eventuated. In my judgment, Rylance and Wickham were haughty, arrogant and overbearing but in a fist fight they would be gutless. Words were their weapons. My main concern was more about setting the panic button off by accident than by any threat of physical violence.

The office of Rylance was actually the board room of a firm of Real Estate Agents in Park Street, South Melbourne. These conmen had hired the venue on a daily basis and tried to pass it off as part of their extensive property portfolio. As mentioned earlier, on arrival at the office I was met by an extremely jovial, immaculately dressed gentleman who was introduced as the "Honourable Phillip". He looked shifty to me. Rylance was an older man who had an air of respectability, a great asset to a conman, but his attempt to assure me wore thin with repetition. When someone feels the need to constantly reassure you they are honest and sincere, the repetition invokes suspicion; at least it does to me. However despite my suspicion I went along with the charade and acted as if I believed all they told me.

Rylance showed me a copy of the Annual Report of my superannuation fund, on page three of which was my photograph. So it seemed someone had made some effort to ensure my bona fides and learn details of my fund's assets and senior Managers. Getting a copy of the Annual report of the fund was no big deal. Twenty or so copies were always available to take away from the reception area.

Rylance modestly told me that he was an "International Banker" of considerable renown throughout the European Continent. The Honourable Phillip heartily supported him. Reticence is a trait unknown to conmen. For the next 50 minutes, these slick swindlers gave me the biggest "hard-sell" that I have ever experienced. They had every "hard-sell" technique practiced and rehearsed so that they confidently expected it was impossible for me to say "no" to their incredible investment proposal. Their knowledge of sales techniques was laudable but the implementation of them was deplorable.

I had a secret weapon on my side. It's called pain. You may remember an early Michael Caine movie called the "Ipcress File". In it, the British Secret Agent Harry Palmer resisted brainwashing by high frequency sound bombardment. He created a painful distraction. Sitting in the back of a Toyota Hi-Ace van, parked near the entrance to the office, the Police used wide "Elastoplast" strips to stick the recorder aerial wire along my side and down my hairy leg. When I got out of the van and stood upright, hairs ripped out whenever I so much as twitched. Walking into the office had been agony and the continuing sharp pains and my concentration on efforts to disguise my discomfort definitely assisted me to stop laughing at the pure unaltered drivel of the conmen.

Their "hard-sell" sales techniques were good but the so called "secret investment protocols" contained so many inconsistencies as to be laughable. Lack of actual experience in the true investment environment made them unaware that they mispronounced words common in the industry. "Arbitrage" they pronounced as "Ambitrage". At times their statements were totally contradictory, of which fact they appeared totally ignorant. For example, early in their spiel the Hon Phillip told me that something was strictly secret but towards the end of the spiel he said the system was "Common Knowledge" in the industry.

Rather than point out errors I sat in silence for most of the time, content to nod as the occasion seemed to demand. To stop laughing I twitched and suffered. The mutual self admiration duo appeared so wrapped up with their own eloquence that they convinced themselves they spoke the truth. The essence of their proposal was that my superannuation fund should act as a guarantor for "Stand-by Letters of Credit" to the Collateral Bank of the World. "There was no risk whatsoever", they earnestly assured me, because the superannuation fund would be guaranteeing stand-by letters of credit for the likes of First National Bank of New York. The guarantee sought from my superannuation fund was simply to comply with World Bank fussy regulations. All major Banks, they claimed, participated in this secret system of enormously profitable letters of credit guarantee. Bank directors had to swear an oath not to reveal the secret before they were allowed to join a bank board.

My superannuation fund was offered participation of a minimum of Ten Million Dollars, and to prove that my fund had the capacity to support such a guarantee, Rylance, on behalf of the Collateral Bank of the World, required a "letter of intent" on the superannuation fund's letterhead signed by a person with authority to sign cheques together with details of the fund's Bank account. The conmen stressed that the $10M would never leave our fund's account or control or be in danger in any way. Mr Rylance gave me his most sincere and personal assurance of the absolute security of the finances of my fund.

In return for the guarantee, the superannuation fund would get interest on the $10M at the rate of 4% per month, (in simple terms 48% per annum) payable 14 days after the end of each month. All this for doing nothing and without any risk at all. "Imagine how happy the members will be", they said, repeatedly. The Hon Phillip said that I would likely be promoted and given a bonus by the Trustees of my fund for my perspicacity in participating in this secure guarantee system. He said that at least ten times during the hard sell session. As I said, repetition raises suspicion. The paper work they submitted was some of the worst chop and paste photocopies I have seen.

Great emphasis was laid upon secrecy because only Directors of banks knew about the Secret Protocols of the Collateral Bank of the World they almost whispered me. In hushed tones they described the "secret ceremony" into which all bank directors were initiated before they were admitted to the secrets of the Collateral Bank's "Stand by letters of credit". The ritual they described sounded like a Masonic initiation. During repeats of their proposal they invited questions so I slipped in a few Masonic phrases. A genuine member of the Lodge would have replied with certain words. There was no recognition at all of the phrases. These crooks had acquired a copy of the Annual Report of my fund, but they had obviously not read it properly. They neglected one piece of primary research. They did not know that, to represent our superannuation fund's investment, I was actually a Director of the Australian Bank. That was stated in the Annual Report. The idiots did not read it. I was a bank Director but had never heard of any secret initiation ritual.

They might have sensed that I was unconvinced. Towards the end of their presentation I was offered an incentive. The "sweetener" offered to me, "as a person of undoubted authority" was an introduction fee of $25,000 payable directly into any bank account I nominated or in cash. My success fee would be payable 48-hours after their company received the superannuation fund letter of intent and bank details. I tried to look impressed; it took an effort. I hoped the effort disguised the disgust I really felt. I deliberately twitched a few times. Did I look like a low-life who could be bribed?

I promised to consider the proposal overnight and departed. They were most disappointed. An unmarked police car was parked outside with the detectives inside but, as arranged, I ignored them and went to my office by tram in case I was followed. On arrival, a relieved Carol was squirming in a mixture of concern and curiosity. I gave a brief account of events to her and my senior staff, picked up my company car from the first floor car park and drove to Police Headquarters in St Kilda Road Melbourne. On the drive I could not help asking myself why the First National Bank of New York, with assets over 2000 times that of my superannuation fund, could be bothered dealing with such a piffling amount as $10M.

At the Police Headquarters the Police painfully ripped off the sticky plaster strips and re-played the tape of the Collateral Bank of the World proposal a few times. A senior detective who specialized in bank fraud joined the group. He said that if I had been deceived and acted to the detriment of my superannuation fund – then there would have been grounds for arrest and charges. But by then the money would have disappeared forever. My wearing the recording device was proof that I was not deceived. At this time a Court case involving a prominent person was in the media spotlight with the defence accusing Police of deliberate entrapment of the socially elevated personage. Police were sensitive of anything to do with traps in the current media climate.

If the Police were to arrange some form of trap, the conmen may have a legal defence of entrapment given that my fund was not damaged. That could have allowed the conmen to stir up more unfavourable media speculation and escape prosecution. Perhaps they could initiate retaliatory legal action. The Police were advised by their legal experts not to lay charges under Sec. 191 of the Crimes Act, "Fraudulently inducing persons to invest money" but to issue a formal caution to the conmen instead. I contacted all Trustees to keep them up to date. They all expressed relief as they were concerned for my safety.

Next morning I returned to the South Melbourne office of the conmen. As I walked in I asked Rylance and the Hon Phillip if some colleagues could attend our meeting. Without waiting for a reply two detectives and a large uniformed constable swiftly followed me through the doors. Some harsh words were spoken, pathetic denials spat out and threats were made to sue. A detective read a legal warning to each and handed out formal written copies. The "Hon Phillip" blustered through wet lips beneath his moustache. He claimed that I was the one trying to steal from them. The detectives and I laughed at that. A short passage of him talking on the tape was played. If looks alone could kill I would have died on the spot. Later that day the conmen were deliberately and conspicuously followed by a Divvy van all the way to Tullamarine Airport for their flight back to Brisbane.

Conmen have many characteristics in common. High on the list is that most are cowards and another is that they are copycats. When one of their unsavoury members is successful in a scam, word spreads throughout the tribe. The attempted theft of $10M from my superannuation fund by Rylance and "Hon Phillip" contained elements in common with the elaborate multi-million dollar fraud, based on Standby Letters of Credit and the Collateral Bank of the World that levelled the prestigious Sydney based law firm Allen, Allen & Hemsley and seriously hurt the Nauru Phosphate Royalties Trust. The conmen who performed that rip off had at least a little panache. But both Rylance and the Hon Phillip were operating in the big league and were failures. No doubt they will return to stealing from vulnerable invalids.

Hoping to impress Ray that I was toughening up I mentioned to him by phone that I helped frighten two crooks back to their Queensland habitat. He asked for their details and said he would sort them out so they wouldn't bother me again. I said I would think about it. Ray worried me at times. He simultaneously pitied and envied me. He loved the poem "Clancy of the Overflow" by Banjo Paterson. I think he pictured himself in the saddle as "He sees the vision splendid of the sunlight plains extended". Whereas he attributed to me "I am sitting in my dingy little office, where a stingy ray of sunlight struggles feebly down between the houses tall". In truth I had a large sixth floor, air-conditioned, carpeted, corner office overlooking the Botanic Gardens. My stable life with my wife, two daughters and a son was the source of his envy. After his divorce, his Ex got custody of the two children. He seldom saw them.

Frisson engendered when I helped Police thwart inept conmen simmered for quite a while. Pressure of daily work, family responsibilities and other distractions dampened the excitement but an ember still glowed. I wondered whether there was sufficient corruption within the industry or from felonious attacks outside of the industry to make it viable for me to one day set up my own forensic accounting investigation business.

Did the conmen teach me anything useful about causes of crime? Not specifically. A Senior Fraud Squad Detective told me that most conmen he dealt with came from middle-class and had loving, if not indulgent families. His experience dashed the theory used so often in mitigation pleas that the convicted perpetrator came from a deprived environment and had an "unhappy childhood". Both hereditary and environment, individually and collectively, seemed to be excluded as causations. More often than not crims began crime at a young age. Petty crimes and vandalism compensated for lack of adulation in sports and academic spheres. Contempt for the law was engendered after lenient sentences, Community Service Orders, suspended sentences, bonds, early paroles, allowed them to walk free from courts. Experienced Legal Aid lawyers often won "Not Guilty" judgments that cost the youth not one cent and engendered a false sense of being impervious to punishment. Tougher treatment at a younger age was the deterrent proposed by the experienced Policeman.

A quote from one of my heroes, Albert Einstein (1879-1955), a mathematical physicist who had insights into the nucleus of an atom as well as human nature:-"Two things are infinite; the universe and human stupidity; and I'm not sure about the universe."

The chairperson of a church social club at Mount Waverley invited me to speak about superannuation at a monthly meeting. I did so for 40 minutes then invited questions for ten minutes after which supper was served. During question time I made mention of my recently acquired investigator's qualification. Whilst sipping coffee a well dressed woman of about 50 asked for my help to recover $40,000. She told me that about three months ago she received a phone call at 9 o'clock at night.

"Congratulations" said a voice that continued in only slightly accented English," You have won $40,000 in the Nigerian National Lottery. "

Her reply was" That's wonderful, but I don't know how I won because I never bought a ticket in it. "

"Ah, our President selects citizens of other countries at random to give a ticket to, and yours won. It's part of a tourist promotional program.

Now how would you like your $40,000 to be paid? By Western Union cash transfer or direct to your bank account?"

"Western Union cash transfer, please. "

"OK your $40,000 is ready to send. We only need you to send 245 dollars Australian, to pay the Government cash departure tax. Do you have something to write on?"

"Yes"

"OK, here are the details for you to send the $245, (woman writes down details) and the sooner you send the tax money, the sooner you get your $40,000'

Twelve hours after the anonymous phone call the woman was at the Camberwell Post Office when it opened. She sent the money by Western Union. Three nights passed and at 9 o'clock the anonymous voice phoned again to say thanks for the $245.

"Terribly sorry to inconvenience you", it said" But our Parliament just passed a law to impose another tax on cash leaving the country"

"Oh dear!"

"Yes, but don't worry you only need to send another $245 and we'll send the $40,000 straight back to you. Do you still have the Western Union details"

"Yes"

"OK I'll be waiting, goodnight".

The woman was waiting eagerly when Camberwell Post Office opened next morning. In her excited anticipation of receiving "her" $40,000 she told the postal clerk why she was sending money to Nigeria. The clerk called the Manager. Between them they more or less convinced her that she was being scammed. They would not process the Western Union transfer.

Right on 9 O'clock at night, one week later the anonymous caller called again.

"What's happened to the tax money? We have your $40,000 sitting here waiting to be sent to you?"

"The Postmaster wouldn't let me send it; he said it was a scam"

"Ach! Don't believe him; he's just envious of your good fortune. Go to another Post Office and send it".

Next morning she caught a train two stations and at the Glenferrie Post Office she sent $245 to Nigeria.

After explaining the background of her problem she offered me $1,000 to recover her $40,000 because six weeks had passed and her money had not arrived. When I politely declined, she raised the ante to $2,000. When I again refused; she sulkily walked to a group to loudly protest that I was a "Dud. "A dud I may be but I hadn't sent $490 to Nigeria. She reinforced my faith in the quotation of Albert Einstein.

Selling something that either does not exist, or if it does exist doesn't belong to the seller or else it is outrageously overpriced, is the basis of 95% of all cons.   Numerically; cons based on overpriced properties top the list. Cons based on tax deduction schemes are second. In the late 1980's overpriced properties and tax schemes merged into a scam that appeared plausible at first sight.   Cons seemed to exhaust the supply of cashed up gullible private investors and switched their focus to that inexhaustible source of money, superannuation funds. Many cons came from Western Australia when the Mining Boom went bust. Some were very good.

In mid-1990 Estate Mortgage Finance Corporation imploded. They had offered to investors an interest rate range starting at 20%. Most deposit taking entities at that time had rates of 7 to 9%. Supposedly Estate Mortgage had superior lending skills, but in fact they loaned money to sectors of the property development industry that banks would not touch. Prior to the implosion ,a W A investment advisor with the name Lowther printed on his business card , visited my office and offered me a bribe of $5,000 in cash(he showed me a wad of notes) to influence my superannuation fund to invest in Estate Mortgage via his investment agency. The large sum he sought would have netted him a commission of around $29,000. I rejected his bribe and had security escort him out of the building. The next day I heard from two Trustees. Lowther told each that I approached him to solicit a bribe. He told the Trustees that he was doing his civic duty by reporting me for trying to lure him into a criminal act. He appreciated that Trustees do not want the confidence of members shaken by Police action, so out of consideration for the members and respect for the Trustees, he thought it best to first report it to them.

He implied that the Trustees could show their gratitude for his exposure of the crooked Manager by making an investment in Estate Mortgage via his agency. Both Trustees told Lowther that if he had evidence it was his civic duty to lodge it with the Police immediately. They declined his investment proposal. No report was ever made to the Police.

In 2001 a company with the letterhead of Mortgage Lending Securities and Surety Corporation of Queensland distributed a glossy brochure that showed high- rise, waterfront, residential properties that were the security for investors. The brochure stated that the company was managed by a person who purported to be named Rawlings. This Mr Rawlings took $2 million from investors in less than 20 days. He absconded with the lot. "Mr Rawlings" screwed up his face when a TV camera crew intercepted him, but I saw the TV program and recognised "Mr Rawlings" as "Mr Lowther". He was only out of prison three months before starting the new scam. Investors were fleeced. None of the buildings pictured in the glossy brochure belonged to the bogus company. Last I heard, Lowther/Rawlings was still on the run.

Chapter Twelve

The Gigantic Commonwealth Superannuation Fraud (That Wasn't)

CHAPTER TEN EXPLAINED MY DESIRE to protect superannuation from thieves and how I came to be a qualified Forensic Accountant. Chapter 11 told how I cooperated with the Police to "warn-off" a couple of conmen. Lest any reader erroneously forms the opinion that I developed dreams of grandeur and pictured myself as today's Sherlock Holmes, let me state categorically that any Forensic Accountant who considers himself as equivalent to a Sworn Officer of the Law is dangerously delusional.

Intensive academic and physical training eliminates many Police recruits. Those who graduate have my admiration. Contemplate the diverse assemblage of crimes they must combat. Crimes against persons are top of the priority list starting with Homicide. Homicide is the all-inclusive term for the killing of a human. Murder is killing "with malice aforethought" or during the course of a crime. Manslaughter usually has two divisions, voluntary as a result of violent passion or severe provocation and involuntary involving killing during an unlawful act. Robbery too has categories, such as robbery with a weapon or by intimidation, threat, coercion or force. Assault can be simple or aggravated. Sex offences include rape, sexual assault and aggravated sexual assault. Crimes against children, molestation, etc are particularly repugnant.

Crimes against Property are one step down the propriety ladder. Burglary, arson and the new crimes against the environment, eg deliberate dumping of contaminating waste products. Only after those two categories does "White-Collar Crime" appear on the priority scale. Included are various forms of fraud. Fraud, the crime that is the most prevalent, includes scores of shades of theft. Identity theft of some type is the start point, usually wedded to computer crime. A later chapter will help you avoid being a victim of identity theft.

Given the vast array of crimes dealt with by Police, the field of investigation of a Forensic Accountant is comparatively small and narrow. Detecting the perpetrators of a fraud against a superannuation fund is relatively simple compared to general Police work. Murders, assaults and sexual crimes directly involving fund staff members are extremely rare. And when crimes affecting contributors happen the Police are there to handle all of the investigations. The superannuation sleuth is only required to do some simple accounting to answer the question of "Qui Bono?" ---- Who benefits? Frauds always leave a trail be it paper or electronic. Identification of the perpetrator(s) is easier than quickly recovering the stolen money before it irretrievably disappears.

One aspect of crime hammered into both sworn law officers, the Police, and unsworn investigators, Forensic Accountants, is that of the "chain of evidence". It is crucial to ensure that evidence is legally obtained and tightly controlled to prevent loss, contamination or interference. Every time the evidence moves along the chain it must remain secure and security independently attested, until the evidence is presented in Court. Proper logging and signatures of recipients can make or break a case. Clear recording and custody of the chain of evidence in the crime trail saved a sizeable loss and led to convictions. Reference to this case was made in the Preface to this book when I said that money attracts crooks like carrion attracts vultures so Australia's massive trillion dollar superannuation industry is under constant attack. Thieves may be offshore using sophisticated electronic techniques or home grown using simple documents falsification.

John, the alleged author of the Bible's New Testament book that bears his name, wrote that Pontius Pilate the Roman Governor of Judea, asked Jesus of Nazareth" What is truth?"Another Roman, Marcus Aurelius, the scholarly Caesar of Rome opined about 170 CE that" Everything we hear is an opinion, not a fact. Everything we see is a perspective not the truth". Jumble those two quotes and the result applies to the mis-named CSS Fraud.

By contrast to the complicated cast of conspiratorial characters the two stage plot seems simple. A hacked secure telephone cable, a fake fax "confirmed" by betrayed codes and "authenticated" by an impostor's phone call. The success of those actions sent $160m to pre-arranged bank accounts in Hong Kong, Greece, Switzerland. Having laid bare the simple plot we enter a maze of mirrors, not conventional mirrors but the amusement park type of distorted images. After the human cast are the innocently involved Corporates. The list looks like a travel brochure. Using ages as at the date of the event, the multicultural cast begins with Gregory Bourchier, a 31 year old employee in the "Trades & Cash" team of J P Morgan who left their employ in early 2004. He was the inside man who is alleged to have stolen or photocopied confidential documents that detailed the procedure to transfer cash from the account of a J P Morgan client to an overseas account. He denied this despite his handwriting being identified on copies of the documents found by Police in the hands of criminal conspirators. It was claimed that Garry Petersen aka "Fat Bastard", introduced Bourchier to "Teflon "Tony Vincent.

The target of the deception was bank account number 28966 of the Commonwealth Superannuation Scheme (CSS) to which eligible employees and agencies of the Australian Government contribute. The target account was held by the Custodian for the CSS, the Investment Bank, J P Morgan. The CSS owns investments, billions of dollars of investments. It outsources management of chunks of investments to asset managers. State Street Global Advisors manage part of the billions. J P Morgan, the Custodian, hold the electronic or physical proofs of ownership of the investments and act as a cash repository. When State Street buys investments for CSS they notify J P Morgan in a supposedly secure phone line conveying a coded fax with phone call confirmation. J P Morgan transfer money from the CSS account they hold to the vendor (s) named in the State Street notification. Vendors can be diverse, Australian or International. The gang of swindlers corrupted the communication between State Street and J P Morgan to temporarily get away with $160 million.

Because the media have enshrined it by repetition in public consciousness, the title CSS Fraud will be used. It may be a bit misleading but that's completely in context with the tenor of this swindle. "Ocean's Eleven" was a tag conferred on the kaleidoscope of crooks as a reference to a Hollywood Movie gang. Even that was wrong because 12 were arrested. The venue for most of the planning seems Hollywood too. Lady Jane's Restaurant and Strip Club located in the Allianz Building at the corner of Market and Sussex Streets Sydney, owned by Anthony "Tony" Vincent. Some plotting seems also to have occurred at an apartment leased by Alexander Roizman in the suburb of Pyrmont. Commonwealth Crown Prosecutor, Mark Buscombe told the Sydney Central Court that "Teflon" Tony Vincent was the brainchild behind the fraud and that planning went on for six months. Here again uncertainty arises as Dallas Fitzgerald, son of Felix Lyle, a Bandido bikie gang chieftain was also named as the mastermind. Still another contender for architect is a shadowy Russian/South African/Israeli man named Arkadi Drisner, a reputed diamond mine heir with oil industry contacts.

Assuming it to be a collaborative effort it seemed a formidable two-stage plan based on treachery of a trusted employee, outdated communication security, complacency and Christmas. Stage one was to steal the money. Stage two was to disperse and launder the "black money" into "white" or useable, without risk cash. Stage one started with the "inside" conspirator, J P Morgan employee Gregory Bouchier on the spot to cover an error by Telstra Technician, Barry Osbourne and a procedure reversal phone call by impostor, Pensioner, Ernst Hupnagl. The plan's contingency protection was insider, Bourchier, who smoothed over several hick-ups and allowed the $160m transfer from the CSS account at J P Morgan. Stage one complete and successful.

It was stage two that unraveled due to the incompetence of two subordinates. Matthew Terreiro and former South African solicitor and part time investigator, Richard Kurland. Terreiro's error in the transfer of $72m initiated the enquiry by Laiki Hella S. A. Bank of Athens that alarmed

J P Morgan. The fax to Laiki mentioned the name of the fake account; Stylianou Georgios but Terreiro inadvertently added "Pty Ltd." A crucial error by Terreiro who should have known better because he helped set up that account. An alert Laiki bank employee sent a clarification fax to J P Morgan. Kurland's alleged error prevented the prompt transfer of $20.6m from his Swiss bank account. He had given details of the account to his Disability Pensioner friend; Leonid Kuris. The money was due for transfer to the Mizuko Corporate Bank of New York. Terreiro was arrested and charged but charges were later dropped.

Court reports of the CSS theft state that a fraudulent five page fax followed by a fraudulent telephone call purporting to be from State Street Global Advisers to the external fund managers directed $160 million to accounts in Switzerland, Hong Kong and Greece and the money was sent. The forged fax was made possible because of the alleged involvement of Gregory Bourchier who had access to security codes and Barry Osbourne a Telstra technician who had a swipe card that allowed him entry to the telephone exchange. Osbourne hotwired equipment to by-pass security on the dedicated line and made the five page fax appear to be properly originated. Even with the right codes, Osbourne sent the wrong date, November 29 instead of December 29. Fortunately for the criminal syndicate, Bourchier was on hand to cover up. The hacking is alleged to have been made during the pre-Christmas holiday lunch time at the Telstra telephone exchange in Dalley Street a short distance from the George Street Sydney office of JP Morgan. A fax followed by a telephone confirmation call was the authentication check. Ernst Hufnagl made the call impersonating a State Street Manager then went to the Lady Jane to report to "Teflon" Tony.

Sections of the media report that an Australian Federal Police spokesman and a JP Morgan senior Vice-President both described the theft as "sophisticated and well organized" but a fax and telephone call authorisation method seems antiquated when electronic encrypted authorisation systems have been available for years. Other sections of the media have also emphasized the word "sophisticated". To my way of thinking the word is misused by the media who are notorious in misapplication of clichés. For example, almost any conman is claimed by the media to a "king-con". That media- conferred title panders to the ego of grubby thieves who are, for the most part only low-life incompetents.

Continuing this pontifical/philosophical vein, a digression from the narrative of this convoluted case is warranted. Texts that emanate from a Court during presentation of evidence are not necessarily the truth, the whole truth and nothing but the truth. The brief of the prosecutor is filtered of facts successfully argued by defense counsel as being "inadmissible". Inadmissible evidence, in laymen's terms is evidence that is deemed unreliable and cannot be presented to a judge or jury. It includes, inter alia, hearsay or evidence illegally obtained or evidence that may take too long or may risk inflaming a jury. That definition offers considerable room for pre-court legal argument as to what a judge or jury can hear in assessing guilt or innocence.

Any regular attendee to the Public Gallery of a Criminal Court quickly notices that answers given by an accused to the craftily constructed questions of his defense counsel seldom sound unrehearsed. By contrast, and in absolute abrogation of their sworn oath, the replies to questions of the prosecutor sound like lies. Scope therefore exists for an observer to exercise caution in determining the Pontius Pilate question when it comes to this crime.

The element that adds spice to the CSS Fraud case is that the Australian Federal Police (AFP) had phone taps on many of the conspirators. They were after illicit drugs. Because the gang used veiled speech, nicknames, etc the AFP did not, at first, twig that they were listening to the set- up of a bank heist. Are phone recordings made on a drug discovery warrant fully admissible in a bank heist trial?

The Sydney Central Local Court was the scene in which the AFP charged three men with conspiring to launder the $160 million alleged to have been stolen from the CSS. Those charged were South African born Richard Kurland of Leura, NSW a former South African solicitor. He was acquitted. Leonid Kuris, pensioner of Bondi was also charged and charges were dropped. Alexander Roizman of Darling Point Sydney, pensioner received a 9.5 year prison sentence. Two other men in their late 30's Jian Ping Wang (6.5 years prison) and Jian Hua Chen (3.5 years prison) were alleged to have assisted in setting up bank accounts in the names of Hong Kong Power Ltd and Lun Tun Trading in Hong Kong. Sydney's Central

Local Court was told that the pensioner, Roizman went to Hong Kong after $30 million was transferred to the bank account of Hong Kong Power Ltd. The disability that entitled Mr Roizman to an Australian Centrelink pension apparently did not impede his participation in gambling that lost $3.018 million on the floating casino cruiser, Captain Omar the Third. Jian Ping Wang sat at the same Baccarat table as Roizman, for the gambling spree, but when quizzed by Police each denied knowing the other.

The CSS thieves were widely reported as being well organized, however all but $3 million of the $160 million was clawed back in five days. Any thief worthy of the appellation "well organized" with that much money for that much time should have made the money disappear. Another non-superannuation based fraud in Sydney, perpetrated around the same time, saw millions of Aussie dollars electronically transferred overseas to a bank not on the Australian Government prohibited list. From that bank the proceeds of crime were transferred to 18 banks that were on the banned list. Recovery was impossible and the entire transfer dispersal took less than one hour. So on media reports alone, the thieves do not appear to me to have been either well organized or in the higher echelon of sophistication, only opportunists and lucky.

Mr Kurland, described as an investigator, worked part time as an insurance assessor for the disability pensioner, Mr Kuris. Is the CSS the only entity being defrauded? It is hoped Centrelink took note of the activities of these pensioners. Being an Aussie with our ability to extract humour from anything, I can't help feeling that the Sydney Courtroom provided the gallery with a laugh. The defence barrister for 58 year old Richard Kurland charged with participation in the fraud told Magistrate Allan Moore that when $20. 6 million appeared in his previously dormant bank account at the Bank Cantonale Vaudoise in Lausanne, he thought it was a genuine transaction. Charges against the pensioners were dropped on the grounds that they were duped. Unanswered is the question: why would a pensioner have a Swiss bank account?

J P Morgan introduced new levels of authentication. The entire superannuation industry scrambled to increase security with multi layered authorization systems. Apart from the fact that conspirators were caught, further evidence exists of my contention that the CSS Fraud was perpetrated by a syndicate that planned stage one in Australia fairly well, but lacked knowledge of the international money laundering aspect to successfully get away with stage two. The gang who briefly obtained the CSS $160 million did not know what to do with it. Nobody seemed to know how the spoils were to be divided.

Conspiracy to launder money carries a maximum jail term of 25 years. Probably the 25 year maximum sentence, which seems steep when compared with some other crimes such as manslaughter and murder, was implemented as part of the toughening-up of the laws to combat terrorism. Nothing is more certain than that superannuation with its enormous wealth will be targeted by terrorists to fund their demonic devastation.

Chapter Thirteen

Super and Illegal Gas

A CONTRIBUTOR TO A MELBOURNE gas company superannuation fund was on the road to riches via an illegal by-pass he made around the gas meter in a large apartment complex. The by-pass was made in a fashionable riverside inner Melbourne suburb. The contentious superannuation issue focused precisely upon what date his services to the gas company were terminated. It may seem self evident, a date is a date, but the contributor, let's call him Eddy, tried to accuse the superannuation of malicious discrimination against him. His bruised sensitivities required the healing salve of a sizable slice of monetary compensation. The actual purpose of Eddy's unfounded accusation was to try to cobble up a creditable counter claim to the parent company's accusations of theft and the State Gas Examiner's charges under the Explosive Substances Act.

Eddy had worked for nearly eight years in a middle rank clerical position at a major suburban gas depot. He was a health fanatic. Every day he brought home-made salads for lunch and raisins and assorted nuts for morning and afternoon tea breaks. Eddy worked out at a local gym during most lunch times and often again after work. His muscular physique dampened derogatory remarks that a less formidable individual who lived on "rabbit food" may have had to endure. Eddy had an opinion on everything and made it known, loudly and at length to everyone he met. He spoke the Aussie language with a slight foreign account. Some of his co-workers called him a Hungarian Count. At least I think that's what they called him.

Amongst Eddy's duties was maintenance of the register of "unaccounted gas" that is, gas pumped into the local reticulation area for which payment was never capable of being received. Unaccounted for gas results from numerous small leaks, particularly in the older parts on the inner city system, where the aged bitumen seals on one hundred year old cast iron pipes allowed small escapes. Each small escape was not dangerous because the small amount of gas dispersed. Cumulatively the numerous escapes accounted for up to 3% of gas pumped into one of the larger ratings precincts. Small leaks are extraordinary difficult to detect.

So long as no great unexplained increase occurred within the regular survey period, no alarm was felt. But there were always penetrations of the gas reticulation system due to variety of causes; such as motor vehicle accidents that knocked down power poles the butts of which frequently fractured a gas pipe as the pole fell. Builders digging trenches with machinery often ruptured the gas system and sometimes burst water mains washed away the soil supporting a gas main and the sheer weight of the unsupported pipe caused a crack in tar filled joint seals.

Unaccounted for gas was also caused by thieves. They uncoupled the gas meter and joined the incoming gas service pipe directly to the resident's pipe system. A dangerous activity. Over the decades scores of would-be gas thieves have died through asphyxiation, burns or explosions. A successful by-pass meant free gas for the householder because the gas meter would not register any usage. Some thieves would reconnect the meter days before the meter reader called. They would go back to the by-pass once the meter was read. The premises of thieves had phenomenally low gas consumption. About 95% were caught and legal action for recovery of the estimated price of the stolen gas was instigated along with Police prosecutions. Some of the shoddy by-passes were terribly dangerous.

Most people never give a thought to the fact that domestic gas is an explosive substance and its use is controlled under State Law Explosive Substances Acts. Unauthorized tampering with a gas line is a criminal offense. Unauthorized tampering with a gas main and/or a service supply line can lead to lengthy jail terms. Twenty years for a main, up to ten for a service. Mains are buried under streets; service lines connect mains to consumers. Gas pressure differs greatly between mains and service lines.

In part, thieves were detected because of monitoring of the unaccounted gas in each locality. For inner city and suburban areas the survey was monthly. For outer-areas the survey period varied depending on the total area useage and varied from three to six months. Eddy participated in the suburban monitoring and recording. When a major rupture occurred he would be required to calculate the volume of the gas escape using a formula based on the size of the ruptured pipeline(main or service), gas pressure in the line at time of rupture and the time between the rupture and the shut-off valve closing down the supply of gas to that line. The calculation provided a reasonably accurate estimate.

Eddy appreciated that the weakest part of the estimate in the calculation formula was that of elapsed time – time leak happened – time leaked stopped. A few minutes variation made a difference in a calculation of the volume of escaped gas and hence its value. Even the most accurate Police reports contained a few minutes of time differences in accidents that resulted in gas escapes. And the time stipulated as "gas escape stopped" in the report of the gas company emergency crew could also be inaccurate by a few minutes.

When muscle-bound Eddy met Lucy at a Health Club it was love at first financial sight. Lucy was divorced and six years older than Eddy who had just attained the big "four o". Eddy's first marriage had failed 15 years ago. He seldom saw his two daughters and terminated all support services payments when his "ex" remarried. Since the break-up, Eddy had been in a dozen or more relationships but somehow that elusive element of stability never eventuated. Lucy had long legs, adequate breasts, small waist and a big bank account. No dependent children and, the clincher, in her divorce Lucy acquired ownership of a strata title apartment in a prestigious riverside block of 30 apartments all of which were connected to the gas system on a "common" basis.

The "common" gas basis meant that only one large gas meter existed for measuring gas used on the premises. A flat charge for gas heating was made based on the area of each apartment and gas hot water charges were calculated from water meters installed near the very large hot water system. In theory, the bulk useage of gas attracted a commercial tariff that allowed a lower cost per apartment even though some tenants may use a little more gas than others. (This system has since fallen into disfavour and only a few such connections now remain). The Body Corporate, the legal entity that managed the apartment block, allocated the gas costs per apartment. The gas company distributed bills using that allocation.

After a whirlwind courtship, probably not exceeding half a day, Lucy was besotted with her younger, heavily muscled lover. Eddy moved in with Lucy. At a poorly attended Body Corporate meeting a month or so later Eddy proposed and obtained permission to negotiate for a better gas deal, without disclosing that he was a gas company employee. Shortly thereafter each apartment owner / tenant received a letter, on gas company letterhead, to the effect that a new deal on gas prices was offered. A further 25% saving on the existing, low, bulk rate would be achieved if each owner / tenant paid cash to the collector who would call each month by prior appointment. It was emphasized the savings could only be given if every apartment in the complex participated. Being good neighbours to each other and always being keen on a discount, all owners eventually agreed. Eddy's road to riches had begun. So he thought.

He by-passed the large gas meter. It was a good, safe, professional by-pass and invisible to all but the closet scrutiny. As Eddy worked in an area where literally thousands of gas bills were processed monthly, his appropriation of a small quantity of blank bill forms went unnoticed. So each month thereafter, he sneaked away from work. He put on his gas company jacket, complete with company logo, and put "gas bills" with an inked rubber stamp "collectors calls (date)" under the door of each apartment in Lucy's residential block. The date being handwritten. There were a few hiccups but eventually most occupants of apartments simply left their gas bills and cash payments under door mats, ornamental plant pots or in mail boxes. They felt secure because they always received back the top part of the gas bill marked "paid" stamped with a gas company rubber stamp. Their savings were considerable. A 25% reduction for cash was a good deal.

Eddy easily covered the "unaccounted for" gas increase due to his by-pass on the large gas meter by altering rupture reports in the area by a few minutes whenever necessary. After sixteen months Eddy had sufficient capital for a deposit of 50% of the purchase price on a 4 bedroom house on the beach in the Melbourne suburb of Edithvale. The house was purchased in Lucy's name with a loan from a bank making up the total price. Rent received from tenants in the house plus his "gas bill" collection soon paid off the remainder of the mortgage.

Even with the best totally legal plan something always seems to go awry, however if it's legal the problem can be rectified. When the plan is illegal and it goes awry, rectification is improbable and retribution is most probable. Retribution, for Eddy, started innocuously with the owners of one of the apartments, a retired photographer and his wife. This sweet silver haired, socially responsible, elderly couple, planned to be away in South Australia for a fortnight. However with the emergence of the beautiful wildflowers in the famous Wilpena Pound in the Flinders Ranges National Park they stayed on an extra week, taking colour photographs.

When they returned they found their gas bill beneath the door and realised it was unpaid. Being concerned not to lose the generous discount for themselves and to avoid adverse ramifications for fellow residents, next morning the photographer took the gas bill direct to the gas company's head office in Melbourne. When he presented the bill and cash payment to one of the cashiers it created some confusion. Because the bill lacked certain information the cashier referred it to a supervisor. From there it went up the chain of responsibility until the experienced departmental Manager thought that it had the characteristics of a by-pass. At day's end a team of engineers were at the apartments to assess if a by-pass was in place and to eliminate any danger of fire or explosion. The by-pass was photographed. Copper pipes and brass fittings were carefully removed as evidence.

Investigators within the gas company swiftly tracked the type of blank gas bills to Eddy as did Police investigators who talked to other residents of the apartment block. Eddy heard by telephone from a distraught Lucy of the appearance of investigators. He fled his desk and escaped immediate apprehension. He hid out using a false name in a Motel in the Croydon area from whence he wrote a letter to the company giving fourteen days' notice of his resignation and stating that he would not return to work before then for "reasons associated with family". He requested that his superannuation resignation benefit and other company entitlements be paid to his bank account of which, incredibly, he provided details.

The letter was cunning. Whether by artifice or luck never became apparent. Like most superannuation funds in the early 19990's the resignation benefit for less than five years membership of the fund consisted of a refund of the member's own contributions plus interest thereon at a specified rate, at the time 5%, compounded annually. However after five years of contributing membership the above sum was increased by a share of the actuarial reserve, ie the accumulated investment assets. In Eddy's case, the financial difference in his superannuation payout, say one day before five years and one day after, amounted to $626.

Eddy was arrested by the Police in a pub near the Motel he had chosen as a bolt hole. Four charges were made initially but others followed. Cash, records, bank deposit books and blank gas account forms, left behind in haste in Lucy's apartment together with items he had carelessly left in his desk or locker at work sewed up that case against Eddy. And in his cunning / stupid letter of resignation, the details of his bank account were a pure gift to the Police.

The gas company suspended Eddy from work, on pay, for one week then dismissed him on advice from the company's lawyers on the day the Police laid criminal charges. No consideration at all was given to Eddy's superannuation entitlements in the process. Eddy's letter advising of resignation to take effect one week later was filed as being superseded by his dismissal. The company simply implemented its standard operating procedure upon detection of a thief. I won't go into detail of the company's and Police prosecutions of Eddy; suffice it to say he was jailed for a total of 5 ½ years and was lucky that several sentences were served concurrently otherwise he would have languished longer. The greatest part of Eddy's custodial sentence resulted from infringements to the Explosive Substances Act. If the by-pass had leaked and a tossed cigarette, for example, had sparked the high pressure gas of the single large meter for 30 units, the whole building could have blown up.

During the Police prosecution process, Eddy's retaliatory legal action was taken against the gas company and the superannuation fund. He claimed that he had been denied natural justice in that his dismissal from the company had taken place only a few working days short of him achieving five years of superannuation fund membership. Had his resignation letter, which pre-dated dismissal, been accepted he would have attained his five years of fund membership. As a matter of principle (Eddy, like most apprehended thieves was very intent upon matters of principle –

provided it was in his interest – and appeared oblivious to any hypocracy). He wanted "his" $626 plus a large slab of cash by way of penalty damages because denial of the payment had upset his feelings.

His claim had to be taken seriously and the company had to spend money on a legal defense while Eddy enjoyed the luxury of a Legal Aid funded complaint. From his prison cell and no doubt spurred on by fellow inmates intent on seeking revenge on society, Eddy's complaints grew to a ridiculous extent. Fortunately the case was resolved swiftly – about ninety five minutes in the Civil Division of the Magistrate's Court. In essence the judgment was that the exact date of Eddy's dismissal resulted from his own illegal actions. The company's actions were consistent with an established procedure and neither the company nor the superannuation fund had any legal or moral obligation to depart from that procedure to enable Eddy to benefit from a greater superannuation payout.

As a frame of reference, the 1993 estimated value of stolen gas was conservatively put at $48,000. Eddy was known to have collected $25,750 in cash. Legal fees for the gas company's defense were $5000. Eddy's Legal Aid case cost taxpayers $7,800, including the cost of his failed superannuation claim action. The house at Edithvale in Lucy's name could not be positively shown to have been purchased on the proceeds of crime so it could not be seized in restitution.

A word of advice, don't try to emulate Eddy by stealing gas. Detection systems, "smart" gas mains, and "sniffer" equipment installed and issued since 1994 can accurately pin point "unaccounted for" gas to within a few metres. Renovations of old gas pipes and new joints have reduced gas losses to a fraction of what it was once.

As an epilogue: Lucy waited until Eddy got out of prison after serving three years of his sentence. Lucy sold her apartment and the Edithvale house. Together they moved interstate to start a new life.

Bradley worked a gas meter reader for a municipal gas works in a large Northern England city from the day after he left school until the day before he migrated to Australia five years later. The day after he arrived in Australia he applied for a job as a meter reader at Victoria's largest gas corporation. With excellent credentials from his previous employer he got the job without any problem and began the induction course on the Monday of the following week. Bradley was a big lad, just over six feet tall in the imperial measurement (189 cm) and a solid frame that someone described as being that of "a study yeoman of England". He had red hair, light blue eyes and few doubted his claim to be descended from Viking stock.

Cricket was his passion and Dennis Compton his hero. He joined a cricket team in Melbourne's Western suburbs and rose by sheer dedication from the "thirds" to the "firsts" by middle of his first season. Bradley could be relied upon to bowl tirelessly all day at a good length and line as a medium fast bowler. His bowling average was 2. 5 wickets per game and he batted at number four, ending his first full season in the top team with the respectable batting average of 31.

Over the next five years Bradley achieved several milestones; he married Rosa, a second generation Australian/Italian girl for whom he would do "almost" anything. By "almost" it is meant that his innate sense of universally tolerable caused him to baulk at barracking for the Collingwood Football team. Instead he supported Carlton and praised their champion Silvagni. That appeared sufficient to Rosa's way of thinking for domestic harmony. Prior to meeting Bradley, Rosa had never seen a game of cricket and thought that "Cricket is like baseball on valium". But love conquers all and Rosa attended every one of Bradley's matches until the last few weeks before the birth of their first baby.

By that time Bradley had been so solidly propagandized as to be heard to concede that Australia's Cricket Captain, Allan Border, might be comparable with his boyhood hero Dennis Compton – an enormous concession for a Pommie; it surely marked the start of his conversion to being an Aussie. Bradley had to move his collection of cricket trophies out to the garage of his rental West Footscray house when Rosa presented him with a son as their second baby. More space was needed in their small house. That dark haired 18 month old daughter now had a red headed brother. The prospect of a future Aussie cricket captain in the family caused Bradley to surrender to the process of being totally Australianised.

So far, the world appeared grand to Bradley. He was saving for a deposit on a home of his own. He made application through the superannuation fund for a home loan and had applied for a more senior job in a rapidly developing area near Dandenong called Fountain Gate. New homes in a new estate were available at a price he could afford. Furthermore, when he made some tentative enquires about local cricket teams, he was flattered to find that his reputation had preceded him and several teams would welcome him with open arms.

Bradley was a reliable and observant meter reader and had detected and reported several unusual occurrences that led to prosecutions for gas thefts by persons illegally by-passing the meter (and in some cases the prosecutions resulted in other charges of interference with a dangerous substance under the Explosive Substances Act). Meter by-passing is often more prevalent in new estates so Bradley's application for a newly created senior meter reader position in a new area was viewed favourably and he was duly promoted. The home loan he applied for from the superannuation fund some 18 months earlier was now available. Bradley, Rosa, and their two young children moved into a brand new home within easy pram pushing distance of both Fountain Gate shopping centre and the local council's new recreation area with its magnificent football/cricket arena. In the off cricket season Bradley worked at home in the evenings to install a sprinkler system, sow a lawn, plant a garden and erect a DIY garage.

Then the cricket season arrived. Bradley trained with his new team. Somewhere, he could not recall later exactly how, the subject of home loans was raised and Bradley mentioned he had a loan from his superannuation fund at 7% p. a. with a repayment deducted fortnightly from his salary – so he had fortnightly rests on the interest. Other members of the team had loans upon which interest rates varied from 12% p. a. to 14% p. a. most with monthly and in one case, quarterly rests on the interest. Bradley had a far better loan by comparison.

Resentment exploded immediately among a group of five team members. These give-everyone-a-fair go Aussies were livid with envy at a Pommie who had scored a better deal than the "born here" locals. The resentment was particularly virulent with team members who held "white collar" jobs and felt superior to a "blue collar" worker. They felt they had a god-given right to treat a blue collar meter reader, especially a migrant, who spoke with a broad Yorkshire accent, as an inferior. Probably jealously of Bradley's superior cricket ability added to their warped actions.

The rotten core of five met after a game where Bradley had been the team's best player. They resolved to "take him down a peg" and over a few beers came up with a plan based on a recent newspaper report. The investigative journalist of a Melbourne daily newspaper had uncovered a real estate agent's dirty trick of selling a run down property at a high price with a low deposit and low weekly repayments subject to the purchaser restoring the property. The rent was supposed to convert to loan repayments when the renovations were done. Hidden in the fine print of the property sale contract were clauses permitting the agent (who it turned out was also the disguised vendor) to reclaim the property if the repayments fell into arrears or the property restoration did not meet certain standards or rate of progress.

After about 18 months, the purchasers, who the agent carefully selected for their vulnerability, were sky high in debt to suppliers of building materials and services to maintain the required rate of restoration progress. As reported in the newspaper article, the purchasers were also in arrears as to their weekly payments to the agent. He treated the arrears off-handedly for a month or so whilst urging more money be spent on renovations. At a time when the agent deemed he had soaked the vulnerable purchasers of as much as possible, the owner and his "strong-arm" associates evicted the purchasers. The purchasers lost their deposit, all loan "repayments" made plus the value of the extensive renovations. They were tossed out on the street without money or assets and still owned large sums in relation to the renovations. They became bankrupt, so the suppliers lost out too.

The agent however won enormously. He had turned a run-down dump of a house into something valuable which he sold at a handsome profit. The victims were the vulnerable purchasers and, of course, the suppliers who could not claim back from the agent the value of the electrical re-wiring or plumbing renewal that went into the house. According to the newspaper report, all debt was attributed to the unfortunate purchasers so no recovery from the unscrupulous agent was possible. The purchasers were recent migrants, a fact that was given such prominence as to later weigh heavily of Bradley. The law caught up with the crooked agent and his licence was revoked but, with the money he had available, he bought himself a top lawyer and so avoided any heavy penalty. Probably as a result of the media's condemnation of that real estate agent's actions, we now have laws that impose far tougher penalties for that type of behaviour.

Media reports of the agent's misdoings, trial and very light fine and Community Based Order as a trifling penalty formed the basis of the plot by the rotten core of cricketers to undermine Bradley. At every training session and at every match they spread their verbal poison, constantly referring to the case of the crooked real estate agent. At times other innocent parties were "inspired" to comment upon the real estate agent's rip-off of migrants. The rotten quirumvirate of cricketers either sensed a flaw in Bradley's personality or hit upon it by accident, but their unrelenting insistence to him that he was being set-up for a real estate fraud that would leave him and his family destitute began to materially affect Bradley.

For the first time, Bradley began to take days off work on sick leave. Bradley, Rosa and two children called in to the superannuation office to politely but firmly request to actually look at their loan account in the mortgage register. Never before had a borrower asked to see the records but the superannuation Manager gave Rosa photocopies of every document and thought little more of the event. A month later the fund Manager received a curious request from a Citizens Advisory Bureau acting for Bradley. They wanted the fund to send to Bradley by Registered Mail, without delay, a "solemn certification" providing full details of his mortgage account. The puzzled Manager responded with a copy of the relevant pages, each certified as being authentic by the superannuation fund auditors.

A similar request was received, shortly afterwards, accompanied by a letter of authorisation from Bradley, from a large Building Society. The tenor of the request indicated that Bradley may be switching his mortgage loan from the superannuation fund to that of the Building Society. Usually this indicated that the member had got another job and was "clearing the decks" before resigning. The superannuation fund staff briefly speculated that the new job would have to be good to compensate for the loss of a 7% mortgage rate when the Building Society rate was 12 ½ %.

Within days a third request was received from a lawyer representing Bradley demanding not only details of the Mortgage but a detailed and audited list of all of Bradley's entitlements from both the superannuation fund and the employer should his service to the Company end by way of resignation, dismissal, death or disability. That letter rang like a Toxin. Why so many enquiries? Was the request for "dismissal" benefits deliberately disguised amongst the request for other benefits? Had Bradley done something so seriously wrong that he was contemplating flight before the dark deed was discovered?

Enquires showed Bradley to be on sick leave. A Doctor's certificate was held in the Personnel Department. Was sick leave being used, as so often it is, as a prelude or mitigation for discovery of some fraud? Or was he in real difficulty? Bradley's Supervisor would not contemplate any consideration of any wrong doing. He trusted him implicitly. The company's Social Worker sought to visit but was refused an appointment by telephone. When she called at the home unannounced one evening, she was refused entry, an act totally uncharacteristic of the jovial Bradley and effervescent Rosa.

The superannuation fund Manager was astounded to receive a letter from yet another lawyer, also claiming to represent Bradley. This lawyer's letter contained an application for disability retirement for Bradley on the grounds of severe depression occasioned, it was claimed, by Bradley's belief that the superannuation fund intended to defraud him. The letter stated that the superannuation fund had not made sufficient effort to dispel Bradley's belief that he was being defrauded and so, it was claimed, the superannuation fund was culpable in contributing to Bradley's depression. Bradley's lawyer conceded that the superannuation fund could initiate its own action because it was being accused of fraud without a shred of evidence. But, it was claimed, the absence of fraud was not in dispute. Rather it was the negligence of Bradley's employer or, failing that, then the superannuation fund in not adequately dispelling Bradley's perception of fraud that was the germane issue.

What a load of crap. How does a superannuation fund dispel a misperception that it did not know existed and was held by only one of its thousands of contributors? The allegation had to be taken seriously lest the superannuation fund be sued. In accordance with established practice it was requested that medical evidence to support Bradley's claim be lodged directly with the Chief Medical Officer (CMO) of the company. The CMO read the psychiatrist's report that arrived a week later. From it the CMO advised that it appeared Bradley had a treatable form of depression with one of several possible causes, maybe, being his concern about the low interest on his loan from the superannuation fund. Obviously the fund could not agree to find favourably towards his application for total and permanent disability retirement when the illness had a high probability of complete recovery. Not could the superannuation fund accept any culpability for his depression. Bradley's disability claim was rejected.

An Inquiry Agent was engaged to check Bradley's meter reading route to see if anything there may have afflicted Bradley. It was from his comprehensive report that a hint of the action of Bradley's vicious cricket team mates emerged. Two were feeling ashamed for their actions. One refused all comment and two seemed pleased they had injured "the big Pommie". Bradley's lawyer made a lot of noise about an appeal to reverse the decision of the superannuation fund Trustees. It was later learnt that a Queen's Counsel was engaged by that lawyer to provide an Opinion in support of Bradley's claim. But the Opinion went the opposite way, which greatly surprised the Trustees because some lawyers seem adept at choosing QC's who opine in favor of the plaintiff. Bradley's claims were not pursued.

At the conclusion of his sick leave Bradley resigned, sold his home, at a good price, paid out the superannuation fund mortgage and returned to the UK. Six years later, with three children now, Rosa returned to Australia and a divorce became final shortly thereafter. Clearly Bradley had some predilection towards persuasion that may have been more acute than average. But the planned, malicious, concentrated plot of five educated, envious, false "friends" ignited a mental conflagration that destroyed a family. Only two of the five exhibited any true remorse. I resolved that if I could do a disservice to any or all of them I would not hesitate. To date I have not had the opportunity but I hope it will come. I never pretended to be perfect.

In the story of the unfortunate Bradley from Bradford I used the term "Pommie" and it is possible that some readers, imbued with over exuberance of political correctness may find my reference offensive. Tough luck it they do! My maternal Grandfather "Jack" Klukosky was a migrant. I still recall how proud he was of the Polish pilots of 609 RAF Squadron who flew their Spitfires so gallantly against the German Luftwaffe during the Battle of Britain in 1940.

And I vividly recall to this day the intensity of the hatred of Grandfather's Polish friends against Germany and Russia who divided and occupied their homeland; the Nazis murdering civilians under a black flag and the Communists murdering under a red flag. Grandfather's friends told me never to forget that the German aircraft smashing bombs into Britain, the homeland of my Father's family, were flying on Russian petrol from May 1940 to June 1941.

As for my use of the term "Pommie" (which derives, so I've read, from the early convict description of "Prisoner of Mother England" P. O. M. E.) I feel entitled to use it because I am descended from Pommie migrants. My paternal grandfather came from Canterbury, Kent, UK. In Canterbury High Street stands the "Alfred Cooper Centre" – dedicated to my great uncle a decorated artist, and built by James G Beany, a surgeon, politician and philanthropist born in Canterbury in 1828. Dr Beaney migrated to Australia and was an early benefactor of the Pipeclay Club the forerunner of the Naval & Military Club, of which I was a member. Being a descendant of migrants I feel racially eligible to disregard political correctness in my terminology.

Chapter Fourteen

Stultifying Statistics

SUPERANNUATION IS BASED ON STATISTICS. Contributor turnover due to resignation, retirement, disability and death are factors that determine the investment portfolio profile. Incidence of dismissal is so small as to be ignored. Law enforcement agencies throughout the world use forms of profiling developed with input from many Universities and Criminology entities and codified by the Federal Bureau of Investigation in the United States of America. Vastly exaggerated in movies and TV but never-the-less sound, though not infallible, profiling is an excellent investigative aid. Meticulous analysis of crime scenes provides behavioral characteristics that may lead to apprehension of an alleged offender.

In the 1980's I managed a Semi Government superannuation fund and was asked by an elected Trustee, a scientist, if, in view of what seemed to be an increase in problems with contributors, it was possible to identify "problem persons" in advance of a problem arising. The Trustee suggested that I report on this matter without too much formality, by which, he explained, I need not include the "usual mass of statistics" that inevitably are given in support of any premise from which conclusions may be drawn. He sought only a conclusion and recommendation.

To properly meet the request the first thing to be defined was just what constituted a "problem person". Many contributors have gripes about certain sections of the fund rules but rather than being "problem people" they are inspirations to change, to keep the fund modern, meeting the contemporary needs of its members within the framework of the various Laws applicable to superannuation. Defining a "problem person" is to a large degree a matter of opinion and that being so the survey period chosen was from the day of my appointment as Manager of the fund, a period of 11 years. Any bias that I have should thus be more likely to be uniform for the period and allowance made for it.

The chosen definition resulted from what turned out to be an intense meeting of Trustees convened with only one agenda item, that of a workable definition of a "problem person". The final selection was "a Contributor against whom the fund takes Police or legal action or against whom a serious threat of such action is made as a defensive move. " For example, those persons who threaten legal action if a disability benefit is not paid and the fund takes or threatens action because it has reason to suspect a fraud, most often by way of an altered, counterfeit or fraudulently obtained Doctor's certificate or false statements made on medical reports. No matter how much abuse a member may direct at the superannuation fund staff, he or she is not classified as a "problem person" until a solicitor or politician makes a formal representation on behalf of that person.

Comment on the results of the survey. The average had been 0.091% "problem persons" per year of total membership for six years and thereafter 0.094% per year for the next five. The increase in actual numbers, not percentage, coincided with the introduction of a non-staff section of the fund. The proportion by which "problem persons" increased was exactly the same in relation to non-staff members as had previously existed for staff members. Both staff and non-staff "problem persons" had increased in the last two years and the percentage of actual members enrolled who pose problems was now 0. 13%. I felt that the increasing number of challenges reflected a change in the mood of society in general, more assertive, more inclined to question.

This extraordinary low figure highlighted two matters. Firstly, that the incidence of "problem persons" in the fund was so low as not to warrant any major changes in procedures at present. Secondly, the incidence was astoundingly low compared with funds of a similar membership and composition. These two matters, led me to conclude that it was precisely because of the rarity of challenges that they receive perhaps an undue emphasis. In some similar funds, challenges by "problem persons" are so frequent as to be routine. If present trends in other funds continued and "challenging your superannuation fund" becomes a national sport; like Income Tax evasion in English speaking countries and revolutions in South American countries; then this fund may need to recruit a lawyer because some of our members will certainly follow the fashion and involve the fund in litigation with costs to the detriment of the majority of contributors.

Four pages of statistics were compiled profiling male and female problem persons. The report was prepared with the help of an Actuary and the Personnel Manager. The Chairman of the fund thought it was great. He wanted to use it to exclude people who complied with the profile from employment. He thought it so great that he gave a copy to the Member of Parliament who was our responsible Minister.

The Minister read it and was appalled. He ordered immediate destruction of the report and that each person involved in compilation of the report, including the typists, be ordered to provide a written statement to the Chairman that they had not kept a copy. He personally phoned to tell me that if I discussed the report's content with anyone, especially the media, he would sack me.

Wow! What a reaction. I concluded that his political supporters and constituents met the criteria of the defective people described in the report. Or maybe it was him.

Premature Inheritance

Albert Einstein said:-"The difference between genius and stupidity is; genius has its limitations".

In his early forties he was smartly dressed, well groomed and pleasantly spoken as we exchanged introductory greetings on the way from the reception area to my office. On first name terms from the start, he was Keith; he politely thanked me for agreeing to see him on short notice. From his expensive briefcase he produced papers and family photographs, each separate batch of papers neatly contained in coloured plastic folders.

From his expensive leather wallet a driver's licence. He politely handed items to me in a logical sequence and waited patiently as I read or looked at each. These proved him to be the son of one of our company's longest serving and highly respected mid-management chief clerks.

Keith's father loved his job and with retirement looming had advantaged himself of the company's Retirement Counselling Program. In the methodical manner that earned respect from his colleagues during his career, Keith's father spent several months of spare time planning his retirement. Many of his friends at all levels throughout the company shared the infectious pleasure that seemed to resonate in happiness waves from Keith's father at his approaching retirement. Selfishly, some were secretly apprehensive about his successor who appeared to be a person of lesser caliber and likely to cause them problems. Any shock of realizing that the "big day" was swiftly approaching all too soon disappeared as he and his wife planned the adventures that full time work, financing, raising and expensively educating a family had precluded.

I jumped to the conclusion that Keith's visit was connected with the preparations just underway for his father's retirement send-off party. Keith's pedantic method of proving his relationship with his father seemed a bit extreme, but initially raised no suspicion only a vague uneasiness. Many times in my life I have been wrong. If goes with the territory of being human. This was another astray moment, but it took a little while before I realized my misjudgment. I'm a bit slow sometimes, that also goes with the territory because I instinctively trust people.

Keith was not interested in his father's farewell. He was only interested in his father's money. What struck me most about Keith was the rapid changeability in his voice and attitude. Looking me straight in the eye he said in a low, stern, tone that he wanted details of all of his father's financial entitlements. Then in an abrupt, whining voice he told me that his father refused to give him any details and that he had a right to obtain information about his inheritance. Before I had fully grasped his supplication request his entire demeanor altered again. In louder tones and increasingly overbearing, he stood to his full 185 centremetres (6 foot, 1 inch) and said that photographs, his driving licence, etc, comprehensively proved his identity so I must comply with his demand, or face legal action that would surely have me dismissed from my job. The import of his words took a few seconds to penetrate my brain and be interpreted.

Even then I was not sure I had fully understood and politely asked him for a repeat. My request seemed to indicate to him that I was mentally deficient so he repeated his demand at greater volume, slowly, with every word clearly articulated as if giving instructions to a retarded child. He showed a total absence of any reticence or embarrassment when using the words "his inheritance". The first question that came to my mind was "Why won't your father tell you about his retirement benefit?", and when I asked this he leaned aggressively forward, both hands clenched into fists on my desk, head thrust forward, the voice deepend and he told me that he was the one with the prerogative to ask questions. He said "You are just a Government Employee and, as such, responsible to the public". As a member of the public that gave him superior status to compel me to answer his questions, not ask them of him.

Only three other people have been so insufferably rude to me in that way in my career in superannuation. In each case their rudeness was designed to provoke me into a reaction advantageous to themselves and adverse to me. I fell for it the first time years ago and suffered. Once bitten twice shy. To my mind Keith's threat and attempted denigration of me made him an immediate enemy and in the Army my instructors in tactics taught me that to attack an enemy head on was inevitably costly. It is far better it distract the enemy in some way, then to hit him with a surprise attack from the rear or from a flank. With Keith standing 10 centimetres (4 inches) taller than me that thought had considerable attraction. A piece of advice I had taken to heart was a saying attributed to that magnificent British actor, the late Robert Morley, who allegedly said "You catch more flies with honey than you do with vinegar". I'm going to buy a copy of his diet book one day.

My response to Keith's rudeness was to be silent. Ticking over in the back of my mind were the suspicions that maybe Keith might be suffering a schizoid fit and, alarmingly that he was scheming to collect "his inheritance" far earlier than his father intended to relinquish it. Should I warn the father? If so, what could I say without causing family disruption? I needed more tangible evidence of Keith's intentions before shooting off my mouth. So I remained silent. It's not easy but once you learn to do it you have a marvellous asset. I adopt what I refer to as my "Buddah Pose".

An inscrutable gaze with fingers folded over my ample stomach and totally immobile. Some people have been rendered into gibbering idiots after two minutes of confrontation with this pose.

Keith appeared to assume that my silence indicated over awed consent to his demand. He was not rendered helpless and immobile, much to my disappointment. His questions continued and were specific about the annual value of his father's pension, how the pension could be 100% commuted to a lump sum, what tax would be deducted, how much was his father's unused long service leave, annual leave, severance pay, how much of the total amount could be paid in cash and how much by cheque. He continued in a commanding tone through the long list, now seated with a pen poised to record the answers he expected from me.

After a further full minute of silence, rather than ask him any question I told him that all payments were made by direct credit to the bank account of the ex-employee on the next business day following his or her retirement date. I said it in almost a whisper. Keith was upset about the direct credit. He wanted to know how he could change the procedure, so again I whispered that he must speak with one of the fund Trustees. The point in whispering was that it made Keith put his unprotected head forward. My right hand now rested on a heavy sticky tape dispenser. I mentioned that the company Secretary was a Trustee and offered to make an appointment for Keith to meet with him. Keith accepted without hesitation. With relief I then ushered Keith out of my office with no other information whatsoever, except with the promise to telephone to arrange a mutually convenient time for a meeting between Keith and the company Secretary. Obviously his expectations were greater than they should have been at the words I used, but I was unmoved to provide clarification.

The company Secretary was indeed a Trustee of the Fund. He was also a qualified lawyer. We both served as officers in the Citizens Military Forces, CMF (now Army Reserve) him in the Infantry, me in Artillery. I called to see him to discuss the situation and obtain the benefit of the thoughts of a legally trained person. After listening and questioning he readily agreed to meet Keith. He told me it would likely be a short meeting before he "threw the bugger out" I felt good about that; it's marvellous to find a legally trained person who also has common sense.

Together we spent some time drawing up a series of questions for the Trustee to ask Keith to try to determine Keith's intentions. We agreed that unless the Trustee uncovered something he considered damaging in discussion with Keith, we could not approach the father. But I was advised to dictate a memorandum of the meeting with Keith for the records, just in case. That was done in the form of a Statutory Declaration, witnessed and put on file, but with the fervent hope it need never be used.

In the event, we need not have worried. The father called in unexpectedly at my office a couple of days later and without any preliminary greeting, which was most unusual, asked straight out in a worried tone if Keith had visited me and what had Keith been told. I replied "Yes" and "absolutely nothing". With a very unhappy face, the father thanked me, apologised for Keith's behaviour and left. Keith never turned up for his appointment with the company Secretary, nor did he phone to cancel it. I never saw or heard from Keith again. At the father's retirement party a couple of weeks later, it was obvious that he felt awkward in my presence so after one drink a quick hand shake and offer of "best wishes" I left early. The remainder of the party went off very well I was told.

The action of Keith is not that unusual. In over forty years as a Manager or Trustee in four different superannuation funds I, or some of my senior colleagues, encountered half a dozen people who were convinced that the superannuation entitlements of a parent rightfully belonged to them. Every family tree has some sap.

My position regarding inheritance is that in world history, inheritance is a novelty that was once the exclusive privilege of a very small number of wealthy people. In Britain and a few other countries, Primogeniture, the birthright of the first born to inherit the family estate, was not a discriminatory "gift" so much as an attempt to preserve intact the "tribal" asset. It was very much in the nature of a contract between generations to shield, preserve or expand the wealth of the family or tribal unit in perpetuity. Many historians assert that Primogeniture amongst the Normans resulted in so many second, third and fourth son warriors without family estates that to keep these warriors out of mischief at home, their fighting abilities were directed towards foreign conquests. Hence the invasion of Britain in 1066 and parts of the Mediterranean shores around the same time. A method of by-passing ancient traditional Primogeniture is detailed in the Bible. Try Genesis Chapter 27.

Today our thinking about inheritance had changed or should have changed. Wealth is far more widely available, albeit somewhat more modestly than that of the "Pharaohs", the "Medieval Popes", the "Indian Moghuls", the "Industrial Revolution Merchants" or the "Computer Technologists" of today and, of course, former Prime Ministers of some countries.

Notwithstanding that enormous broadening of the "wealthy class", many heirs still impatiently covet an inheritance, focusing upon being the recipient of bequests with little consideration they may one day be the bestower of a bequest. Many kill to achieve inheritance. Arsenic once had the nick-name of "inheritance powder".

Greedy grabbers need to be told that inheritance is not an entitlement. I have done my share of trying to disseminate that message but I am aware from questions asked, that only the decent, responsible members of the community will understand it. The greedy will still covet cash they have never earned.

The Big Break

Buckets of tears all this week. At home as well as the office. Carol was leaving after 14 years. Her husband, an Industrial Chemist, was promoted Vice President of a Canadian company. Carol and he were going to live in Montreal. Carol had three send off functions; 100 plus in the company board room, 20 plus at my Club and the last with her husband and my family at my home.

I dithered about a replacement. I wouldn't steal one of the wonderful secretaries of any of my six section Managers. Instead I employed temporaries from an executive agency for seven weeks while I tried to resign from the company. I wanted to run my own outfit. Carol's departure did not precipitate my move but it was an influential factor. I accepted the offer of the company Chairman. A consultancy that included my appointment as a Trustee of the fund I had managed for 20 years. I suspect he had a hand in my being offered two other paid superannuation trusteeships, one of a government and the other of a large industrial company. I discretely advertised my services as a "Private Detective" working exclusively in the superannuation industry by direct visits to prospective clients. I got a lot of knock backs, met some very nice people as well as scathing skeptics and had to ward off depression, but persistence pays and at the end of a long seven months my first three retainers were from two banks and a large insurance company. A prime factor in every service contract was total confidentiality.

Assertiveness

Ten centuries after the Vikings, the Northmen, ceased raiding Britain, the Book of Prayer of the Anglican Church still contains an entreaty to the Lord to preserve believers from those raiders. I totally identify with the spirit of that prayer save that I substitute for "Northmen" the words "people who have attended Assertiveness Training Courses". As Vikings were a scourge to the Britons, so graduates of Assertiveness Courses were to me. Assertiveness training courses are probably great for mentally balanced people who benefit from learning techniques designed to correct minor deficiencies within their personalities.

But it seems to me that people who have some personality imbalance misinterpret the aim of assertiveness training. And it also seems to me that a disproportionate number of people with personality defects are attracted to assertiveness courses. It tips them even further from equilibrium. With disequilibrium comes delusion. Delusional superannuation contributors seem convinced that superannuation Managers are fair game. Several threatened to have me sacked unless I would instantly accede to their demands. No matter that the demands be illogical, illegal or in breach of the Trust Deed.

During my years in superannuation, I was threatened with dismissal a dozen times. Many of those people appeared at first sight balanced, but each betrayed their delusion as soon as each opened their mouth. And usually they opened their conversation by announcing that they were graduates from an Assertiveness Training Course. If the declaration was an attempt at intimidation it failed. Oh how I loathed that type of announcement as it inevitably preceded a demand for something screwball that would advantage the assertive announcer and disadvantage everyone else.

Dion was employed for such a short time that a contribution to the superannuation fund of his employer had not yet been deducted from his salary. Dion telephoned to request an appointment and was invited to my office later that day. He was somewhat casually dressed, probably just complying with the lower limit of the company's acceptable dress code. He declined to sit but as I sat he put both hands on my desk, learned forward and with a penetrating look from beneath abundant eyebrow told me that he had just completed an Assertiveness Course at the Citizen's Centre in Box Hill. "Bloody hell", I thought, "another nutter". I am sure I instinctively winced.

From his facial expression and body language it was obvious that he thought his statement would shock or intimidate me, so he further asserted himself by talking the visitor's chair from in front of my desk and moving it so it was on my side of the desk. A rude and threatening gesture, encroaching into my space. He was right – I was threatened by his action, I missed his next few words whilst I quickly worked out how best to physically immobilise the bastard should he become violent. As I recall, this quickly contrived plan involved my stamping the left heel of my solid brogue shoe on the canvas top of his right trainer shoe whilst my right hand picked up the heavy sticky tape dispenser and hit the right side of his head with a force I hoped would not be lethal. I have a penchant for sticky tape dispensers. If he detected any change in my demeanour he clearly misinterpreted it as awe in his presence, because he demanded that I immediately give to him a copy of the fund's $980 million investment portfolio.

Painful personal experience and the observation of others taught me that when confronted with weirdoes it is best to contemplate a protective plan as a shield should the weirdo become violent. Otherwise to speak as little as possible until the full story is laid out or the nut case runs out of puff. Accordingly I inclined my head, smiled as well as I could and opened my hand as if to encourage further conversation. It worked. Dion, it turned out, was anti-war, anti-nuclear, anti-logging, anti-alcohol and anti-commercial medicine. He was for organic food, free love anywhere and anytime and free marihuana. He told me that his group intended to do away with all Police forces, law courts and lawyers. He wanted the portfolio to see if the superannuation fund had investments in any of the activities he was anti.

Dion stared into my eyes from a range of about 25 cm (10 inches) and told me that if any such investments were discovered, he would initiate action for my immediate dismissal and impeachment before the Parliament of the Trustees. I was shocked. Not by what he said but by his bad breath and watery eyes. I guess I flinched. Encouraged by my reaction he stood up and began a tour, reading aloud my framed qualification certificates hanging on the office walls, the fund's company registration certificate and peering at memorabilia on my bookshelf as if he were Sherlock Holmes looking for clues about a crime. He curled his lip at the photo of my wife and children and ranted for a few minutes about the disadvantages of marriage.

I let him walk around a bit; anything to get his bad breath away from me, then told him that the standard operating procedures of the fund required that requests for portfolio information must be in writing addressed to the Chairman of Trustees of the superannuation fund and state the reasons for the request. He was advised that our portfolio was only otherwise released on a commercial-in-confidence basis to our panel of brokers or to consultant actuaries employed to advise the fund. I smilingly suggested that he leave my office so he could begin to write his request and I rose and opened the door to remove any impediment to his departure.

He did leave, and his parting words were that, because of my refusal to comply with his request, immediately, I should contemplate being sacked very shortly. How he intended to achieve that he declined to say. Over the next few months he verbally sought a copy of the portfolio several times, each time threatening to use his influence to have me sacked for refusal to "comply with the demands of the workers". Dion refused to put his request in writing. He claimed that to do so could be construed as cooperating with the establishment's system of control of the workers, and he was anti-establishment. He continually reminded me that he was a graduate of an Assertiveness Course.

I doubt he knew the meaning of work. In his late twenties, he had no qualifications, no assets, and no focus in his life and, in my opinion, no ability to achieve anything worthwhile. If the company had not been growing so rapidly and in need of more employees, I doubt he would ever have got the job, he tried to stir up trouble with the employees in his own section and with his Union but got nowhere. Dion told the on-site Union Representative that paying Union fees contravened his beliefs, he joined under sufferance. The member-elected Trustees of the superannuation fund held positions in some of the Unions and they were not keen for delusional Dion to get his hands on the investment portfolio. Eventually it was Dion who was sacked not me. His pre-marihuana leanings caused him to be absent, late and accident-prone when "high" once too often. His fellow workers were pleased when he left as he was anti-soap and anti-water too.

The Trustees resolved not the make the fund's share portfolio generally available because past experience of doing so caused problems. They had once included it with the quarterly report to members. Some members passed it on to Brokers who inundated us with advice to sell or buy. Much of the advice looked like "churning" designed more for the benefit of Broker's commissions than for the benefit of the fund. A Manager just cannot cope with thirty Brokers all giving advice that was often contradictory. The superannuation fund settled on a panel of five. We reviewed the panel annually based on the success or otherwise of the advice they gave and dropped the worst performer off and appointed one new Broker each year. That way we spread our business around and introduced new tactical investment techniques whilst maintaining our strategic aim. We made the Brokers accountable for the advice.

It must have worked because when I left the superannuation fund, of which I was General Manager for nearly 25 years, it had a robust actuarial surplus. Indeed within its industry group it was the only fully funded fund to be solvent.

Another natural idiot who believed surviving an Assertiveness Course was a pre-requisite to domination of the populace was, let's call him Lionel.

A mediocre white goods appliance salesman, Lionel, lived with his wife and one young child in the suburban home of his wife's parents. They loved their daughter, idolised their granddaughter and tolerated him, just. In a laudable attempt to better himself Lionel attended evening classes in salesmanship, but he seemed unable to fully comprehend the finer points or unable to apply the lessons to any great effect because his sales performance never significantly increased. Lionel became frustrated at his inability to improve his sales and one manifestation was an urge to leave the city and relocate to a country area. It seemed that he had sublimated aspirations to be a big frog in a little pond.

Perhaps he also wanted to get away from his in-laws. He applied several times for sales jobs in suburban branch offices of the large company but was by-passed because, he thought; his technique at the job interview was inadequate. Determined to improve his prospects Lionel enrolled in a twelve week "Self Assertiveness" course. A good idea, because "education is no load to carry" as my Mum told me when I was young. (My Mum's advice was good except for one item. That involved me purchasing a bust of Beethoven because Mum said I must get ahead in life).

Towards the end of the assertiveness course, Lionel went for another interview; a sales job in a sizeable country town. He was successful. There were several other applicants and Lionel's success cemented into his mind that assertiveness worked. He applied himself ever more diligently to the assertiveness course homework required for the last couple of sessions. But, as mentioned in connection with a salesmanship course, Lionel, regrettably, always seemed to get the wrong slant on some aspects of the teaching. And so it was that he saw assertiveness as his key to solving every problem in his life.

And he did have problems because, as he had been unexpectedly successful in obtaining the new job, he now had to move out of the home of his in-laws and find accommodation for himself, his wife and young child in a sizeable country town that he had never visited before. He had not given any thought at all to a residential relocation. Some might say that Lionel was adventurous; others less charitable might say he was stupid. If you subscribe to the stupid assessment then you support my contention about attendees at assertiveness courses. Lionel had about three weeks to find suitable shelter before starting as the new area salesman.

His employer generously granted him time off on pay to scout out a new home. Lionel and his wife spent a day looking around and concluded that no existing home available in the country town suited the lifestyle to which they intended to become accustomed. They found a vacant block in the area they liked and that very day impulsively committed their entire savings to purchase that land. They decided to build a new home using the land value as part of the security for a building loan from a bank. Lionel decided he would reside in a local boarding house pending completion of the building of their family dream home. His wife and child would remain at the home of the wife's parents in the meantime. Lionel would accept the inconvenience of driving four hours back to the city at weekends to visit him family.

So far all appeared more or less manageable – some risk and some sacrifice are often rewarded later. As a domestic appliance salesman, cookers, hot water services and room heaters, he had contact with builders' From somewhere he obtained copies of an Architect's plan for a large house. Lionel and his wife fell in love with the plan. They tackled the task to estimate the finance required to acquire their dream. Sadly the estimate revealed that the total cost of the expensive new home outstripped Lionel's ability to meet the repayments on the bank loan in a climate where the prevailing home loan interest rate was 12%. He was loath to compromise on size, design and fitting of his dream home, or to consider building it in stages. He wanted his dream to be fulfilled and he wanted it now. Most of us can empathise with him in wanting to achieve a dream.

Sometimes you just have to compromise, at other times you can succeed simply because you refuse to compromise. Part of success in life is recognising the times when one should compromise and not compromise. Lionel saw his problem as being the cost of construction. He concluded that if he were to be the builder, that is, if he coordinated the work and placed sections to contractors, he could save a sizeable amount of money. So he bought a "self help" manual on how to build a house. Lionel was courageous, ambitious and definitely moving out of his comfort zone – good luck to him – so far.

About the time Lionel was wrestling with this problem, the superannuation fund Annual Report to members was distributed. For several decades the Trustees of the fund had allocated a fixed percentage of the total amount of investment finances for home loans to contributors. The pre-requisites and procedures for lending were well and clearly communicated to members in half yearly reports. The main sections are summarised as follows:-

A contributor to the fund must have a minimum of three years membership prior to becoming eligible to submit a home loan application request and first mortgage security was essential.

1. Applications to be considered, when a member became eligible, may be lodged with the fund. All are dated, numbered in order of receipt and sent on the same day to the fund's Legal Office, together with copies of relevant documents.
2. The loan to the contributors must not exceed 66% of the valuation of the house and land as valued by one of the panel of independent valuers, approved by the fund.
3. Loans are made only on completed dwellings which are owner occupied (ie no holiday homes or investment properties) and for which a Certificate of Occupancy issued by the relevant municipal authority was issued (ie the fund will provide no bridging finance).

The effect of the rules resulted in, on average, the time between lodgment of an application for provision of the finance and actual payment being 14 – 18 months. This meant that the contributor who received a loan had around 4 ½ years of service with the parent company before receiving a loan. That period of service was viewed as a comfort to the Trustees who were disinclined to make low interest loans available to persons who departed the employer's employee after a short time. The loans were genuinely low interest and much sought after as the interest rate was 7% p. a. compared with the currently obtainable bank first mortgage loan rate of 12% p. a.

Lionel's brain slipped into top gear when he read the interest rate in the Annual Report. With him being his own developer thus resulting in a lower cost for his dream home plus a 7% rate of interest he convinced himself that his dreams for a 30 square 2 storey, triple car garage residence was achievable. The only three hurdles appeared to be the superannuation fund "waiting list" of 14 – 18 months and the fact that he had less service by 11 months than that required for being eligible to lodge his loan application, and that loans were only made for completed residences. But to a man with dreams and an assertiveness course under his belt, these hurdles were trifling.

Lionel phoned for an "urgent" appointment with me, as fund Manager, on the grounds that he had to travel down from the country. He was adamant that he had to meet me face to face – the telephone was not acceptable to him, he said. Being a reasonable kind of chap I offered to meet him at our most Northern suburban branch to save him an hour of travel. I'm like that, cooperative. Bad mistake. In the assertiveness course Lionel had learned the positive power of dominating voice inflection. Lionel was employing his voice inflection technique over the telephone and my offer to save his travel time convinced him that he had achieved moral superiority over me and that Lionel's dominance had compelled me to offer to reduce his travel time. I'm really a dill because I did not detect his "power voice" technique. If I had given it any I thought, I would have guessed it was a bad line and he sounded a bit distorted.

So Lionel, his confidence boosted by his first" win," met me, gave me the full force of his dominant handshake (which again I did not notice because I have a fairly large hand) and proceeded to loudly tell me that he was an Assertiveness Training Course graduate. I think I shuddered and stifled a groan at what I knew would follow, ranting from a relentless ratbag! But I had agreed to meet him and so I must endure. He told me what he intended to do and what he expected me to do to ensure his demands were met. Lionel told me that he wanted an immediate loan by way of bridging finance to be drawn in installments each time the value of the progressively erected building warranted.

During the course of our one hour discussion I iterated and reiterated, in increasingly firmer tone, that home loans were limited, time in service counted, other members were waiting so must he, no queue jumping was allowed. Lionel attempted to denigrate me by claiming that he was positive, I was a negative and that the positive must prevail. The fund only loaned on completed dwellings, I stressed many times, all apparently to no avail: I could not politely find a chink in the "Assertiveness Armour" upon which Lionel replied to obtain immediate bridging finance in preference to other employees in the queue.

After an hour I realised I was talking to an egocentric nutcase at least as far as his "assertiveness" attitude was concerned. My last words to him were that he must wait his turn. Under no circumstances would he be permitted to jump the queue. He must not rely upon an immediate loan. The incomplete loan application he claimed he sent to my office the day before, but which I had not seen, would not be processed for about 2 ½ years. Lionel's parting word to me (no thanks for saving his time at the expense of my time) were that his superior determination would prevail, even if it caused me to become unemployed. Faced with that attitude can you blame me for contending that it be compulsory for all Assertiveness Courses to conclude with a session on the attractiveness of voluntary euthanasia?

Later that evening Lionel told a work mate that he was a mentally stronger person than me. How often is tolerance mistaken for weakness? Despite my sternly delivered caution about precipitate actions, within a week Lionel went to a timber yard in the country town with copies of the house plans and materials quantity schedule. He ordered a "house lot" of timber, including orders for the special windows, the semi-circular internal staircase and three extra-wide automatic roller doors for the garages. Lionel showed the timber merchant a copy of the superannuation fund home loan application, claiming it was an approval. He signed the timber merchant's delivery contract. On the "payment" section of the contract he wrote – "finance to be provided on request after delivery of ordered items by superannuation fund "and signed it. Only a raving ratbag would do that!

The first I heard about this action was many weeks later when the fund's Accountant brought in the timber merchant's invoice and request for payment. The Accountant said she was puzzled. When I read it I was furious. Enquires were made with the timber merchant and I told him that payment was refused. I did not try to talk to Lionel, rather I handed the matter to the Legal Office. Lionel was informed via a registered mail letter from our company's Legal Office that he was ineligible for a loan. Especially without prior valuation and without any paperwork and that if he sought to involve the fund in any expenses, then legal action against him would be undertaken.

In total defiance of the printed rules, Lionel's reply came via a lawyer in the country town who claimed a verbal contract existed because I, the fund Manager, had promised Lionel the money. My failure to honour my "promise' clearly made me a reprehensible person who deserved to be sacked. But even the country lawyer must have known that his client was on shaky ground. That letter was a bluff. Whenever a lawyer claims that you are "reprehensible" take heart, it means he hasn't got a fact to fan his face with. The letter ended with the claim that I was guilty of "reprehensible conduct". All up, three reprehensibles! Not bad for a bush lawyer.

Lionel's claim was a ridiculous lie. He was floating in a cloud of dreams and misplaced reliance on his assertiveness-induced moral superiority. I felt sorry for him at first, but not too sorry, because any allegations by a contributor meant that I was suspended, on pay, until the matter was resolved. I took these lying allegations very seriously because I treasured my reputation, who doesn't? Lionel persisted with his false claims. In a short time I looked at Lionel as my enemy. The head of the company's external auditor firm conducted the investigation. It took three days to gather and process all information. One question he asked was "Qui Bono" "Who benefits?" Only Lionel. There was no benefit for me whether I had promised Lionel or had not promised. The auditors reported to the Trustees that Lionel was unreliable, untruthful and seeking to gain an advantage without consideration of his reckless and mendacious assertions. A good decision. I was immediately reinstated.

The company Legal Office was asked to consider whether or not Lionel's actions were grounds for dismissal or even Police intervention. It is noteworthy to mention that Lionel had reported his grievance to his Union and several members to the Union executive conducted their own independent enquiry. Over 200 members of that Union had home loans with another 15 on the waiting list. Four contributor/unionists were due for loans in the next couple of months. Lionel was trying to push in ahead of them. The brief report to the Union main committee was "Lionel is a bloody lying bastard and we recommend no Union support for him".

Lionel had a dream and nothing was going to stop his attainment of that dream by fair means or foul. The damning reports of auditors, refusal of support from his Union were shrugged off by him as irrelevant. He wanted something and was determined to get what he wanted. His assertiveness training caused him to believe in success if he persisted. Whist the Legal Office were contemplating Lionel's dismissal, he lodged a claim with the State Discrimination Tribunal. The basis of the claim was religious discrimination against the company, the superannuation fund and, of course, me.

To better explain the basis of Lionel's shoddy claim, I state that for many years I was a director of the Early Planning for Retirement Association

(EPRA) which owed its establishment in a large part to the Secretary of the State Electricity Commission (SEC) Superannuation Fund, Stuart Morris, Jim Peddlesden of ACOSS (now COTA), Sir Willis Connolly, Chairman of the SEC, Murray Buxton of McPhersons Ltd, plus others. I was privileged to be in that exalted company and to be a foundation director of EPRA. In that role I organized "Retirement Counselling" meetings throughout Victoria; in fact EPRA even had a film made. It was entitled "The Big Day" and I had a speaking part in it.

One of these EPRA meetings was an "Open to the Public" meeting in Dallas Brooks Hall, Masonic Centre, East Melbourne. The hall was packed. Around 2200 people attended. Sir Rupert Hamer, the State Premier, was in the audience as a special guest and I was the principal speaker on the financial aspects of retirement. Being near the "first" in retirement counselling, meant that the event attracted got a lot of publicity. The Masonic Lodge publication "The Mason" devoted several pages to reports about the meeting conducted in their venue including my part as the speaker on finance. The report mentioned that I was a Freemason.

Lionel obtained a copy of "The Mason" and using that as a basis concocted a story that I had unlawfully discriminated against him by refusing his loan application solely because he was a member of the Roman Catholic Church and I was a Mason. He telephoned me and offered to drop his religious discrimination action if he was granted an immediate loan. I told him what he could do with his offer and reported his telephone call to the Legal Office. Despite the telephone record, Lionel denied that it occurred.

Lionel lodged a complaint and I was summonsed to appear at a hearing. The members of the Government Discrimination Tribunal listened to Lionel's argument for about 25 minutes. He was alone. His parish priest declined to speak on his behalf. The Tribunal was not impressed so Lionel's "assertive" techniques must have waned. The employer / fund lawyer spoke in my defense, for about seven minutes. She distributed copies of Lionel's incomplete and undated loan application, the fund rules, the timber merchants' account, etc. She did a concise, thoroughly professional job and is a really lovely, intelligent Italian / Australian young lady. I still recall her bright white shirt and grey business suit as she addressed the tribunal. Her attire was adorned only by a gold chain with a gold crucifix.

Until I received that discrimination allegation notice, I never knew what religion Lionel adhered to and even if I had known – so what? As an EPRA member I had spoken about retirement counselling at many Roman Catholic functions, including one to Priests at St Patrick's in Melbourne. The funds rules applied to everyone, equally. The application form had no space for religion of an applicant.

The Tribunal cogitated for about two minutes before dismissing Lionel's complaint as "frivolous and mischievous" and the Chairperson delivered quite a dressing down to him. Costs were ordered against him, a somewhat unusual practice. They did not amount to much, so he was lucky.

With no cheap interest rate home loan immediately available, the burden of getting Lionel out of his financial mess fell upon his unfortunate in-laws. They had to remortgage their paid- for home as security for the money loaned to Lionel. Lionel's dream house was never completed, at least not by him. Lionel's dream grew into a ragged nightmare. His sales techniques lost some of their effect. He resigned from the company after five pugnaciously uncomfortable months and went back to the city to work in Real Estate. He chose the right profession, at the right time and the right product – city town houses – and made enough money, so I heard, to repay his in-laws for the loss they sustained when the uncompleted country house was sold.

Lionel walked away protesting to all who would listen that he had been victimised. His claims were totally unjustified. Consider the situation from an unbiased viewpoint. Lionel's allegations to the Tribunal were unaccompanied by any proof other that his unsupported word. His financial commitment was minimal. Had Lionel won he could reasonably expect cash settlements sufficient to solve his self-inflicted financial crisis. When he lost he forfeited only $150 in cash and had to withstand a two minute admonition from the Chairperson of the Tribunal. From my position, the corollary to Lionel's win would be, in the then intensely politically correct climate, instant dismissal. I faced ruin with an enormous loss to my family of benefits greater than Lionel's potential win. I doubt he ever gave me a thought when he told his lies about me.

Yet he continued to claim the status of victim of years thereafter. At meetings of the Property Council of Australia our paths crossed occasionally and he conspicuously snubbed me. Friends told me that Lionel made comments about me that they considered to be slanderous. Apparently not too many members of PCA believed him because I won election to every committee position for which I nominated.

My unfortunate experiences with assertiveness course graduates who wield their graduation as a means of intimidation caused me to equate assertiveness with irresponsibility. Graduates who truly absorbed the learning have no need to flaunt it. I hope any experience you have is happier.

Different Coercions

Exhilarating but at times irritating, that's been my experience of superannuation. There are lots and lots of lovely contributors who manage their lives lawfully and responsibly. My staff and I departed from our comfort zones many times to help to our utmost when misfortune occurred, traffic accidents, heart attacks/strokes, drowning, serious sports injuries and other deaths due to murder and suicides. The parent company's ethos was decidedly paternal as was its superannuation fund. A small percentage of contributors were irresponsible and tried to fracture the law for their own greedy satisfaction, be it money, sex, drugs or just revenge on society. These irresponsible contributors involved the fund in complicated legal and unpalatable family matters. Never-the-less when I finally left the company to hang up my own shingle as an investigator it was with a deep feeling of sadness. Strangely, it was the defeat of the ploys of the irresponsible that I was to miss most.

At the start of a new financial year I accepted an appointment as a consultant to a group of superannuation funds. The first fund in the group as established in the early 1960's by a local company that made pressed metal parts for the motor vehicle industry. Over the next 25 years, the original employer company had merged with other companies making components for cars and a couple of years later that company was itself taken over by the Australian subsidiary of an international conglomerate. For reasons that must have appeared appropriate at the time, the superannuation funds of the various business sectors were never merged. The newly-organized automotive industry entity had employees contributing to six different funds with different contribution levels by employees and employer and different level of benefits. These disparities were sources of irritation to employees at all levels. In an industry renowned for industrial disputation, new management was merging all the Funds into a single entity, firstly because it was equitable and secondly to preempt industrial unrest.

Although my appointment was as a consultant I was also to act as the management appointed Trustee on the board of each of the six funds for a specific period, with the mission of substantially contributing to the merger especially in the area of member consultation / information. Four months after being appointed as a consultant, the superannuation project team I headed developed merger conditions for the group acceptable to all nine unions and management. The team planned information sessions necessary to inform and persuade the various sectors to obtain contributors' consent. Given the spread of locations in three southern States of Australia, it was quite an effort. Draft copies of letters, brochures, and comparative benefit schedules were ready for printing and the new Trust Deed and its appendices were well advanced in the process of receiving legal and actuarial approval. That's the administrative technical part of the superannuation merger and preparation thereof was to me absorbing.

But it is the people connected with the industry that makes superannuation exhilarating. They are often amazingly unpredictable. Adrian was one such person. He was 30 years old, almost half my age, and about my height and about my spreading build too. Unmarried, he lived with Mummy and Daddy and despite an expensive private school education could not hold a job anywhere for more than twelve months. Since entering the workforce at age eighteen he had dozens of jobs. Family connections allowed him to start his career in a Stockbroker's office. That was his pinnacle because thereafter each subsequent job was a step lower down the salary scale.

Currently, Adrian was employed as a general hand in the parcel dispatch section mainly sending out motor car suspension parts to repair shops. At times he delivered the internal mail in the Administration building. He learnt about my role partly from notices on the canteen noticeboard partly by way of the usual inter-company gossip grapevine and partly by unauthorized opening and reading of the external and internal mail he delivered to the superannuation fund merger project office.

Adrian opened the door to my office without knocking, walked in and sat down uninvited. He opened his presentation by introducing himself as an Assertive Program graduate and a member of one the groups of funds. "Bloody hell", I thought, "Another nut, I'm getting too old for this crap" I am nothing if not consistent in my depreciation of these graduates. Statistically I guessed it was time to meet another because it was about six years since my last confrontation. Adrian warned me against trying to remove him personally and psychically or having him removed because as a graduate of a TAFE Assertiveness Training Course, he knew how to "exert moral authority", he said. At least "moral authority" was something I had not heard before. It confirmed that I was dealing with another nut case. He told me he had a proposal of great benefit to us both. It was imperative that I hear immediately.

My first impression of him was that he had been exposed to an overabundance of American TV sitcoms and maybe was in the early stages of schizophrenia. But I have been too hasty in judgment other times in my career so I decided to give him the benefit of the doubt, I did not answer, as was my customary practice when confronted with an imbecile, but waved an open hand to indicate he could continue.

Adopting an exalted lecturing tone, Adrian told me that, as a former Stockbroker he knew how the Australian financial system operated. Also that he knew I was a Trustee of the company's self-invested fund, because he frequently read my incoming mail and out -going memos. He knew that I had access to investment information superior to that available to the general investing public. Rambling on and unashamedly dropping the names of eminent people I was sure he did not know, he claimed to have an extensive knowledge of superannuation and also an enormous degree of influence with the Federal Government and with his co-workers. I doubted both assertions but kept quiet and listened.

He claimed that his fellow workers respected his exalted intelligence and would follow whatever direction he gave them. Exalted intelligence? A thirty year old mail-boy? Whilst enlightening me, Adrian had risen from the chair and began pacing across the office using his hands in elegant sweeping gestures to emphasise his principal points. The only interruption to his hand waving occurred when he paused to clean wax from his ears with his car keys. I still had not uttered one word however my original assessment of Adrian as a nutter was re-enforced and I wondered whether he spent time sniffing fumes from the Necropolis chimney. He seemed to think that that I was more impressed with him than he was with me.

Adrian finally came to the crux of his proposal which was that I provide him with timely "secret" stock market information from which he would prosper. In return he would ensure the company's plans to merge the numerous superannuation funds into one fund would proceed without a hitch due to his influence with Federal politicians and within the local work place. Should I not willingly and enthusiastically cooperate with his eminently reasonable proposal, unprecedented industrial unrest may erupt due to unfavourable reaction to the superannuation merger. He surmised that the cost to the company of a failed merger of the Funds would be considerable, and that my reputation in the industry would suffer. He said that I must realise that it was cost effective to concur with his proposal. The cost of my relaying investment information to him was minimal whilst the cost of a failed superannuation merger could have a deleterious effect on the company's finances.

I now broke my self -imposed silence. Softly, politely and with a deliberately deceptive smile I told Adrian he was fired for mail tampering and attempted coercion. I escorted him to the Personnel Department to have the sacking put into effect immediately. He seemed stunned and made no effort to resist as we walked fifty metres to the Personnel Department. On the way he said "But it's my word against yours" several times. I suggested we test the strength of our relative credibilities before a panel consisting of the company's management and the senior Union representatives. The lessons of the TAFE Assertiveness Course seemed forgotten because he meekly declined my offer, signed the resignation form I put in front of him and was gone from the premises less than 45 minutes from entering my office.

Adrian's fellow employees never seemed to notice Adrian's departure.

This chapter opened with comments on statistics, a profile of "problem people", drawn on an eleven year base specifically related to the Australian superannuation industry. The results of that profile correlated closely on 60% of its results with the published FBI profile of criminal propensity. The difference being that some crimes, murder, assault, etc, are insufficient in numbers in superannuation to gather meaningful information. That report was destroyed by political order. But I remembered enough of the conclusion to categorically state that Keith, the early inheritance seeker, Dion the anti-everything merchant, Lionel the liar and Adrian the would-be financial genius all fitted perfectly in high risk, irresponsible, sector of the statistical profile.

Chapter Fifteen

Caught by Statistics

SUPERANNUATION IS BASED ON THEORIES of statistical probability codified by that admirable English gentleman, Sir Edmund Halley, a mathematician and astronomer who correctly predicted the exact date of the return of the comet in 1680 CE that bears his name. Over the last 335 years Halley's demographic /mathematical base has been improved, modified and made accurate to an amazing degree, especially since the introduction of computers – which themselves owe something to Halley's mathematics and a lot to another English World War Two code-breaking mathematician ,Alan Turing.

In the decades since *1960* superannuation has grown exponentially as an industry. Covered by superannuation in Australia are ten million people and total assets of the industry are astronomical, exceeding a trillion dollars today. Wherever there is money there are thieves. The thief in this fraud was detected because of the way superannuation funds apply Halley's demographics. It may be a slow process at times, but it is inevitable that irregularities are discovered.

A superannuation Corporate Trustee company that administered many funds was based in Melbourne. An irregularity was highlighted on the computer list of one of their NSW "Defined" funds during a regular 3 yearly review known as an "actuarial review". The Trust Deed of the fund required a formal review at least every three years to ascertain the precise financial status of the fund. Like many long established funds the Trust Deed of this old NSW fund had not been updated to reflect the revolution caused by sophisticated computer programs and societal developments. The regular review revealed an unusual number of males dying in their late eighties leaving very young relicts. I will avoid elaborating on the comments of the male computer staff who speculated on the causes of death when the records showed that men aged eighty-plus died soon after marrying twenty year old brides.

The dictionary term of "relict" means a widow. Within the superannuation industry a relict refers to the widow of a superannuation pensioner and the relict is entitled to receive a lifetime pension at a rate, usually about 60% of the full rate, upon the death of her husband. By far the majority of Australian superannuation funds pay a continuance pension only to relicts who were married to the superannuation fund pensioner **prior** to his retirement date. But up to the mid 1990's several NSW based defined benefit superannuation funds paid continuance pensions to relicts of earlier contributors irrespective of the date of marriage. After 1990 that provision was discontinued for new entrants to the accumulation sector of the fund.

An Actuary is a highly qualified mathematician. So highly qualified are actuaries that they are one of the few professions permitted to give expert evidence in a Court of Law about predicted future events. An Australian Actuary can tell fairly accurately how many people will die in Australia next year. In Saddam Hussein's Iraq, an Actuary there could likewise tell how many and also give you their names and addresses. Using a program produced to fulfill the requirements of the actuary to the fund, the computer produced actuarial predictions about future pension benefit payment levels. In part, these predictions were based upon the demographics of Australia which show, for example, that when an 80 year old plus, male pensioner dies, his relict is predicted to survive him by 3.4 years on statistical average.

Calculations of future payments to relicts are budgeted on that basis. However the computer print outs in the case of this NSW fund revealed irregularities far beyond any acceptable standard deviations. Additionally suspect was the concentration of young relicts in one geographical area. This old style fund had once drawn its contributors from a major transport workshop located nearby, but the geographical concentration of the anomalies still looked suspicious.

Past experience had demonstrated to Trustees of superannuation funds that irregularities in any specific area should not be investigated by the Manager in charge of that area. Trustees prefer to have an independent specialist accountant investigate and report directly to them. Recent changes in Accounting Regulations, Corporations and other Laws place responsibility for fraud prevention upon Trustees, so the use of specialist accountants and Private Inquiry Agents has increased. By employing a specialist outsider to investigate problems, the Trustees comply with sections of the new regulations. In so doing they acquire a high degree of immunity if a fraud is uncovered.

I had been operating as a Licenced Inquiry Agent for some time when I was engaged to investigate the recently revealed irregularity. Because the NSW superannuation fund had its Head Office in Melbourne and they appointed me as their investigator, I could operate interstate on the basis on my Victorian Inquiry Agent's licence. I commenced with a study of a list of personnel employed at the Parramatta NSW Branch office of the Corporate Trustee to see if I was known to any of them. No name registered.

In particular I checked the qualifications that each claimed to have earned. My check went back five years. Experience clearly shows that persons who lie on their employment applications or embellish their achievements too greatly have a higher propensity for criminality. (You can gild the lily a bit but making an orchid out of a weed is too much to be tolerated) The check did not show up anything significant, so I decided that a visit to the NSW branch office was indicated. I contrived to be credibly introduced to the branch office staff as a specialist lecturer and journalist. I was involved in writing a series of articles on the NSW division of their big superannuation fund administration service. There was an element of truth in that subterfuge as an article I had written appeared in a recent superannuation magazine. Several copies of the magazine were distributed shortly before my arrival. There was always the risk that a person participating in a fraud might be alerted by my arrival. Sometimes that's disadvantageous. At other times it's advantageous because it applies pressure and pressure leads to mistakes and mistakes lead to detection.

This time my carefully worked out plan came unstuck near the start. To introduce myself as a journalist to the maximum number of employees, I chose morning tea time in the staff canteen. At this time I did not know that a problem had occurred with a computer earlier in the morning and just as the Manager finished an introduction designed to induce in the staff a warm, woolly, happy cooperative mood, the contracted computer repair engineer, after completing the repair, entered for a cup of coffee. His name had not appeared on the personnel list I had vetted. I did not see him enter. I got an unwelcome surprise when I heard his voice boom from out from behind me.

His name was Mark and we had worked together extremely well to foil further fraud on a major Credit Union in Victoria some months earlier. Mark was a delight to have around when investigating possibly dangerous frauds. Mark was huge. He had fabulous muscles and incredible reflexes. His sports were kick boxing and women at both of which he excelled. To match his "incredible hulk" frame he had a loud voice. He used the voice to affectionately greet me then told the twenty four members of staff that we had caught crooks together in Melbourne and that I was the smartest Private Detective in the business.

My masquerade as a journalist fell away in shredded tatters. My masquerade as a journalist may have vanished but over the next few days I found myself forced into the role of a priest because many members of staff came to my temporary office to confess. Most were minor misdemeanours or to return items of equipment, including two PC's which they tried to convince me that had inadvertently borrowed. One lady said she was sorry for not returning a PC earlier. She took it home to help her son with his homework and forgot about it. I found it was missing for close to two years. Some homework! I thanked each employee for their actions, promised no repercussions then sent each off with absolution and advice to sin no more but to ensure that I was given their complete, confidential cooperation in my enquiries over the next few days. I got it too. I promised the Manager to keep all reference to the recovery of those items strictly to us. No mention to Head Office. That soothed his sense of affront at not being told in advance who I truly was and my purpose.

In less than five days sufficient highly persuasive evidence existed to confirm that the irregularity was definitely a large scale and surprisingly patient long term fraud. I formed the opinion that it did not involve collusion with any superannuation staff employee. . The five W's and an H is the way I conducted an investigation. What, When, Where, Who, Why and How. Computer printouts told me What, When, Where so I had a solid start. I needed to determine Who, Why and How. In anticipation of criminal proceedings every item of uncovered evidence had to be recorded. The pain-staking and boring task was essential. The old adage "If it's not recorded it didn't happen" applies equally to Police and Private Investigators. And recording must be in a set format otherwise it gives the defense counsel of an accused a lever to claim the evidence gathered about his client is inadmissible. Even a slight error can lead to a claim that the privacy of the accused was violated. So my recording had to be accurate and detailed. It was time consuming but necessary. My biggest concern was that the swindler may be alerted, accidentally or deliberately. My concern proved groundless.

My investigation revealed the prime suspect was a cunning employee of a large hospital who saw a weakness in the system and exploited that weakness. The hospital had a special accommodation wing for elderly, infirm patients, a palliative care facility. As it transpired, the fraud was this; being a hospital administrator, the perpetrator had access to the records of patients admitted. He checked for widowers who were members of any of the three NSW superannuation funds with a deficiency in their Trust Deed definition of "relict". The widowers in palliative care became his targets, especially if they had no close family.

With unrestricted access to their private information he could easily obtain a birth certificate, tax file number, superannuation account numbers, etc, sufficient to create a "clone" of the invalid patient. He stole the identity of the help-less, trusting, bed-ridden patients and used several accomplices, an elderly man to impersonate the bedridden patient and several younger women. The hospital administrator would accompany a couple to the Parramatta Marriage Registry and a marriage would be enacted between the male impostor using the name of the bedridden hospital patient and a much younger woman.

When the elderly patient died, the crooked hospital administrator would apply for a continuance pension for the relict. Naturally he would take most of the relict's pension as his commission. He was caught by

Halley's mathematics because after 5 marriages in 6 years the computer showed relicts (say average age of 25) with life expectancy of 60 years, so 5 relicts x 60 years = 300 years against the statistical survival term of an elderly relict of 3. 4 years, so 5 x 3. 4 years = 17 years predicted.

In round terms say an average pension for the recently deceased elderly pensioners was $24,000 p. a. (460 p. w.), then each relict was "entitled" to 66. 66% thereof or $16,000 p. a. for life (females life expectancy being 85 years). So $16,000 x 60 years = $960,000 x 5 widows = $4,800,000 without indexation. With CPI indexation the sum approximates $16. 8M. The original actuarial estimate of costs was 3. 4 @ $16,000 p. a. = $54,000 x 5 = $272,000, a lot less than $16. 8M. The swindling administrator got the lion's share on an automatic monthly bank transfer from the account of the relict to accounts he had established in the name of his unknowing relatives. Assuming the swindler lived to his statistical average age, he could expect to collect around $6. 6 million. Not a bad rip-off.

It took me another five painstaking days to investigate, acquire and document sufficient information to justify a very tight formal complaint to the proper authorities. With cooperation from every member of staff I had applied the five W's and the H test to the records of each of the five suspect marriages. Every staff member was eliminated as a suspect in the fraud. The evidence in the files clearly showed that whenever the superannuation fund received a notice of the change of circumstances of an elderly ex-railway worker pensioner, all administration procedures were properly followed. Notices of changes of address, Powers of Attorney, Marriage Certificates and bank account relocations were recorded or checked precisely as required by management rules.

The glaring consistency was the participation of the hospital palliative care administrator. The glaring inconsistency was the administrator's notifications of events that, with the full knowledge of properly collated facts were improbable. Assume, purely for illustration, that notification of admittance to hospital of a pensioner was received on a Monday. On Tuesday the superannuation fund has what purports to be a genuine Power of Attorney exhibited at the reception desk together with a change of details of the bank account into which the superannuation pension is paid. On Wednesday a Certificate of Marriage of the 88 year old male to a 23 year old woman is shown at the reception desk. On Thursday the fund administrator is notified of the death of the pensioner and on Friday a not-too distressed "Widow" lodges a claim for a life pension of two thirds of the sum paid to her recently deceased husband. True, that's a condensation, usually the time frame was three to nine weeks. Most of the notifications were accompanied by a letter on the letterhead of the reputable hospital. My first impression was that the hospital was very good at attending to the needs of its patients.

Repetition breeds suspicion. The local Marriage Registry was a busy place. It processed 25 civil weddings per weekday, more at weekends. For a fee any member of the public could obtain photographs of groups taken by an automatic camera. Images were kept in a computer since it was installed many years ago. I got the luck that comes from hard work. I paid the fees and collected five photos a few days later. Surprise! Surprise! The "groom" in each photo was the same, as were two of the brides. Interestingly a tall rather distinguished man was a witness in all marriages. One identified female was a bride in two marriages and a witness in another. One female was a bride and also a witness in two others.

A visit to the hospital general records, using a superannuation fund letter as an "authority" yielded the information that all five pensioners never stirred from their beds from date of admission to date of death. A bit of snooping around revealed that the administrator of the palliative care wards was the distinguished gentleman in all the marriage photos. I had pushed to the boundary my privileges under my Victorian license. To go beyond risked having all evidence collected so far being declared inadmissible. I would not jeopardise the fund's objective to cease false pension payments and recover stolen money.

The Chairman of the Management Company flew into Sydney to receive my report and to look at the computer printout evidence He listened and looked with growing astonishment. He called in the local lawyer who oversaw local legal matters. He, in turn called in a Sydney Licenced Private Inquiry Agent to investigate further. My Victorian PIA licence was adequate to investigate the NSW branch of a Victorian superannuation fund, but not to operate as an investigator in a NSW hospital. More admissible evidence was uncovered by the NSW PIA, acting the role of a hospital public relations consultant. The NSW investigator and the fund lawyer presented their evidence to both the Federal and the NSW Police.

The swindler was charged as were the 5 "ladies", each with a raft of Federal and State offenses. Note the word "ladies" is in inverted commas. They readily agreed to the" marriages "because of the novelty of being paid for doing something when vertical not horizontal. The 78 year old impostor, the perennial bride groom, died before the trial. Rumour had it that he was paid "in kind" not money. Death by over indulgence?

Convicted of fraud and several other offences the swindling hospital administrator was sentenced to over eight year's jail (he served only 5 ½ years all up, including time in remand). I was disappointed to hear that only part of the $372,000 he stole before being caught was recovered. The ladies were convicted, and were given a variety of sentences from suspended to 3 years in custody.

All pensions were stopped. About 30% of the stolen money was recovered from the sale of assets registered in the names of unknowing relatives of the swindler. He promptly filed for bankruptcy. He made two appeals, one against conviction and when that failed another against the severity of the original sentence. That failed too. Taxpayers funded his appeals via Legal Aid. The carefully recorded reports of the NSW PI and myself were attacked by the defense lawyers several times from many angles but withstood every assault. Statistics and meticulous records prevailed.

Chapter Sixteen

Tainted Trustees

I WAS EXCEEDINGLY LUCKY THAT the Trustees of each of the superannuation funds in which I served firstly as a Manager and later as a Trustee were people of very high moral calibre. Never had I cause to be concerned that any one of them abused their Trusteeship to obtain personal gain. Perhaps because of the high moral yardstick they set during my formative time, I expected Trustees of other funds to be of the same level of high principle. But, alas, we live in a venal world and I was deeply shocked when colleagues in the superannuation industry told me of their tribulations with tainted Trustees. In the 70's, 80's and early 90's it seemed to some of my colleagues that no satisfactory avenue existed for reporting the corrupt actions of some Trustees.

One manager of a self-investing fund based in Melbourne came under heavy, almost daily, pressure from one newly appointed management Trustee to put an exorbitant percentage of share purchases and sales with one Stock Broking firm instead of spreading the business amongst a panel of several. Most funds used a panel of five or six or sometimes more Brokers depending on the size of the fund's investment portfolio. This diversity allowed Trustees to obtain the advantage of advice from various informed sources. In the instance to which I refer here, the harassed Manager sought a private interview with the Chairman of the Trustees and put his case of pressure to abandon established practice in favor of a bias that could be detrimental to the fund. His trust in the Chairman was monumentally misplaced.

The "old boy's club" solidarity came into operation and the Chairman, despite highly persuasive evidence that an unbiased observer would concede warranted serious investigation, curtly dismissed the matter and was uncomplimentary to the Manager. Shortly thereafter a special audit was sprung upon the Manager. No fund, no matter how good, is without blemish in some capacity no matter how insignificant.

The special audit report was sent direct to the Trustees without prior discussion with the Manager a highly unusual practice, used seldom and only justified when serious issues such as fraud by the Manager are suspected. The report listed over 20 transgressions. These transgressions were insignificant, dubious, and petty. Some were based on a totally incorrect interpretation of comments made by junior members of staff about matters of which they had little understanding.

In short, the Manager was pilloried for having the guts to bring to the attention of the Chairman the improper activities of a management appointed Trustee. That Trustee and his family were members of the Chairman's peer group. As well as management appointed Trustees ,that superannuation fund had member elected Trustees. One wonders what may have been the outcome if the Manger had complained about the activities of one of the elected Trustees – say, the shop steward for the Union of the manual labourers.

My Manager colleague now experienced poor treatment by other Trustees and also senior colleagues within the company. The Manager was crucified by innuendo of an undisclosed type. Life became miserable for about three months, the time it took the Manager to get fed up and find another, commensurate, job in the superannuation industry. On his estimation, it took him over five years before his reputation in the industry was restored.

Years later we heard rumours of the enormous financial "kick-backs" (ie cash and other valuable presents) that the tainted Trustee of that fund accumulated. In the mid 1970's he was on fees of $18,000 pa as a Director of the employer company as well as $40,000 p. a. on kick backs from the Broker. Plus the tainted Trustee operated his own family business offering advice to superannuation funds, for which the family company received substantial fees for seemingly little effort.

Ostensibly that Trustee was a respected Melbourne businessman. But word spreads within the superannuation industry even though it was slow. His family company fell into disfavour.

When he sought to be appointed as a consultant to a company of which I was Chairman, I was pleased that another on our list submitted better credentials so I could happily and properly reject the tainted Trustee. It would be fitting if I could write that the tainted Trustee was brought to justice but life is not like that. Crime often pays if you have the right social connections. He lives in luxury and to his children and most business acquaintances he is a pillar of morality and a member of prestigious clubs.

Another tainted Trustee stole not money but authorship. That Trustee "robbed" several superannuation Managers, each more than once. His reputation within the industry eventually became so poor that few would willingly talk to him. But that did not stop him from talking to them. He was only tolerated at annual conferences of the Association of Superannuation Funds of Australia because his unsuspecting wife was a truly luminous personality. The tainted Trustee had an impeccable political pedigree within the Melbourne establishment which he and his blood family exploited to have him placed on Company boards. His positions were all sinecures. When the other Directors appreciated his lightweight or even negative contribution he was shunted into subcommittee type Board jobs, such as the company superannuation fund or the executive remuneration committee where he could be relied upon to vote whichever way the Chairman indicated.

The annual conferences to the Association of Superannuation Funds of Australia (ASFA) were very well organised events conducted at venues spread throughout Australia to reflect its national membership base. ASFA was a great "school" for newcomers to the industry and a great inter-active networking opportunity for those with more experience. Its social aspects were beneficial and not to be under rated. It was the social events that attracted this tainted Trustee the most. His wife shone in the carnival social atmosphere and was a valued participant in the Ladies Business Sessions. He liked to bask in her radiance.

His tainted method was this. To raise and maintain his profile within the industry he regularly requested the superannuation fund section Managers to compile reports to the Board of Trustees on various subjects. With scant alternation, these reports would appear in the major superannuation publications, SUPERFUNDS, and SUPER REVIEW as contributions of his own work. No mention of the actual author. Just the name of the superannuation fund. The two publications were oblivious of his duplicity.

Furthermore, to reduce possible criticism, he prevailed upon his fellow Trustees, in the interests of saving members' money, to allow him to be the sole representation of his fund to ASFA. The superannuation fund "working" members, the Manager, section heads such as the investment accountant, had their membership revoked or at least not renewed when it expired. That effectively cut them off from important information sources, and the tainted Trustee was selective about information he gathered, so the fund's information access on many matters was impaired.

The tainted Trustee still required reports to be written by the Managers on subjects he nominated, ostensibly for benefit of the entire board of Trustees. These well researched reports were published, without attribution; in such a way that a reasonable reader would assume the Trustee was the author. Sickeningly he claimed not to have himself named as author out of modesty. The Chairman of Trustees was privy to the plagiarism and he condoned it by refusing to stop it or to demand appropriate accreditation. Even the greatest idiot can learn when regularly fed digestible parcels of wisdom by professional Managers so this tainted Trustee made a name for himself for quite a while. In the early 1990's his fund was merged with another and he retained a seat on the new superannuation board for over a year before the other Trustees realised that he was claiming credit for reports written by others. They squeezed him off.

At least two other deserving Managers I knew had similar sad experiences and one was so bitter he left the industry. Other Managers had better success, albeit at a cost to members. Some "inherited" Trustees as a result of company mergers or "acquired" Trustees through a ballot and sometimes these Trustees were lounge-lizard liabilities. Some Trustees only wanted the prestige of the position without the responsibilities. They were easy to get on with and attended only the social functions were they could get a free drink. Generally they were a nuisance, rather than tainted. Most did not last long.

Trustees are supposed to be above reproach; persons of high ethical standards, immune to temptation. But many are far from that, despite legal penalties. Some were parasites, following the investment activities of the fund investment managers with an eye to making money for themselves. One such tainted Trustee, one of five on the Board of Trustees, let's call him Ian, demanded daily reports of the investments. His justification was that he assiduously monitored the progress of the fund in the interest of members, an assertion difficult to refute. I'm surprised that other Trustees did not question Ian's demand. He was on the mechanical equipment side of the company business with no known investment or accounting qualifications.

On one occasion the superannuation fund was persuaded by a member of its Broking panel to take a short term punt. Usually the fund invested for a longer horizon but the Broker was reliable, the investment commitment not too great and the stock involved was one that was within the fund's investment specifications as likely to be included.

The fund made a purchase of $80,000 and that was duly reported to Ian. Using the maiden name of his wife, Ian also made a purchase, using money borrowed from a bank, supposedly for home extensions. One month later the stock had risen on the prospect of a take-over. The fund sold for a $90,000 return. Not bad, $10,000 profit in 30 days. Only one week later however, that stock's price plummeted below the fund's original purchase price on the ASX. The anticipated take-over, which caused the share price to rise, did not proceed. The predator found the victim company had "poison pill" provisions in its senior management employment contracts that were deemed unacceptable.

Whether Ian was experiencing a bad hair week, or some other event distracted him, he either mis-read that the fund had sold out of that stock or he held the view that the stock still had further to rise. Whatever his motive, probably it was greed – he did his shirt as they say in the business when he was forced to sell at a loss. He lost about $16,000 that he could not afford. The loss so upset him that he decided to vent his spleen on the fund Manager. He made several undeserved abusive and accusative telephone calls to the Manager. At the next monthly meeting of the Board of Trustees,

Ian got so wound up by his hurt feelings and bust bank account he got carried away with his condemnation of the Manager. Unintentionally he revealed far too much about his own stock market activities.

The other Trustees were appalled by what they heard. The Chairman of Trustees quietly asked the Manager to leave the room and wait outside. A short time later when the Manager was recalled, he passed a florid-faced Ian stalking out through the same doorway. The Chairman quietly directed that Ian's resignation be recorded in the minutes. Nothing else was ever mentioned about Ian who left the company's employ at the end of the month. Congratulations to that Chairman. By far the majority of Trustees are trustworthy, the few that prove otherwise taint the reputations of all.

Not all Trustees are conscious of their responsibilities. Two directors of a Queensland based superannuation fund Trustee Company appeared to look upon the fund they were entrusted to administer as a gold mine from which they could extract about $10 million for their own benefit. The Employees Productivity Award Superannuation Funds, EPAS, managed the assets of Queensland hospitality industry workers. According to Judge Hall in the Southport District Court and Judge Healy in the same Court, later, John Kenneth Shields and Terrance Robert James breached their duties of trust. One judge noted that the members had a right to rely on the utmost probity of the Trustee whist the other judge commented about the great deal of distress caused. Reports from ASIC and the Sydney Morning Herald state that both Shields and James gained advantage by making reckless loans from EPAS to companies in which they had an interest and they picked up "borrowers fees" of $180,000 and $248,000 respectively in the process. Loans made to the companies defaulted resulting in EPAS having to write down its assets. What happened to the missing $10 million is unclear but obviously the members suffered from the actions of these tainted Trustees.

In another fund, successful ASIC action resulted in the Trustee, Stephen Nightingall, being found guilty of illegally acquiring $103,000 from the superannuation benefits of ten clients in 1999 and 2000. Colin Frederick Quarrel stole or lost large sums from superannuation funds. He was convicted of obtaining property by deception in the sum of over $2. 2 million and one charge of theft in excess of $1. 7 million. Earlier a fellow director of Sentinal Financial Management, Allan McDonald Healy was sentenced to a five year jail term.

The Czech who wrote himself a cheque for Four hundred and fifty million English pounds from the UK Daily Mirror Newspaper employees' pension fund deserves a dishonorable mention when talking of tainted Trustees. He was named Jan Hoch at his birth in Czechoslovakia in 1923. During World War Two he escaped from Nazi concentration camps, became a Captain in the British Army and served with such distinction as to be awarded a Military Cross. After a few name changes he was known as Robert Maxwell. Although he shook off several names he never shook off speculation that he was, at best, a sympathiser with the infamous KGB (the Soviet Secret Service,) also the British MI6, and another theory advanced is that he had connections with Israel's Shin Bet. Maxwell took on Aussie Rupert Murdoch in a financial battle for two British newspapers and lost. The London Stock Exchange branded Maxwell a liar. But like a rubber cheque he bounded back and acquired control of a left-leaning UK Newspaper, the Daily Mirror.

Ignoring all elements of stewardship, Maxwell used financial methods as murky as anything attributed to any of the Secret Services with which his name was linked. He stole Four hundred and Fifty million British Pounds before disappearing from his luxury yacht in the Mediterranean. His body was found at sea. Murder, suicide, or accident? No one knows for certain. Until the body was located, speculation had it that he staged the disappearance. What is not speculation is that thousands of UK pensioners and would-be retirees were left lamenting for their disappeared benefits. I took personal umbrage at his assumption of the name Maxwell because one of my heroes is James Clerk Maxwell, renowned for his theory of electromagnetic radiation. Hoch disgraced the name.

Trustees have been tainted or derelict in their duties as stewards of the assets of others. When it comes to stewardship the quote from the Bible, First Corinthians, Chapter 4, verse 2, seems appropriate, "Moreover it is required in stewards that a man be found faithful". I'm not religious but I subscribe to that admonition.

To Australia's Stock broking fraternity, the Managers and investment Managers of self-investing company superannuation funds were prized property in the three decades from mid 1960 to mid 1990. Possibly Managers have lost a lot of their attraction these days. Specialist funds Managers administering billions of dollars of investments in stipulated criteria portfolios have supplanted them. There are now less numbers of sizeable company self-invested superannuation funds. During those halcyon three decades, a decision making or substantially influential fund Manager could rely on at least one luncheon invitation and one evening "seminar / presentation" per week. The Stock broking and major share issuing companies would be the tab- paying host. As Manager of a large self-investing superannuation fund, my wine appreciation education blossomed.

Stock brokers who did not take clients to lunch at least three days per week were frowned upon by their firm's principal or partners. One Stockbroker told me that his partners considered him derelict in his duty if he arrived back at the office before 2. 30 pm and sober. Peculiarly the Managers felt compelled to accept the generously extended hospitality of the Stockbrokers. Rejection of too many invitations meant exclusion from market information that Managers relied upon to maintain or enhance the performance of their fund's investment portfolio.

The Festive Season was extraordinary. Not wishing to offend any firm of Stockbrokers meant at least 30 functions between St Barbara's Day (6th December for those readers who do not know St Barbara is the patron Saint of the Artillery) and Christmas Eve. By courtesy of Stockbroking friends I enjoyed lunches and dinners served by in-house caterers at every Broking firm in Melbourne, several in Sydney and a few in each of Adelaide, Brisbane and Perth. Many of the Brokers were men of extraordinary wisdom, character and achievement. I am eternally grateful for their friendship, advice and example.

The interstate based Brokers moved heaven and earth to entertain fund Managers who attended conferences of the Association of Superannuation Funds of Australia, (ASFA) in their respective States. To counter-act any attenuation of loyalty the local Brokers had hospitality suites in the ASFA conference venue hotels. You knew where you stood in the industry pecking order by the number of invitations and gifts you received. The gift had to be innocuous and not of such value as to be considered bribes, so I have a great collection of port and whiskey pottery crocks, now empty, key rings, key wallets, up market ball point pens, pocket calculators, nick-knacks and ties. My grandchildren find them fascinating.

When not at conferences and at times other than the festive season. The invitations, as mentioned, remained steady. Events held after normal business hours at a Broker's office usually meant meeting about 40 of your colleagues / competitors in the industry. Frequently, items associated with ASFA were sorted out at these functions because almost the entire Victorian Division Committee would be present. I was a Victorian Division ASFA Council Member for over 15 years and thoroughly enjoyed the opportunities to chat with esteemed colleagues and sort out ASFA administration matters over a convivial glass of vintage red. I was honored when an ASFA Distinguished Service Award was conferred upon me. These Broker's functions were an accepted part of your job. If you were absent from too many you fell outside the information circuit. When in the information circuit you learned a lot about the inner working of the Stock Market, future floats and, from time to time, learned enough to prevent investments in dodgy enterprises.

In early 1980 an invitation, hand written with a nib pen in mauve ink with an expense deckled edged envelope personally addressed by the senior partner of a "boutique" broking house was hand delivered to me. The "boutique" Broker was newly established in Melbourne having been a minor interstate "family" business for three decades. By marriage new blood was introduced into the firm. A fifteen year old bottle of Dimple Scotch whiskey accompanied the invitation. As was customary in my office, to the bottle of Scotch I had a raffle ticket affixed and it was placed in the "Christmas Hamper" as were most gifts given to me during the year. Just prior to Christmas, numbered raffle tickets butts were drawn by staff members who took as their present the items bearing the same number as they had picked in the draw. This sharing of gifts usually meant at least three items per superannuation fund staff member for the festive season, and contributed to my departmental staff loyalty program. It helped prevent me from succumbing to dipsomania.

The boutique Broker's hand written invitation promised something "excitingly original". Curiosity made it seem worthy of exploration and on the appointed date, place and just a few minutes late, I arrived. At first I thought I was in the wrong place. Only five other fund Managers were present not the usual gaggle of 40 or so. I made the number up to six. The youngish, impeccably tailored senior partner of the broking firm was the only other person present and he was reeling off a string of very blue but very funny jokes. My arrival completed his guest list. After ensuring we all had drinks, the senior partner suddenly recalled he had to leave for an urgent engagement elsewhere, but he was certain that his staff would entertain us. With abject apologies to the six surprised fund Managers, he departed through one door with the speed of a startled gazelle.

Barely, and it is an appropriate term, had the door closed when his "Staff" entered via a door at the other end of the room. The "Staff" consisted of six beautiful young ladies, elegantly if only partly clothed, who navigated across the ankle deep jet black carpet to each fund Manager with the unerring trajectory of a homing torpedo.

"My" hostess was about half my age and weight and 15cm shorter. She appeared to form an instant attraction to me, was solicitous in topping up my drink and could hardly wait to hear me tell her of my exciting life as a "mover and shaker" in the finance industry. She was an absolute stunner. Snow white skin, low cut black dress, long black eyelashes and carmine red lips. The lips seemed to match the colour of the simple ruby necklace. She was very beautiful. She took my hand and we sat down together on one of the soft black leather divans. She moved in close so I could better benefit from her perfume. She stared deeply into my eyes and listened intently to every word I spoke. Mention by me of my wife and children were dismissed with a quick shoulder shrug that severely tested her cantilever verandah support which, when it slipped a bit far down, was not adjusted.

One of my best business friends, Barry, a chap with whom I had shared a CMF Officers Training Course, was one of the other attendees. He caught my eye and we both imperceptivity shook our heads. "Never allow yourself to be compromised" was a dictum drilled into me, firstly as a Lieutenant at the School of Military Intelligence at Neutral Bay near Sydney and later as a Captain at the same School when it relocated to Woodside near Adelaide. Barry was one rank above me in the Army Reserve (CMF) and either he had attended the School or his inate common sense made him wary. I was able to point at my watch and hold up two fingers, not in any rude gesture but in the Army sign language manner. He nodded to let me know he understood we would both make a break in two minutes. I made the most of my two minutes; mild manual indiscretions were encouraged, not rejected. Barry and I sneaked looks at the second hand on the ornate, black and gold wall clock over the well shaped shoulders of our respective "ladies".

Other guests seemed far less reserved than we two and as the drinks went down they seemed to have advanced from verbal intercourse with the luscious lady staff members, towards a more physical association. In the two minutes before my get away, "my" staffer told me that she lived in an apartment in the suburb of Jolimont, a short taxi ride from where we were at present at the "top" end of Collins Street. The girl she shared the apartment with was interstate for a few days. She was lonely. She thought I was handsome and strong (I thought she must be nuts, drunk or blind).

As the second hand on the square wall clock reached our two minute limit Barry and I both stood up and asked direction to the gent's toilet. His "staffer" told him not to hang out there too long. "My" staffer gave me a grin and asked if I wanted a hand. Barry and I strode with unhurried regal dignity or as much of that attitude as we could muster, out through the richly carpeted reception area. Each recovered his briefcase and then we BOLTED!

Later at a CMF Army parade night, Barry told me that "his" staffer had the same story as mine, ie lived in a nearby flat, the girlfriend who shared was away, and she was awfully lonely and instantly infatuated with him. Over a drink in the Officers Mess, Barry and I speculated upon what might have been and whether any ardent exploits would have featured on hidden camera 8x10 inch photos or perhaps on colour video. I know that in the espionage business it is called the "honey trap". I never took any of the telephone calls that came in the next day from my gorgeous "staffer" nor any of the dozen or so calls during the next week from the senior partner of that broking firm. His broking firm went into liquidation about four months later.

What's the saying, the virtue of virtue is virtue? Alas.

Owen was the well regarded 42 year old ex-serviceman Manager of a superannuation fund whose contributors were employees of a large Australian diary food manufacturer. Owen's defined benefit superannuation fund Trust Deed, in relation to death in service, provided to dependants of a deceased contributor, a lump sum of three times of near-final average salary as at date of death . However if there be no dependants, the balance of the deceased member's account ie the former member's contributions, plus interest thereon, would be payable to the Estate of the deceased.

As an example, for a young employee on a salary of $20,000 pa, the death benefit payable to dependants was $60,000. But with only a few years of contributing membership by the young employee, the payment to the Estate may be around $4000. It may seem a large discrepancy but there are valid reasons for it in a defined benefit type of superannuation find. From the 1950's to early 1990's it was the norm in most large "defined" superannuation funds. The word "parent" did not appear in the definition of "dependants" in the Trust Deed of Owen's fund, so a "parent" was not automatically entitled to a dependant's cash sum payout and therefore could only be considered as a dependant by lodgment of proof of dependency or by exercise of discretion by the Trustees if certain circumstances existed.

A man who had migrated to Australia in his early teens, left the family home shortly after his eighteenth birthday. Not long after his departure he got a job with a dairy food company located 210 kilometers from home. His job entitled him to voluntary membership of the superannuation fund that Owen managed and the young man exercised his right to join. Evidence presented later under oath by his work mates and friends at the Coroner's Inquest made it clear that the unfortunate young fellow wanted nothing to do with his parents, both of whom were working full time elsewhere. The unfortunate young man never told workmates of the reasons for the split with his family.

Close to the fourth anniversary of him leaving home the young man committed suicide in his room at a house where he was boarding. He used a point twenty-two calibre rifle. During the years he boarded, his parents never visited and the landlady testified that he never received any mail from them. The disturbed young man left a signed note that accused his father of unspecified abuse. After the Inquest and after making efforts to locate dependants and making all inquiries that were reasonable to determine no dependant existed, the sum of around $4000 was ready to be paid to the estate of the deceased. No member of the family of the deceased appeared at the Coroner's Court and the fund had no reply to letters sent to the address of the parents.

There being no Will, friends of the intestate deceased took it upon themselves to wind up his affairs and donate the balance of the $4000, after expenses, to charity. Out of courtesy they informed the parents. Clearly some attitude change had occurred since the Inquest. The family was incensed. They claimed to be advised by a friend who had read a copy of the concise superannuation fund booklet (not the Trust Deed) that on his calculations the sum of $60,000 was payable. The parents either genuinely misunderstood or deliberately chose to misunderstand the function of a superannuation fund. The parents of the deceased contributor claimed that they considered the $60,000 to be compensation for their lost son. By offering only $4000 they said that they felt that the Trustees were denigrating their son or trying to cheat them because they were of ethnic origin.

A lawyer took up their case on the fee- share basis (or whatever the legal nicety of that is called). The lawyer made legal claims on no less that fourteen grounds and in each claim ethnic / racial discrimination was the cornerstone. Attempts by the fund to mediate were rejected. Considerable skewed vilification of the Trustees was deliberately leaked, pre-hearing, to some sections of the media. Threats of strikes by one of the militant Unions to "encourage" the company to pressure the Trustees to find in favour of the family of the deceased were made. The matter came to the Civil Division of the County Court a year after the suicide. (The Superannuation Complaints Tribunal was not operative until 2002).

The fourteen grounds for claiming the $60,000 amount had by then been reduced to one – that is, that the Trustees had failed to properly interpret the definition of "dependant" in the Trust Deed because they, the Trustees, were motivated by malice towards ethnic people. The trial sought was by judge only. Legal advisors to the fund expressed surprise because they expected their legal opponent to opt for a jury trial. The opening two days were taken by Counsel for the complainant arguing about the numerous ways that the word "dependant" could be interpreted. His exposition on the various facets was very good. Witnesses were called to testify of the alleged malicious attitude of the Trustees to ethnic people.

In every case the complainant's so-called evidence was tested by the superannuation fund Counsel and shown to the totally worthless. Not one of the witnesses had ever met any one of the Trustees. Several witnesses retracted elements of their statements claiming mistakes due to language misunderstandings. A judge, fast growing impatient, told the complainant's Counsel that had the witnesses not promptly retracted, he would have charged them with perjury. Counsel for the complainant spent time trying to argue that financial dependence was not the sole criteria to be considered. All parties agreed on that point, but the parents could not satisfy any measure about financial, religious, emotional, transport or home maintenance dependency, nor could the prime claim of ethnic discrimination be proven. Counsel attempted to have accepted, as a fall back position, that the decision of the Trustees was sufficient, in itself, for a reasonable man to infer malice intent by the Trustees.

The judge was unimpressed with that argument and said so, acidly. The judge was more active than customary in the questioning process and many times indicated displeasure at tactics of the Counsel for the complainants. The judge spent some time questioning the court interpreter about the precise responses to a great number of questions. After three days the Court was recessed and a few days later the judge handed down a decision in favour of the Trustees. The judgment stated the no dependency, be it financial, emotional or spiritual had been proven between the deceased and his parents, nor had one shred of credible evidence been advanced to prove malice, ethnically based or otherwise, by the Trustees. Accordingly, the payment of $4000 to the Estate of the deceased would fully and completely fulfil the responsibilities of the Trustees.

During the period of these events Owen was subjected almost daily to threats and abuse. He had Telecom install a recorder to trace the threats made by phone to his home and some prosecutions followed that monitoring. Not all of the pressure came from outside. One Trustee whose latent theatrical ambitions were awakened by a late-in-life, small but exhilarating role in a Light Opera company production became a real nuisance. As his ambitions blossomed his ability to make decisions wilted. He was upset at the amount of time he was required to expend reading reports. It distracted him from theatrical pursuits. He blamed Owen. "Just pay them off and get rid of them" he urged daily. It seemed to Owen that other Trustees felt the same way. Even if they did not directly complain, their cooperation was lukewarm. Exhausted by the constant pressure, Owen resigned from the company, sold his house and with his wife, daughter and two sons, moved towards the sunshine.

Completely changing his vocation he teamed up with another man, a friend of some years, to form a fencing company in Miami on Queensland's Gold Coast. He enjoyed working in the sunshine. His eldest son joined the company later. Owen is now my fittest, healthiest, sun tanned, ex-superannuation fund colleague. His business is booming.

At a conference of the Association of Superannuation Funds (ASFA) my wife and I had lunch with a colleague who, like me, was a member of his State's ASFA Council. At our table were my colleague's wife and two other ASFA members each with their respective spouse. Someone raised the subject of superannuation fraud and a lively discussion took place about audit procedures and alternation of staff duties to allow independent checks and so limit the prospects of fraudulent practices.

Probably I was aged in my mid- twenties at the time and the person I refer to as a colleague was double my age. I liked and respected him for the sound advice he offered at ASFA Council meetings and the assistance he gave to me, a relatively new boy on the scene, about the already vast and rapidly growing superannuation industry. Truly he was a mentor to me and many others. His real name was Ralph and I use that in this book as my grateful tribute to him as, regrettably, he is no longer living. Ralph was uncharacteristically reticent during the lunch time discussion of fraud. Given his background as an accountant and auditor in a very large Australia wide conglomerate company I recall remarking to my wife as we were walking away from the table that Ralph was not his usual sparkling self at lunch. I said to my wife that I hoped he was not suffering an illness. I did not know at the time that Ralph had recently been diagnosed as having cancer; however it was not his fatal illness that prevented him entering into the discussion about fraud.

At the conclusion of the day's presentations many conference delegates took a cold drink out to the elaborately decorated first floor pool side area to exchange ideas about the afternoon's workshop sessions and I found myself again with Ralph. He indicated that he wanted to chat privately and we stepped towards the end of the balcony out of earshot of others. Ralph astonished me with his revelation about a fellow in his mid fifties who was sitting at our table at lunch time and who had joined in heartily with the condemnation of frauds in the industry. Ralph told me he refrained from joining the discussion for fear that he may inadvertently make a maladroit remark.

Let's call the lunch guest Dick, a computer department manager with a Government entity. Ralph told me that Dick was currently under investigation both by a large independent audit firm and the Australian Taxation Office. Ralph admitted he was breaching a confidence by telling me of the investigation but that he did so out of friendship because Dick appeared to be a predator looking for prey and Ralph felt that I needed to be warned in view of my inexperience. Ralph told me that Dick was on the look out for people with a need for money. Dick would promise to solve the money problem with what he claimed as an undetectable rort. Dick would take a percentage.

Ralph was right. The next day Dick singled me out at the morning tea break. He tried to question me about my personal finances. Forewarned by Ralph I avoided meaningful answers and took advantage of the proximity of the other colleagues to whom I introduced Dick and thereby stifled any further personal conversation. For the remaining day of the conference I avoided Dick but I noticed that he had conversations with several younger members of the Association. At the conclusion of the conference my wife and I returned to Melbourne and Dick returned to the capital city of his State and I soon forgot him.

It was in the early part of the following year that Dick achieved prominence in the newspapers. He was arrested by the Police. It was alleged that he operated two separate frauds using the relatively new computer technology. The first involved the insertion of twenty or so "phantom" pensioners into his superannuation fund's roll of close to

12,000 genuine pensioners. Each month after pensions were paid into nominated bank accounts of the "phantoms" Dick would take a few hours off work on some pretext and withdraw cash from each account. He was collecting around $7000 per month over the sixteen or so month's duration of his fraud. It was alleged that Dick had tried to corrupt Managers of other superannuation funds by offering to show them how to set up an undetectable roll of phantom pensioners.

Dick's second computer-based fraud involved the "wiping" of long service leave records. He would select people who were close to retirement and who had used up all, or nearly all, of their long service leave. Dick would arrange to "wipe" their usage so that when they retired they would be paid the long service leave entitlement due of the basis of length of service. As an illustration, let's assume that an employee approaching retirement after 30 years service was entitled to 1. 1 weeks of leave for each year of service, a total entitlement of 33 weeks. If the employee had used, say 28 weeks during his working career, then on retirement the employee could receive the difference, between leave accrued and leave used up, ie five weeks salary. And a favourable tax rate applied to that cash payment. Dick's offer was that the 28 weeks already used would be "wiped" courtesy of his computer expertise. The employee would thus be paid for the full 33 weeks upon retirement and Dick would receive half of the increment in cash. He apparently collected about $35,000 per annum from this scam for at least four years.

Evidently something went wrong and Dick faced charges related to long service leave record removal. He could afford expensive legal representative and he got a good one. Although he was charged, his lawyer argued esoteric points about admissible evidence, introduced psychiatric attestations about Dick's susceptibility to irresistible temptation and sought numerous postponements. Close to three years after his arrest he finally faced court. Then the three year time lapse was used in mitigation. Dick was out on bail the entire three years. The original twenty or so charges were reduced by negotiation to eight. Although he was convicted of defrauding his employer on the long service leave fraud and was also convicted for the "phantom pensioner" frauds on the superannuation fund, the jail sentences were ordered to be concurrent. That meant that, of the three and half years jail on each of those charges, total of seven years, he was required to serve in custody only half that time, three and half years. With good behaviour, etc, and the 8 months "inside" on Remand he walked in two years.

The sentences handed out for white collar crimes sometimes leave me exasperated. I freely admit that when it comes to the Law, I'm an ignoramus. I fail to see why an expensive Court trial finds a person guilty of several offences and the penalty, for, say, eight charges, is rolled into the same as if there was only one. It seems to me that the thief escapes penalty in relation to the other seven charges. The message such sentencing sends wrong. It tells thieves not to stop at one crime because the penalty for several is the same as for a single!

Spice

The English language is reputably based on logic and if that be so then it follows that as "mice" is the plural of "mouse", then "spice" is the plural of "spouse". Spice is usually revealed, in the superannuation context, when a contributor dies and two widows (or relicts) lodge claims to collect the death benefit. Most of the time the discovery of the "other woman" causes instant and deep desolation for both "widows"(but not always) and creates a delicate problem for superannuation Trustees and Managers. My first taste of spice occurred when a 15 year contributor dropped dead while a spectator at a Saturday afternoon cricket match in South Melbourne.

On Monday morning I heard of the death via a phone call from a work mate of the deceased. After checking, I contacted the widow to offer condolences and assistance. She said that the family had the matter in hand, thank you, but would appreciate a written copy of the superannuation entitlements. I had a statement prepared and delivered to her that day.

When my puzzled Secretary, Carol, told me that another widow was in reception, visibly annoyed, I too was puzzled. This second Mrs. X(X2) had been shuttled to me by the supervisor at the depot of her late husband and again by the Personnel Department of the company. She was somewhat justifiably upset and indignant that she learned of the death of her husband only indirectly and that his employer was giving her the run-around. She had dozens of questions that I was reluctant to answer. She eventually left, unhappy, to attend a meeting that I helped arrange with her lawyer an hour later.

Perplexed and concerned, I contacted the first Mrs. (X1) to try to find out anything that might clarify the situation before reporting to the Trustees. I did not learn much so I resorted to mumbling gibberish about possible changes to the superannuation statement that I now regretted having sent so soon. I advised her to see a lawyer immediately and have him contact me. Both lawyers phoned and I informed both of the double claim situations. Each agreed to study the legalities, inform their respective client and set up appointments.

Mrs. X1 came in looking as if she had been crying for days but bravely applied cosmetics to best advantage. I asked her if her lawyer had apprised her of the changed circumstances and she shrugged her shoulders and nodded a "Yes". I didn't press but mistakenly assumed that she now knew of the other Mrs. X2. As gently as I knew how I outlined an approach that the Trustees and I had agreed upon to resolve the unusual situation. She sat stunned. Wide eyes stared at me and in an ascending shrill voice she asked "What other family?" Her lawyer chickened out. He did not tell her about the other wife and family, as he had promised me to do.

Embarrassed, unsure what to do and desperate not to add to the existing burden of grief I supplied tissues and Carol brought in cups of tea and womanly sympathy. There was no retreat. In the barest possible detail I told her about the other wife and children. Those 45 minutes were one of the hardest times I had in the superannuation industry. But my consternation was nothing compared to the additional grief of widow X1. Fearing her collapse, I contacted the medical centre and the duty nurse came to her assistance. Carol drove her home in my company car.

Benefit payments when there are more dependants than normal, "Who gets what?"Some superannuation funds had very greatly detailed Trust Deeds that sought to cover every possible human eventuality. A good friend of mine believed strongly in that approach. Other funds had Trust Deeds that were basic and vested a considerable amount of discretion in the Trustees. I was a supporter of the latter on the grounds that I preferred contributors to have a document that they could understand, not a Trust Deed so voluminous that it was too heavy to carry. Trustees may have wide discretion but they are bound to act with "the prudence of a reasonable person" as per the Trust Act. The lawyer for Mrs. X2 took the initiative and the problem was solved by mutual consent. The dependent children shared 60% of the commuted lump sum; each widow accepted 20%.

Bigamy used to be a crime, the punishment for which was prescribed in the Crimes Act as level 6 imprisonments (5 years maximum). Why do bigamist men die early? Exertion? Someone suggested it was 2 mothers-in-law. The lawyer who chickened out and failed in his duty to advise his client handled quite a bit of property conveyancing work for the Credit Union of which I was Chairman. I stopped it and gave it to the lawyer for Mrs. X2.

Chapter Seventeen

Identity Theft, the Core of All Fraud

EVERYONE IS A TARGET. EVERYWHERE there are thieves waiting to steal your money your identity and your credit rating. And your superannuation. What is Identity Theft? It occurs when thieves illegally acquire sufficient personal information about you to create a mirror image or clone of you on electronic and/or paper information storages. The thieves use your personal information to open bank accounts, obtain credit cards, fill out legal forms, steal superannuation and run up massive debts at the betting agencies, casinos and retail shops, to name but a few of their predatory actions. In more than one case they have mortgaged and/or stolen the family home without the real owners being aware until too late.

In telling you about thieves I used the plural because most identities are stolen by gangs. The independent loner such as the "catch me if you can" thief Jodie Harris, who taunted Police in three Australian States while on the run for theft using stolen documents, are rare. Gangs rule today's Identity theft (ID) scene. ID theft is predicted to be the epidemic crime of the 21st Century. Senior law enforcement officers have described it as a new crime, but it is not. Identity theft is the modern, high tech version of a 4000-year-old fraud.

A full description of the modus operandi, (M. O.) of an identity thief is provided in that classic chronicle of corruption, sex, murder & genocide; the bible. Jacob, in collusion with his Mother, steals the identity of his twin brother Esau. Using a goat skin they deceive the blind Father, Isaac. Jacob cheats Esau out of his inheritance (Gen. 27). Its well worth reading because it clearly demonstrates that human nature has not altered over the last 4000 or so years. It's only the technology that has changed. The computer has replaced the goat skin as the instrument of deception and taken the crime world wide.

Having your identity stolen hurts. I know. I've been a victim. Someone did it to us, my wife & me. That rotten thief temporarily robbed us of our reputation as honest people. We couldn't even get a card from Victoria's biggest retail store. At a time when Myer Cards were so easy to get, one was issued to a prankster using the name of cowboy film star, Hoppalong Cassidy. We were refused a credit card from every bank and it took seven years before the Credit Reference Agencies removed the false information about us in their databases. This was despite me giving them certified copies of records of the Magistrate's Court showing we were innocent victims. . Thankfully the law has now changed.

We became aware of the start of our seven years of credit deprivation when a bank Manager telephoned my wife while I was at work to enquire if I lived at that address. We lived on a 2. 4 hectare (10 acre) hobby farm 45 km from the city centre and were not listed in the Melbourne telephone directory. Our phone number was listed in a rural directory. My wife answered "Yes" whereupon the bank Manager became abusive. He complained to my wife about how much time he had expended to locate me and that now he had tracked me down legal action to recover large sums of unpaid credit card money would be initiated that very day. He demanded that she give him my work address and telephone number. He said he did not have a reliable contact. Although upset by the bank Manager's attitude and his threats to sue us for debt, my wife told him that she would contact me and ask me to phone him. She wrote down his number.

The banker threatened Police action and mentioned the shame that he could bring upon us in the eyes of our neighbours, if I did not phone him back immediately.

Lady readers, imagine how you might respond if an irate bank Manager telephoned you regarding large debts that your husband has allegedly incurred. Some of the debts, he said, being incurred in "houses of ill repute" as they were once politely called – how would you feel? Gentlemen, image trying to convince your upset partner that you had not spent a lot of money in brothels.

Tuesday mornings at 9.15am I held my weekly senior staff meeting. Six section Managers attended. Carol, by now my Secretary for five years, knew that short of Nuclear War or an urgent call from the company Chairman, no interruption was permitted. Twenty minutes after the meeting started, Carol came in, pointed at the telephone and said "It's your wife. You better take it" I wasn't game not to. My wife told me of the bank Manager's call. I spent quite a bit of time convincing her that we were not in dire debt and I had not spent $6000 in brothels. To this day my six section Managers rate that Tuesday meeting as the most interesting they ever attended.

Under our system of law, an alleged perpetrator is innocent until proven guilty. But with identity theft, the victim more often than not is viewed as guilty until proven innocent. I give you an assurance, based on experience, that back then it was very hard to prove your innocence when you didn't know precisely of what it was you were supposed to be guilty. Better options for proof of innocence are now available.

One great advantage of the superannuation Industry is that Managers develop a network of contacts with other superannuation fund Managers. I phoned my opposite number at the bank's superannuation fund, told him of the alleged threats and debts, and assured him of my innocence. He was apologetic about the branch manager "overstepping the mark" and promised to contact the bank's investigators and vouch for me. A true friend indeed, I remain most grateful to him. Several anxious days followed before the branch bank manager, who had previously been abusive to my wife, phoned her to soothingly apologise for what he claimed was a "mistake". She graciously accepted his apology.

As it transpired, the bank investigators uncovered a fraud perpetrated against several banks by one of the contributors to the fund of which I was Manager. What that crook did was simple. The "parent" company of our superannuation fund encouraged the formation of a Credit Union and I became a foundation Director. For 20 years, from the 1960's to the late 1980's, Victorian State Government regulations required Credit Union Annual Reports to include details of each Director and Manager. That meant the publication of full name, date of birth, place of birth, occupation and home address of each. The intention of the regulation was to allow depositors/members to have confidence in knowing details of the people who had control of their money. The theory was alright but it was compiled by honest legal draftsmen. The professionally dishonest scoffed at it; in fact it benefited the unscrupulous.

Copies of the Annual Report were mailed to 15000 members of the Credit Union. That's how the identity thief got my details. He started in the northern Victorian town of Horsham, which had five banks. Using the information from the Annual Report, he opened an account with each bank in the name of each one of the five Credit Union directors. Every bank made a credit check on the "new" customer and approved credit cards with high limits. Next day the swindler lodged a change of address notice from Horsham to another country town, Stawell. He advised the bank he had been promoted, so all cheque books, credit cards, etc were sent to that new address. No information about the falsely opened bank account ever reached me. Shortly afterwards he changed the address again, to Ararat.

Over the next few months the swindler spent hugely. He made the minimum monthly payment on each credit card often using another credit card. During that time, to further confuse the issue, he sent fourteen more change of address notices to the banks in respect of me and the other Credit Union directors. He travelled between the country towns in a top-of-the-range, leased; Mercedes Benz. It took eight months before the thief was caught by the Police, on information provided by the bank investigators. During that time he spent $360,000. ($11,000 per week). My colleague at the superannuation fund of the bank followed, with interest, the investigation and apprehension of the swindler. He was outraged at the prodigious spending spree. On the phone he said to me," Who does he think he is, a Labour Government Federal Treasurer?"

That thief using my name, obtained higher credit limits from the other banks than I got from my own. That really cheesed me off!

Still there were two positive aspects. Firstly, in part, this ID theft and its publicity led to the acceleration of the introduction by the Federal Government of the 100 points identification system. (Financial

Transactions Reports Act 1988). The same Act makes it a criminal offence to conduct a bank account in a false name. Secondly, the Victorian State Government repealed that part of the Credit Union Regulations requiring full details of Directors and Managers to be published in Annual Reports. But despite the public benefit, my wife and I had seven years of denial of credit and embarrassment. The memory is still painful. So when I write about ID theft I know what it's like because I have been there.

A superannuation fund contacted me in my capacity as a Licenced Private Investigator, about an "irregularity", nothing to do with a popular bran-based breakfast food. "Irregularity" excites me because I never know whether I'll find a simple clerical error, a den of thieves, a crooked hospital administrator or a murderer. This irregularity involved a Trustee who refused to allow a retirement cheque to be issued for superannuation of a long-serving 62 year old employee of a Victorian based trucking company. Let's call the employee Lindsay.

Lindsay took four months Long Service Leave and went to Europe with his wife. A fortnight after his departure, his employer received a letter of request for early retirement effective ASP. In that letter the Australian born Lindsay said he wanted to retire in Italy, the land of his parents. He would not return to Australia after the expiry of his leave. "His "letter gave directions for payment of his sizeable superannuation and other benefits to his bank account, details of which were supplied. The signature on the letter appeared genuine. Enquiries by the superannuation fund staff revealed that Lindsay's family home was being cared for by an adult son and daughter. A clerk in the Personnel Department of the Transport Company made a phone call to the home and a male, who identified himself as Lindsay's son, confirmed that his "father" wanted early retirement, so the payment process was started. But a Trustee of the superannuation fund, who knew Lindsay quite well, was not convinced that Lindsay would live overseas because Lindsay was devoted to the Carlton Football Club. The Trustee wanted further confirmation before a payment was made.

To placate that Trustee it was, somewhat reluctantly, decided by the Manager to engage an investigator. That's when I was called in. Half of the time of an investigator is to find a start point. Seeking one, I questioned the company office staff and learned that mail sent to Lindsay's address received a prompt response. The local Post Office told me of the approximate daily time that mail was delivered in Lindsay's area. From my car I watched the mail box. I saw a Courier Van park in the driveway and a well built man in his mid-twenties unlocked the front door of Lindsay's house. He reached inside and brought out something that turned out to be the key to the mail box. He opened the box, took the contents and disappeared back into the house, leaving the front door open. I knew the man was not Lindsay's son who was aged 44. Shortly afterwards a Ford car parked behind the van and a slim, good looking brunette in her mid-thirties rushed in through the open front door which was loudly closed. I had my start point.

A talk with Lindsay's son about visitors to the home of his parents provided the next step for answers. In two days the identity theft fraud was uncovered. The Police were informed by the lawyers of the superannuation fund based on evidence in my report. In catching this identity thief I wasn't particularly smart, it was easy because he was so over confident, one could say even cock-sure, and dumb. He smiled at the CCTV cameras in the Commonwealth Bank, Oakleigh, Victoria when transferring Lindsay's bank account. In the waste paper bin beside Lindsay's desk the Police found screwed up sheets of paper on which the thief had practiced forging Lindsay's signature. An arrest was made and the thief who stole Lindsay's ID was remanded in custody. Bail was refused.

What happened was this; Lindsay's 33 year old married daughter had keys to Lindsay's house. The family knew this but what they did not know was that the daughter also had a boyfriend. His nickname was "Blondie". To facilitate their illicit liaison, the daughter gave duplicate house keys to Blondie. When the daughter was not there, he had a free run of the house. It was not what the daughter intended, but Blondie had his own ideas.

Lindsay kept all his financial papers immaculately filed in a two drawer cabinet. Blondie "sprung" it open, ie twisted the sheet metal cabinet so it opened without a key. Blondie read all of Lindsay's personal papers including employment, superannuation, bank, investment and tax records. The dishonest Blondie saw Lindsay's signature and practiced imitating it until he could make a passable forgery. It was Blondie who sent the forged early retirement application to Lindsay's superannuation fund. (Blondie had ordered new credit cards and was trying to sell Lindsay's investments too) By luck, it was Blondie who answered the call when the company clerk telephoned. The brazen boyfriend claimed to be Lindsay's son.

It was Blondie who opened a bank account in Lindsay's name at another branch of Lindsay's regular bank and changed the address (a fault in the 100 points system, since corrected). Lindsay was eventually contacted by telephone in Perugia, Italy. He was appalled when he heard the news and returned home immediately. His $280,000 of retirement benefits was saved, but at the cost of the ruin of a holiday of a life time. Lindsay and his wife were terribly shocked at their daughter's frolic with Blondie in their bed. The entire family were embarrassed. The husband of the daughter was livid. But as no money was lost and to save further embarrassment and publicity that Blondie threatened, Lindsay prevailed upon the superannuation fund and Police to drop the charges. Blondie gave me a big smile and a two finger salute when leaving the Oakleigh Police station. As the saying goes, you win some, you lose some.

Alan, the successful superannuation thief from Melbourne and the crooked hospital administrator from Sydney both used stolen identities to steal. They had easy access to information because of their positions of trust. The thief who stole my ID had easy access to my details because they were public knowledge. Blondie indulged in burglary and went into history as the first identity thief to be foiled by love of a football team. The above examples confirm what the experts predict. The next world wide crime epidemic will be identity theft.

Here are some tips for your protection. Remember that practically no one is immune from the concentrated attention of a gang of thieves, so your first protective measure is to avoid being selected as a target. Regular computer users should heed the numerous cautions that appear on their screens and if they are frequent buyers, I recommend the use of PayPal. Otherwise have a separate bank account with no overdraft capacity and only sufficient money in to cover purchases. Use a debit card for purchases not a credit card. Don't use your name in full – give the bank a statutory declaration as to why you do not want to use your full name. Instead of James use Jim and no middle initial. And for businesses I recommend the Business Security Kit issued by the Victorian Police.

Thieves search for victims amongst the vulnerable, the unaware, the careless and the greedy. They look for soft targets so shield yourself and avoid being identified as potential prey. My tips assist you to do that and avoid being seen by ID thieves as vulnerable, unaware and careless. My tips make you a hard target.

A word of reassurance. Will your precautions indicate to ID thieves that you are a target of value? No, say the Police. On a risk / benefit analysis, the extra effort by thieves means extra risk for them. Thieves will leave you alone; they will go for easier targets. My tips seem so simple you may wonder at their effectiveness. They work by cutting off easy access to the information needed by the ID thieves. Make yourself a hard target. When you make it difficult for thieves to access to your data, they don't dally; they can't afford to pause because time is the greatest enemy of the "hit and run" thief.

Your protective strategy is simple; create delay and increase the risk for the thieves. Tactics you adopt to create delay are simple too – here are the simple tactical tips.

Tip 1: Have a lockable letter box

A quick grab by a thief of letters sticking out of a letter box often yields a bonanza of information. Contemplate what you receive by mail – bank statements; dividend payment advices, credit card statements, actual credit cards, pin numbers, Medicare cards, taxation notices, pension notices, Issuer Sponsored Holding statements from share registries and superannuation statements, to list just a few. Any one of these items offers basic information to thieves looking for an identity to steal. Your easy to get at letter box is the first objective of ID thieves.

From your letterbox the financial pirates can obtain your full name, address, bank, bank account number, bank balance, credit card details, including your limit, investment information including your shareholder and / or superannuation identification number, the size of your investment and maybe even your tax file number. All this from quick dips in your unlocked letter box.

Specialised gangs rule the Identity Theft business. Many visit from overseas to work a season in the Australian scam scene. Equipped with stolen information about you, thieves assess the prospects of their gain by robbing you. They decide on further action to acquire more information. Methods vary and I do not want to provide a blueprint on identify thief so I'll stop the precise commentary here. Sophisticated thieves, using complex computer intrusions will concentrate on sources of immense wealth, so most of us are safe from them. For the majority of us, foiling the "average" thieves is our objective and it's as easy as having a suitable size letter box that you can lock.

If the letterbox is lockable but too small for the mail you receive, the hanging out envelopes neutralize the advantage of a lockable letterbox. So have a letterbox of an appropriate size so that your mail falls in fully. Lots of letterboxes still in use today were designed for post WW2 letters. Our mail today in much bulkier. The thief that walks your street stealing mail must move speedily to avoid being seen, reported and apprehended. A lock gives you an advantage because thieves almost never stop to force open a locked letter box. As mentioned, one reason is that it takes time. Another is that when they are caught, the plea of a thief of mail from an open mail box is often explained to a Magistrate as "a spontaneous and uncharacteristic lapse into temptation caused by an easy opportunity". The lawyer for the thief will seek to shift the blame to you, the householder, who presented the irresistible temptation to her / his poor client. In a society conditioned by trial lawyers to believe that there is an explanation for every crime, this defence of "uncharacteristic, impulsive yield to temptation "repeatedly seems to result in a lenient penalty.

However, if the thief has busted a lock to steal letter box contents, that defence is impossible to sustain because the householder has taken reasonable precautions. Damage exacerbates the crime as it proves premeditated larcenous intent. The hoary old exculpatory bleat that the lock was a provocation is no longer accepted in Courts.

Theft of postal items is not a State Police but a Federal Police matter, and Federal offences result in stiffer penalties. Under Sec. 471 of the Federal Criminal Code Act 1995, "Tampering with mail receptacles"
A person is guilty of an offence it the person dishonestly:
    a. opens a mail-receptacle; or
    b. tampers with a mail-receptacle.
Penalty: Imprisonment for 5 years.
A person is guilty of an offence if:
    c. the person intentionally opens a mail-receptacle; and
    d. the person is not authorized by Australia Post to open the mail-receptacle; and
    e. the person does so knowing that he or she is not authorized by Australia Post to open the mail-receptacle.
Penalty: Imprisonment for 2 years.

So a simple lock on the mail box is, in reality, a very powerful deterrent tactic.

Tip 2: Invest in a shredder

The first target of ID thieves is your letterbox. If thieves find sufficient evidence of wealth or an easy track to identity theft in your letterbox, their second target is your rubbish bin, your green "Wheelie bin". Its contents can be a gift to thieves.

Which discarded financial document is found intact and most useful to thieves? Proxy forms! Lots of people who hold shares do not vote at the AGM of the company in which they hold shares – they simply throw away the proxy form intact, often with SRN and other details, including barcodes, into a "wheelie bin". Thieves adore proxy forms. They are current and can be used to verify a change of address. A change of address is usually a precursor to a rip-off. Don't make it an easy trip for thieves. Use a shredder for every bit of paper you throw out that has your name or any personal or financial details of you and your family printed on it. That includes bank statements, investment information, pension notices and bills, such as gas, electricity, municipal rates, etc. Shredders are cheap, lightweight, easy to use and safe. The Post Office sells shredders for as low as $50. 00.

Admittedly, painstaking thieves with infinite patience, plenty of time and glue sticks can restore shredded material, but how many ID thieves have those attributes? On a risk / benefit analysis it is simply not worth the time of a thief to reconstitute your old accounts to use them as evidence to obtain, say, a library card in your name. Yes, thieves steal books too, using someone else's name. An account from a utility or municipal authority with your name and address on it is sufficient for the issue of a library card. In 2003 as part of another investigation I learned of a 48 year old female who stole over 5000 books from libraries in three Council areas.

Thieves, like military guerrillas, must hit and run. They never have leisure to devote to making a collage of your shredded credit card accounts. Even supposing they did, the risk upon apprehension is magnified. As explained, thieves may try the "spontaneous and uncharacteristic lapse" defence if caught with your intact credit card statement. But that defense is impossible if the statement is reconstituted from shredded paper. That's a certain admission of guilt and conviction will result in a heavier sentence, because of a deliberate premeditated act. So potential identity thieves will not spend time sticking together your shredded credit card statements.

Financial statements that are simply torn up once or twice provide no protection. They can be easily and quickly put together. Use a shredder, it tells the thief you are cautious and so you are not an easy target. Thieves don't persevere with hard targets, they thrive on unaware and vulnerable people so when they see shredded paper in your green top or yellow top wheelie bin, they will move to someone else's garbage and you are safer. Persons more expert that I in identity theft safeguards advise that a lockable mailbox and a shredder, combined, give you a level of protection of 90% against ID theft. That is an incredible level of comfort for such inexpensive precautions – say $6 for a padlock and $60 for a shredder – total $66 – unbelievably cheap insurance.

Most recent reports are that ID thieves are using stolen legitimate credit card numbers to purchase expensive items on-line from internet retailers – computers, cameras, jewellery, cartons of expensive wines and other liquor. The range of value of up to $5000 seems to be popular. Thieves then advertise the stolen items on-line for say, $3000. When sold, the $3000 is sent to their bank account and cash withdrawn ASAP. The item involved, computer, jewellery etc is re-directed to the legitimate purchaser. If not immediately detected, the thieves now have established their bona-fides with the $3000 purchaser and try continue to sell other stolen items to that purchaser, until they detect investigation. You are stuck with a credit card statement showing a $5000 debit that you either pay or try to explain away to your credit card provider.

Same with gambling – using stolen credit card numbers thieves gamble heavily and collect winnings but leave you with the debts when they lose. Sometimes thieves target a seven race event using 21 stolen credit card numbers to bet on combinations. Mathematically two will win for them many thousands of dollars. They losses are left with the owner of the other 19 credit cards.

Tip 3: Never participate in door to door, telephone or mail surveys.

I have seen mail surveys that offer prizes to persons who complete and return survey forms or respond to "get rich quick" adverts. Tear them up – many have suspect origins and they provide ID thieves with a lot of information to make theft of your ID virtually certain. Telephone surveys that usually happen when I have just sat down at the table for my evening meal, receive a polite but firm "No, I do not participate in surveys". Never say "sorry", it makes you appear weak and the thieves may have another go at you. – Just firmly say "No" then hang up. I confess to having a vindictive personality. Like to get even? Press Hash # five or six times before you hang up, it mucks up the computer telephone numbers program and the telephone thieves are inconvenienced by having to re-set.

Internet surveys, unless I am absolutely certain they are genuine, I avoid like the plague. One internet survey in Toronto, Canada, asked the questions, hidden amongst many other innocuous questions, "Where are you going for your next holiday, for how long and when do you leave?" Over 400 people who responded had their homes burgled when on holiday. The surveyor sold the information to a gang of thieves for $60. 00 for each name, address and phone number. Those types of surveys have already started here in Melbourne. I understand the desire of some industries to have surveys and doubtless surveys have community benefit. For me, I will only respond to the official survey such as that of the Commonwealth of Australia Census.

Currently fraudulent medical schemes are circulating in Australian cities involving an unsolicitored letter, a questionnaire for medical self diagnosis –complete and return the questionnaire and get a free health check report and a free tube of "cure all" cream. Don't be lured in by the word "free". The miracle cream is (petroleum jelly) Vaseline coloured by Condy's crystals. You get the eighty cent cream. They get details of your bank account.

Included in my recommendation of surveys to avoid I must emphasise, very strongly, the coupons put out by some astrologers and horoscope analysts. If the clairvoyant wants your credit card details, give them a miss. It begs the question: if the clairvoyant can really read your mind why bother to give any details? If you respond, the clairvoyant may sell your name, address and details to other dubious enterprises and highlight you as a gullible potential target. I have evidence that some clairvoyants, fortune tellers and horoscope readers are linked with pornographic magazine and video distributors. So apart from making you a target for thieves you could find your name on an extremely perverted porno mailing list.

Beware of unsolicited mail seeking your bank account details. The" Nigerian Scam" reappears with monotonous regularity as do fraudulent notifications of lottery prizes, many of which emanate from Spain and/or Holland. How long has this type of letter scam been going on? There is ample evidence of it during the Crusades, about the year 1100. A written record exists dated 1588, it was known as the Spanish Prisoner scam. With all the changes that have taken place some people find comfort in observing that human nature has not changed over the centuries – we still have thieves.

Tip 4: Beware of strangers

Strangers have no right to information about our finances. When we were children we were taught to be wary of strangers. It is prudent to still maintain your guard. We all need to be wary. Alf was an 80 year old gentleman from Seymour in Victoria who took pity on an apparently deserving young lady he met when she sat down at his table in a railway station café. Alf was having a cup of tea while waiting for his train.

The young woman was extremely respectful and polite. She was well spoken with an educated accent and started a conversation with Alf. At a point in the conversation, tears welled up in her eyes. She told Alf of her marriage break up and of her vindictive husband, a solicitor, whose legal actions had deprived her of all her money and furthermore prevented her from opening a bank account. Without a bank account she could not cash a cheque that her parents in Tasmania had sent her to help her. If she couldn't cash the cheque she wouldn't be able to pay her rent next week and so could be tossed out on the street. She said she wasn't asking for money but asked if Alf could help her cash her parents' cheque through his bank account. As the 80 year old Alf had only $50 in his Pensioner Savings account at the bank, he figured that if he was robbed then $50 would be the limit. He was prepared to take that gamble to help a young lady who had all the signs of being genuine but had struck a bit of bad luck. After all, it was she trusting him with her money. The lovely, lonely, young lady was not trying to get anything from him.

So after finishing his cup of tea Alf walked with the young lady to a nearby branch of his bank where she helped him pay her cheque into his account. In a friendly chat on the way to the bank she learnt a few of Alf's personal details such as his date of birth. Alf was pleased he could help his new-found attractive, young lady friend with the low neckline and big brown eyes. (No impure thoughts please gentlemen).

A few days later Alf went to his bank and withdrew in cash the amount of her "parents'" cheque. At the railway café they met, as arranged, and Alf gave the cash to her. She offered to give some of it to Alf to cover his bank costs and compensate him for his time, but Alf graciously declined the kind offer. Alf then simply forgot about the incident. Later he vaguely recalled that his regular quarterly bank statement did not arrive but he did not think much about it.

Some months went by and one day Alf answered a knock on the door of his humble cottage. There stood a local Police constable, an affable fellow with whom Alf had often chatted about local events. But this time the Policeman as unsmiling.

Very formally he asked Alf is he was Mr Alfred ...., and when Alf said "Yes" in a puzzled voice, the constable introduced Alf to a well tailored gentleman making enquires for AUSTRAC. Alf was told AUSTRAC was nothing to do with the railways but rather AUSTRAC was the short name of the **Australian Transaction Reports and Analysis Centre** – a Federal Government Agency that "tracked" (hence its abbreviation) the paths of large sums of money, particularly Australian money being dispatched overseas.

Alf thought these men were at the wrong place but tolerantly allowed them to enter. Alf began to worry when the Austrac man produced papers to show that Alf's little bank account in the country town of Seymour had been transferred to Melbourne City. Records showed that, over a two month period, $600,000 had been transferred from Alf's little savings bank account to several banks in Nigeria. The $600,000 that passed through Alf's account was the proceeds of dozens of credit card frauds.

It didn't take long for the investigators to realize that Alf was another victim. They helped Alf to close down his bank account and open another. They got as many details of Alf's lady "friend" as the 80 year old could remember (he mentioned big brown eyes and long eyelashes and said she reminded him of Paris; when he looked at her he got an Eiffel) and they promised Alf that he would not be prosecuted.

Alf was pleased he still had his $50. It was just as well because Alf's second shock came when Centrelink stopped his pension pending an enquiry into how this aged pensioner had acquired and spent $600,000 that Centrelink's regular bank account surveillance revealed. It took a couple of months to have the Centrelink matter finally sorted out and Alf's pension restored, backdated. Fortunately Alf had a supporting family or he might have starved. It's not only the money that is stolen by identity thieves, it's the enormous stress felt by honest people when their trust is betrayed. Alf was deeply hurt. Alf's life became a nightmare. He seemed to be endlessly filling in statutory declarations and other forms. Paperwork had never been his forte; he had always been an outdoor worker. He never recovered. Alf died soon after filling in the last form.

As mentioned earlier, Alf is only one of thousands of Australians targeted by ID thieves and his story reinforces my fourth tip – beware of strangers, no matter how convincing their story may sound. Should you be approached by a young lady with a similar story to that which suckered Alf, send her to the Salvation Army, They can arrange for cheques to be vetted and ,if genuine, cashed.

Lately there is evidence of ID thieves using adverts in local paper "Talking Friends" to get your personal information. Protect yourself by being a hard target. Beat the ID thieves. They will ruin you financially, despoil your reputation and destroy your willingness to trust. Don't think that your superannuation is safe from these thieves. To them, your super is just another asset to plunder, so ensure you shred discarded superannuation statements. Never talk about your finances to a stranger or to anyone who does not need to know.

A new Federal Government initiative is the Australian Criminal Identity Register ACIR. It lists names of stolen ID victims reported to it and assists in restoration of your credibility (not necessarily of recovery of stolen property). When it comes to ID thieves, every one of us is a target. But if you follow the four easy tips you can guarantee yourself a large degree of protection from the predators.

Let's run through those tips again.

1. Install a lockable letterbox of a suitable size.
2. Use a shredder on all private papers before you put them into the Council rubbish bin.
3. Never respond to questions asked by door callers, telephone or mail surveys and
4. Protect your personal information, especially from strangers.

All four of these precautions give you about 99% protection and that's an enormously comforting percentage compared with the zero percent of an unaware person.

Next time you see on TV or read in the paper about an ID thief or fraud, you may recall that ID theft is on the increase. Resolve to act now. Lock your letterbox, shred personal documents, don't respond to surveys and beware of strangers. Don't be a victim in the crime epidemic. Be secure and defeat the ID thieves. Let's not be losers, let's all be winners.

Chapter Eighteen

Restitution or Retribution?

CONSIDER TWO HYPOTHETICAL SCENARIOS. ONE is lawful the other unlawful. Decide which is which. Then decide which is just.

Scenario One

A superannuation contributor, let's call him Bert, is told on the day he retires that the base rate $500 pw pension he expected for the rest of his life will only be $250 pw. A thief stole a lot of the assets of his superannuation fund. The Trustees suspected something was wrong and hired a Private Investigator. The PI's report pinpointed the thief. The Trustees referred the matter to the Police who apprehended and charged the thief. A judge sentenced the thief to 42 months in a minimum security prison for "nice" offenders, computer access, a library, tennis court, conjugal visits and opportunity for further education at State expense. The excellent facilities will rehabilitate the thief, it is hoped. With good behaviour concessions the thief will be "out" in 28 months. His obligation to society is fulfilled. The missing assets have never been recovered. Bert's life expectancy is 19 years. He must live on half the pension he expected.

Scenario Two

Bert attains retirement age and receives a base rate pension of $500 pw. Over a retirement celebratory drink a Trustee tells Bert a fairy tale. "Once upon a time" he started, and then related that Trustees of a hypothetical superannuation fund were concerned that a significant amount of assets of the fund may be missing. They hired a Private Investigator. The PI reported that a trusted manager may have "borrowed" some assets. The PI suggested an avenue of restitution. Upon receipt of non-recorded approval, the PI arranged a set of circumstances and confronted the "borrower". A sizable percentage was repaid immediately. The "borrower" re-mortgaged his home plus re-mortgaged the home of his consenting but disappointed parents. The "borrower" avoided prison and now works two jobs to pay off both mortgages. The fund lost nothing. Bert got his full pension.

I reiterate, these are indicative, over simplistic and hypothetical. How did you answer the questions? Which of the two is illegal? Does scenario two allow a miscreant to escape the penalty of a Court conviction or is it more just? Just for whom? Bert or the "borrower?" If you were a Trustee, which scenario would you authorise? And if, as a Trustee you pursued scenario two, would you tell your fund members about it? If you tell the members are you subjecting yourself to possible charges of "Perverting the Course of Justice?" If you do not tell the members are you not in breach of the Trust Deed requirement of disclosure? Or will you be comforted by the disclosure provision that only "significant" items must be advised and that you have the power to decide what is or is not significant? If these scenarios were true, any PI involved must exercise considerable caution in writing a book relating details of similar events, if they ever happened. Negotiated retrieval of assets invariably involved comprehensive Confidentially Agreements. Because no Court was involved and because it is difficult to disguise details, defamation is a danger should an identity is disclosed.

Whenever an investigation results in a Court case and conviction, a PI or an author who tells the story and remains relentlessly within the official reports has no worry about defamation when naming people and their transgressions. Examples are as follow.

Mr Atan Ona Kassongo of Castle Hill, NSW was convicted under secs 62 &202 of SIS for not maintaining the Kassongo Superannuation Fund (KSF), a SMSF of which he was a Trustee, in accordance with the sole purpose test. A sum of $4,055,043 from 56 complying superannuation funds representing 192 superannuants was paid to KSF's bank accounts. Mr Kassongo was aware of his obligation to preserve these benefits. He extracted $605,000 as commission.

Mr Sonatane Haitoni Hafoka (aka Tane Hafoka, aka Jonathan Hafoka, aka Johnny) is alleged by ASIC to have assisted Mr Kassongo with at least 80 rollovers and received commission in excess of $300,000. Both were convicted. Mr Kassongo was sentenced to two years imprisonment, to be released after eight months on a three year good behaviour bond. Mr Hafoka was given a six month suspended sentence.

Mr Gerard Karl Little of NSW was convicted of offenses similar to Kassongo, under secs 62 &202 of SIS related to the Little Super Fund (LSF). A total of $3. 5 million from eleven complying superannuation funds representing 121 superannuants went into LSF from which Mr Little got $685,000 as commission. His sentence mirrored that of Atan Kassongo, two years imprisonment but out after eight months with a three year good behaviour bond.

Mr Travers David Loy was found by ASIC to have fabricated false claims, mainly relating to income protection, allowing him to receive $1,224,936 fraudulently. In 2013 he was permanently banned from providing financial services.

ASIC alleged that Mr Kovelan Bangaru fraudently obtained over $19. 8 million and fled to the USA from whence he was extradited, tried and sentenced to eight years and six months imprisonment with parole denied until he has served six years and four months. The Commonwealth Director of Public Prosecutions prosecuted at his trial. ASIC have not commented about any recovery of the $19. 8 million.

Swindlers don't look like crooks. Well most of them. That is part of their success. On first acquaintance would you suspect that a prominent Melbourne Lawyer, a partner in a firm with offices throughout Australia, UK, Europe and Asia was a swindler? From 1993 Max Green, a lawyer in a Melbourne legal firm, was involved in frauds that totalled about $42 million. Max was defrauding many people in a tax dodge scam based upon non-existent equipment hire for the construction of toll roads. Included on the list of potential "suckers" were several superannuation funds. Max had an appointment with the investment Manager of one of the superannuation funds of which I was a Trustee, but he never kept the appointment. He was murdered in a Cambodian hotel.

The Australian Securities and Investment Commission (ASIC) the commercial cop that enforces the Corporations Law in Australia (it has no jurisdiction overseas) estimates that over 100,000 people have been swindled over the last ten years in a vast variety of con tricks. That's 10,000 people each year, or 28 per day. And that's only the victims who have reported being swindled. Many accept their loss without reporting. Don't become a statistic, ask questions, that's your best initial defense as stated earlier. Where can you ask questions? If you have shares, I suggest the Australian Shareholders Association (ASA) is a friendly first contact for information. ASA offer a range of membership options starting with $120 a year for individual membership of this not-for-profit association and that's tax deductable for investors. They have a phone referral service for members. The ASIC website www.scamwatch.gov.au is another source. It's entertaining and educational. Make it a regular monthly viewing practice. Among other items it gives details of the Australian Consumer Law (ACL) that offers, inter alia, protection by way of warnings against misleading or deceptive conduct. Large superannuation funds have a multitude of protections against fraud. Since the failed CSS Fraud protective screens were updated and tightened throughout the industry.

Clearly the weakness within the industry is the smaller Self Managed Superannuation Fund. SMSFs with less resources, especially the DIY stand alone, ie not professionally managed SMSFs. The Australian Securities and Investments Commission (ASIC) is the prime watchdog of SMSF auditors, a role it shares with the Australian Taxation Office. Auditors must pass an exam to gain registration. They act as the "gatekeeper" between the authorities and the SMSF members. In December 2014 the registrations of over 400 auditors were cancelled. To me, the removal of so many is disturbing. Disconcerting also are the enormous numbers of people and entities shown on ASIC's list of permanently disqualified superannuation trustees.

Particularly for a Manager of a Self Managed Superannuation Fund (SMSF) is for a written, approved, Product Disclosure Statement (PDS) to be studied before any investment. Don't be too eager to part with your money, always ask for time to consider, do not be pressured. Remember the adage; if it's not in a written report, it didn't happen. Indeed if you are pressured, its highly persuasive evidence of the tactics of a con artist. Your own solicitor, never the vendor's "free" solicitor, should be consulted before signing any legal documents.

One couple paid their own solicitor $60 for advice and saved their life time earnings in their SMSF. The solicitor's advice saved them from handing over $340,000 to David Gibson, a crooked investment adviser who operated in the Melbourne suburb of Brighton. Gibson ripped off about 600 trusting clients of over $40 million before being convicted and sentenced to 12 years in jail. Gibson offered "tax free" investments to retirees and vulnerable older people. He cultivated a high reputation for integrity and most victims were referred by word-of-mouth. His reputation was a façade. Never- the -less it was precisely that high reputation that shielded him for so long. People felt it impolite to question such a distinguished person. After he was caught and put in jail, many victims wished that they had summoned up the courage to seek an independent second opinion. At Gibson's trial the Judge castigated him for his careful and manipulative cultivation of vulnerable clients. Gibson considered himself a pillar of society but he was just another gutless thief who preyed upon the gullible.

This case should serve as an object lesson to anyone inclined to try to beat the tax system. Gibson's investment schemes had the aroma of "tax dodge" so some people refrained from asking questions because they just did not want to know. A few did ask about the "tax free" aspect and received a glib explanation; however that explanation would not have withstood the scrutiny of an independent solicitor or accountant. The victims paid a high price for not asking questions and maybe for trying to cheat on taxation. Many of the clients of Gibson were overcome with shame and guilt at being fleeced. They blamed themselves and did not readily seek to admit their losses to the investigating authorities. A fair number were justified in blaming themselves as they deliberately sought to dodge tax and / or wrongfully disguise assets to enhance their Centrelink entitlements. Those genuine people who were deceived have my sympathy. Those who invested with half-closed eyes to either dodge tax or deceive Centrelink get no sympathy from me. I reserve that for the truly vulnerable.

One of my mentors in the superannuation industry told me that a financial advisor in the Eastern suburbs of Melbourne bought an expensive eight berth motor yacht. My mentor saw that extravagant purchase as a signal to immediately withdraw his business. He retrieved his investment several months before the financer's company was put into liquidation. The same principle may have helped others if they had known of Gibson's exorbitant investments in racehorses.

So, when it comes to SMSF investments, be honest with yourself and expect others to be also, but never neglect to ask questions. APRA, ASA, ASIC, your solicitor, your SMSF Manager, your accountant, and your bank can assist. Don't be led like a lamb to the slaughter or deluded by a reputation, charming manner or pressure. Any truly reputable adviser will be pleased to meet your solicitor, accountant, bank Manager or an astute friend or yours and provide full information in writing about any investments being recommended. If your best friend is your advisor, matters can be difficult, but insist that business and friendship remain separate. Insist also that all dealings are documented. Professional ethics and standards must be maintained. If your friend is truly your friend, he will adhere to that separation. If not, reassess the relationship without delay.

Details of each of the seven aforementioned fraudsters were publicly aired and serve as examples. Even an edited list of superannuation scammers would fill several volumes. By contrast negotiations for restitution of "borrowed" superannuation money are strictly private. Fraudsters do not want to be named and shamed. That gives a PI some small amount of leverage. Trustees of affected funds do not want to disturb the confidence of contributors. If no money is lost, Trustees are loath to make a report. No report, it didn't happen. The Iceberg Principle in practice. It works.

Most "act alone" embezzlers never offend again, so I guess negotiated restitution had some rehabilitation quality. There are always exceptions. Offenders are known to have changed their name by Deed Poll so probably they get "under the radar" of the superannuation protectors. I would not have recognised a re-named, re-offender if her lawyer had not sent a mildly threatening letter to the Trustees of one fund reminding them of their "vow of silence" pursuant to a Confidentially Agreement. The recidivist was caught defrauding another entity. A Trustee referred the lawyer's letter to me to me purely as a matter of interest. I was not a signatory to that Agreement.

Intrigued, I made enquiries, and sat in the Public Gallery of the Court on the day of her trial for an almost identical fraud of $80,000 to that which she had perpetrated earlier against a fund that now paid me a retainer. During a recess her lawyer sent a clerk to ask me to leave the Court because my presence was unsettling his client. I refused and the clerk left. The lawyer then approached me and said I must leave or the judge would be asked to evict me. I told her to "go ahead" knowing that any eviction would have to entail the lawyer giving details to judge of the earlier attempted fraud. Nothing happened. The judge never even looked at the Gallery. The 42 year old spendthrift female was convicted under Sec. 82 of the Crimes Act: Obtaining financial advantage by deception.

The defence and later mitigation plea sounded pathetic to me. Dispensing with the vocal verbiage, the essence of the defense was that the accused was actually the victim due to the neglect of the Trustees of the superannuation fund. They omitted to specifically include in her job description that she could not temporarily relocate money to her private use when she was under financial pressure. A puerile pretence of a defense I know, but I should have anticipated it. Upon apprehension, every swindler I encountered claimed it wasn't "his / her" fault. His crime was always the fault of someone else or caused by something else. This assertion is top of the list of the shared characteristics of conmen. Each denied all responsibility for their actions. Even in jail swindlers still complain that their crimes were not their fault. Sadly, I think they said it so often that they became victims of their own self-delusions. And this "it's not my fault" propensity for self-delusion would definitely be on the list of conman characteristics following closely on their copy-cat characteristic.

Three swindlers apprehended for almost successful crimes, in three different superannuation funds each tried to convince me their crime was my fault. Because, each said, the benefits offered by the superannuation fund of which I was a Trustee were so good they created an irresistible temptation. Every swindler claimed to be the victim, there was always someone else to blame. Mothers, fathers, other relatives, schoolteachers, bosses, priests, shop assistants, even the victims of their theft – you name it, it was always someone else's fault. One 40 year old man strenuously claimed that his three month compulsory National Service, when he was aged 18 ruined his life. He tried to enlist my sympathy but desisted when

I told him I was a Natio and I reckoned it was great. Conmen never admit any fault.

Several times I heard swindlers have the effrontery to directly address judges and juries in an attempt at self-justification by trying to spread the blame. They invoked the biblical "Let him without guilt cast the first stone". Their lament usually goes along these lines – "There is no such thing as an honest person because everyone here has done something dishonest at some time so you have no right to sit in judgement over me simply because I was a little misguided". An accountant who stole over $18 million over a ten year period from vulnerable clients said that, almost word for word. It was the only time I saw a judge laugh in court. I totally refute the bleat of swindlers because Mr Average who may occasionally acquire something illegal or fiddle a bit on the tax return is in an entirely different category to someone who makes theft and deception his chosen career. A conman is a thief with a monstrous ego and contempt for other humans. He deliberately searches for and then contrives traps to catch the gullible, vulnerable and defenceless. He not only destroys finances, he destroys our capacity for trust. We should be responsible for our lives and our actions, not weaselling out of responsibility for criminal behaviour.

When I was very young I recall a man who stole money from a Post Office claiming it was the fault of the greyhounds on which he bet. Another thief stole money from the Cathedral Hotel (that once stood on the corner of Flinders Lane and Swanston Streets Melbourne) and said his theft was the fault of Walter Lindrum. Mr Lindrum was a billiard champion who owned an establishment in Flinders Street where people could hire time to play on billiard tables. The thief claimed he was addicted to playing billiards all day long, so his theft of the Hotel's money to assuage his addiction was the fault of Mr Lindrum. He, the thief, tried to claim the status of a victim.

Others have blamed the racehorses and when "Tattersall's" arrived in Victoria, thieves blamed "Tatts" for their crimes. Frankly I get tired of these lame excuses, but what really aggravates me is the constant stock of people in high places who seem to readily add to the noise of the blame-deflecting bandwagon initiated by thieves, with barely a kind word for the tragic victims. Recently a former Mayor of Geelong was convicted of stealing. One of his victims was a paraplegic. But in the newspaper report a prominent clergyman added value to the music of "I am blameless, poor me!" by joining the thief and his friends in a condemnation of Crown Casino. Which of these two do you think I consider is the least reprehensible? Most of us have or should have by the time we are adult, an innate perception of right and wrong. The conman allows his ego to over-ride that natural perception and that, clearly is the difference between an "honest" man and a predatory conman. By far the best, "I am the victim" claim I've ever read about was that of a convicted thief, tax cheat and adulterer – former Queensland politician Senator Bob Woods. He blamed his obsession with the late Princess Diana for his crimes.

"Always watch a snake" Cleopatra lisped as she grasped her asp. Good advice if you opt for the restitution route. Ensure that your lawyer includes "escape clauses" in any" Confidentiality Agreement" in case a "snake" signatory tries to abuse its purpose. I retain use of the nomenclature of "Confidentiality Agreement" even though documents of a similar import are titled "Contracts .... , Deeds of ...... Statements of ...., etc. The snake is the nickname of a man I refer to who defrauded a marine engineering company superannuation fund of over $100,000 whilst acting as an assistant to the Accountant. Detected by the company auditors he offered restitution in consideration of non-prosecution. His family rallied around to raise the repayment. A Confidentially Agreement was signed by the snake, the company directors and the superannuation fund Trustees.

Ninety five days later the company was served with a writ claiming $150,000 in damages for unlawful dismissal. The snake contacted several officers of the company to warn that clauses in the Confidentiality Agreement meant it could not be used by the company in any defence of the unlawful dismissal claim. A Senior Counsel engaged by the company reluctantly agreed that the Confidentiality Agreement was deficient.

The saviour of the company was Industrial Relations Law of that State. The claim had to be submitted to an Industrial Relations Mediator prior to registration with a Court. The powers of the Mediator were extensive. He pondered, aloud, at a meeting of the parties, as to whether he would settle the matter by setting aside completely the Confidentiality Agreement and inviting and opinion from the Police Fraud Squad. He also mumbled something about "Champerty" in relation to the family of the snake who financed the "unlawful dismissal" claim in expectation of recovering the $100,000 loaned plus a "dividend". The Mediator called a brief adjournment for snake to consult his solicitor. The solicitor turned green when he heard of the cogitations of the Mediator and snake's claim was rapidly withdrawn.

Lesson, make certain your Confidentiality Agreement is drawn up by a specialist in that area of law. Afterwards I consulted The Concise Oxford Dictionary and found that, at that time, the crime of "Champerty" was defined as "Action of assisting a party in a suit in which one is not naturally interested, with view to receiving a share of disputed property". I am still uncertain whether or not Confidentiality Agreements in relation to restitution of purloined investments are legal or not.

Stopping swindlers provides great satisfaction to superannuation fund managers. Part of the thrill is to pick which six out of every hundred disability retirement applicants are swindlers. Six percent seems to be the industry average and remarkably it appears to have remained constant over the last 30 years. Another part is to pick your way sagely through the law that, regrettably, seems slanted towards over-protection of those parasites who least respect it. Swindlers / frauds / conmen, call them what you will, all have immense egos that are perpetually stimulated by a sympathetic media. Despicable they may be, but conmen provide the media with news and reporting of news is what provides the media with the basis of their income. Every grubby conman has bestowed upon him by the media the sobriquet of "King Con". A most misleading description. There was nothing regal about any conman I ever met.

One conman I encountered flew out to Queensland leaving his room at the Ibis Hotel in Therry Street Melbourne, that's near the Victoria Market, in a most disgusting mess. He appeared to have had a problem distinguishing between the bed and the toilet. Several others each left their rented premises like pig sties – discarded food scraps, styrene containers, bottles, and a sink full of unwashed crockery, soiled underwear, newspapers, pornographic magazines and overflowing ashtrays. In public, each conman was immaculately turned out; expensive suit, double cuff shirt, gold cuff links, hundred dollar tie,(a couple of times an old school tie was undeservingly worn) mirror polished shoes, manicured nails, barber shop shave with ample expensive after- shave lotion. That was the public image. But "at home" many were filthy people and it strikes me as a pity that the media continue to pander to the ego of each conman and elevate them rather than show them for the grubs they really are.

Conmen sucker the public by reversing the truth. They play on sympathy by assuming the role of the victim and adroitly make the real victims and the police appear as unprincipled persecutors. Conmen cunningly exploit the "Ned Kelly" syndrome that pervades our society. I deplore the purveyors of the Ned Kelly "Hero" myth as much as I do the conmen. Conmen are heartless criminals and Kelly and his gang were murderers and thieves. Let's bury the myth.

When I was a young seller of newspapers outside of a Yarraville pub, my friends and I would giggle with glee when we heard of a brazen and ingenious conman who robbed some pompous, arrogant, rich, greedy members of the "upper class". Some of the pretentious class made minor fortunes as wartime black marketeers. The reputation of that conman would soar as his exploits were described and embroidered over millions of glasses of beer in pubs during Melbourne's infamous six o'clock swill. (Pubs closed at 6pm then). Conning the rich was considered an, almost, honourable occupation. For a long time I believed in the old "honour amongst thieves" adage when told of the actions of several tough Yarraville wharfies who were the biggest uncaught thieves south of the Maribyrnong River.

With World War II nearing its end, a conman from the suburb of Spotswood operated a despicable con on the families of servicemen who were reported as KIA – Killed In Action. The unscrupulous reprobate scanned the newspaper obituary columns then wrote to grieving families of the dead soldier, sailor, airman or merchant seaman stating that he was a returned member of the same unit /ship as the deceased. He was home for a short while recovering from battle wounds. He claimed that his dead mate owed him money and spun a hard luck story about returning to action soon to induce the family to discharge the debt to him.

That conman made quite a bit of money from the heartless scam for longer than a year. He made the mistake of writing to a family close to one of the wharfies who realised it was a con. The wharfies traced the conman. He worked as a meter reader for a municipal electricity authority, a reserved occupation, and had never served in any of Australia's armed services or the Merchant Navy. Nor had he sustained any wounds, at least until the wharfies called on him. After their visit he was incapable for reading meters for longer than a year.

This story illustrates that conmen who duped and robbed the rich were applauded but low life conmen who preyed upon grieving and vulnerable people were summarily dealt with by elements of the criminal fraternity. A sense of fair play permeated the community. It was not law but it was justice in the opinion of many.

Today it's not like that. The conman has lost any lustre and is no longer revered. The people viewed as targets today are seldom the pompous rich but honest hard working members of society. They are likely to be your vulnerable ageing parents. Conmen have no remorse. When they steal the life savings of a half blind, partly crippled 85 year old widow they consider themselves worthy of an award for gallantry – that's their level today. The level of scum.

Should any reader think I condemn too harshly let them reflect that my attitude results from my experience. It is hard to help victims left financially and emotionally destitute. The majority of the frail never recover. The sunshine of their later years disappears behind a permanent dark grey cloud.

The late Spike Milligan told those gathered at a luncheon of former Artillery members (Gunners) that there are no new crimes, it's just that today the old ones get more media coverage. I did not properly hear him because, like many former members of the Royal Regiment of Artillery, I suffer with some hearing loss. It's known as gunnerear.

Chapter Nineteen

Is Your Super Secure?

HOW SECURE IS YOUR SUPERANNUATION? Any answer depends entirely upon the type of superannuation fund to which the questioner contributes and how gullible is the contributor. If the contributor is a member of a major fund and a major fraud is perpetrated against that fund then it is highly probable that the contributor is 100% secure. The Superannuation Industry Supervision Act 1993, (SIS) has provisions to allow the Federal Treasury to reimburse the defrauded major fund.

Note that word "major". It seems that a contributor to a minor fund against which a minor fraud is perpetrated may still suffer unreimbursed loss. The scope is wide open because the SIS provisions remain largely untested. No one knows the answer. What happens if a minor fraud causes loss to a major fund or a major loss to a minor fund?

And if a loss permeates through the system of a multiple choice fund to the disadvantage of a contributor will there be adequate safeguards to enable the contributor to seek full restoration? Or can (or maybe should) the defrauded superannuation fund management attribute proportion of a loss to only one class of the contributors? Imagine a massive loss occurs with, say, the High Growth elective investments sector of a fund. Will that loss have repercussions for the contributors who selected the Conservative and Balanced investment sectors? Maybe a clearer answer can be given if the loss was due to the actions of conmen or shonky investment spruikers external to the fund, but what happens if the fraud is perpetrated from within the fund, say by a senior Manager or a Trustee?

"Heaven forfend that a person occupying such a responsible position as that of a superannuation fund Trustee should ever be crooked" was a statement made at a meeting of ASFA. Perhaps it was uttered tongue in cheek. All who heard it laughed. The Disqualification Register of the Australian Prudential Regulation Authority. (APRA) lists over a thousand companies and persons as disqualified under SIS from involvement with superannuation funds as Trustees and financial advisors.

The security of your future retirement may depend upon which of the main types of fund to which you choose to contribute. Banks and Investment companies promote major Retail Funds. These accumulation funds offer membership to all comers. They offer numerous investment options and are popularly recommended by Financial Advisors, who receive a commission and the promoters aim to make a profit by way of fees. Retail Funds are professionally managed in a competitive environment.

Industry funds are "not for profit" entities originally established for employees in a particular industry. Profits remain in the fund to enhance member benefits and almost all have low or mid-range fee schedules and almost all are "major" and allow non-industry members to join. They offer less investment options than Retail but the options seem adequate and most are accumulation with a few longer established funds still managing a few "defined" schemes.

Public sector funds are for Government employees, Federal and State. Newer funds are accumulation, older ones defined, and their investment options are limited. All are "major". Most Corporate funds are run by companies for the exclusive benefit of employees. Larger funds are self-managed by a Board of Trustees appointed by the employer and/or elected by the employees. Again, new members are in accumulation funds, some older members in defined. In some funds parts or all of the management functions are sub-contracted to Industry or Retail funds and Investment options can vary widely. Eligible rollover funds (ERF) hold money for inactive or "lost" members, usually with low account balances. MySuper accumulation funds have similarities to ERF's and are likely to replace existing "default accounts" that are the repository of the superannuation of employees who do not direct any balance to a particular fund when they leave employment. Retail, Industry and Corporate funds can offer MySuper accounts. All of the above have a greater degree of trained, professional managers. They are wary of attempts by frauds to get at your money. That's, in part, how they justify the management fees.

And now, the "must have" fashionable fund, The SMSF, The Self Managed Superannuation Fund. Any adult can set up and manage a SMSF but must adhere to regulations monitored by the ATO. Regulations include; act as a Trustee with all the legal duties applicable thereto; apply all investments to retirement benefits; follow an approved investment strategy; maintain comprehensive records and have an annual audit by a qualified SMSF auditor. It is definitely not a task for unskilled or time-short people. Scores of self-managed SMSFs are deregistered by the ATO each year, many operators are heavily fined.

Fortunately we now have a number of reputable professional organisations who manage SMSFs for people who want control over their financial future. A wide range of optional services are available from initial establishment through administration, custody, full or part Trustee service, taxation, etc. These professional organizations clearly specify what constitutes approved investment choices that they will implement on behalf of a client SMSF and just as clearly list the types of investments that are debarred. It's worthwhile to remember the axiom "If you pay peanuts you get monkeys".

"Welcome to my website said the spider to the fly". A colourful website highlighted the following:-

"Is it fair that you are exploited by a superannuation fund that richly rewards its many employees and pays exorbitant commissions from your earnings? No! Take control of your own destiny. Retire rich".

The proprietors of that site sucked in several dozen people to set up SMSF's. All were robbed blind. The proprietors spent time in prison and their names can be found among the hundred on the "Companies you should not deal with" list published and regularly updated by the Australian Securities and Investment Commission (ASIC).

Probably the victims never had time to consider facts such as fees, performance, service and probity of the "switch" proposer. Positively, not one of the victims had attended any of my lectures on "Identity Theft and Frauds" otherwise they would have recognised one of the "Earmarks", I call them "Arsemarks", of the scammers, which is the hustle tactic, "Must act now" is one weapon in the arsenal of the fraudster. Others are: - Above average and speedy returns, Tax free benefits, No risk, access to Inside Information. All have glossy brochures so full of glowing endorsements that no space was available to print the Australian Financial Services licence details. Superannuation is not simple. Many feel bewildered and are easy targets for someone who professes to solve their problems. Promises of quick and easy access to preserved superannuation benefits mesmerises a lot a people who impatiently want "money now" not in the future.

Returning to the question, how secure is superannuation? In the foregoing chapters about tainted Trustees, contributors lost only a little money in dribbles from kickbacks. No monetary loss was involved with stolen authorship. By contrast, in 2001 cheque frauds on C+BUS, The Timber Industry Superannuation Scheme, Host-Plus, JUST and Motor Trades Association Super Funds are understood to have ripped off $2 million. What may be lost from future attempts by criminals will depend upon the circumstances and the degree to which diligent fund administrators address their risk management controls. Scares will emerge from time to time.

For example several media reports mentioned that Auscoal Superannuation lost $1.6 million in "rollover" cheques following a raid on their Post Office box. Auscoal and Australia Post denied the report to the relief of members. Someone did open Auscoal's Post Office with a key to steal some mail but an alert Australia Post employee changed the lock soon after the unauthorised removal. The following weekend another attempt to access the Auscoal Post Office box failed. No loss to the members occurred. It is interesting to speculate what may have happened had a loss occurred. No doubt action for recovery would have eventuated, with the possibility that some feral member would be inspired to sue the Trustees for negligence and claim a large sum of damages. The Australian Prudential and Regulations Authority (APRA), the Federal Government superannuation monitoring entity, spurred by the failed fraud on Auscoal and others, has tightened controls to increase the integrity of the industry.

Refreshingly a new legal breeze is stirring the judiciary. Over the last few decades the public could be forgiven for concluding that personal responsibility for your own actions was a trait that had vanished. If a person felt disadvantaged or peeved about something then that person or their relatives bleated loud and long. Some entity or other would be accused of some form of moral failure or hind sighted omission and coerced into compensation that the agitators seems to obtain in a manner lawful but loaded with doubtful moral justice.

The underserving obtained rewards to which they should never be entitled were it not for the threat of taking selectively edited accusations to a media outlet. The accusations were welcomed by those media elements that specialise in being professionally outraged and indignant on behalf of the public. Those elements seem to want to perpetuate the Ned Kelly myth that the so called underdog is always right and any organisation is always wrong. In siding with the so called underdog many apologists shy away from asking the question about Ned Kelly. "If Kelly and his armed gang had not been stopped how many more horses would have been stolen, how many gold coaches bailed up, trains derailed and how many more Policemen killed". At least Kelly died game. His apologists seem to me to lack that gameness when whitewashing Ned with the benefits of hindsight.

For me, a recent Coroners Court decision in the case of the drowning death of men who ventured into a rough sea in a small aluminum open boat near Barwon Heads, Victoria, signified the swing in the legal breeze. Coroner Lewis Byrne found, in relation to a drowned man, this his own risk-taking contributed to the death of one of the men. The Herald Sun headline "Killed by his own stupidity" seems to effectively halt any claim that may eventuate.

And as most crimes against superannuation funds contain an element of identity theft, Trustees will obtain a higher degree of protection. Many who work in the industry testified that Trustees were regarded as "sitting ducks". If a disgruntled claimant could show one fault in the supposed omnipotence of the Trustees, then a courtroom tactic was to argue that the insignificant fault destroys the entire credibility of the Trustees in a defense. Any unbiased observer can see the error of the argument. But the tactic was not applied equally to the complainant's indiscretions. And with ID theft now rampant the legal breeze is blowing up a more level playing field. If contributors can sue Trustees for negligence or neglect, then the same criteria are now becoming available to Trustees in their defense. What's good for the goose is good for the gander. The Trustees of the industry's governing empire can now strike back. Trustees are increasing security measures.

One example is that funds will no longer accept written directions from contributors unless other confirmatory evidence of identification is provided. Foreshadowing the trends towards greater protection for Trustees is that of a superannuation preserved benefit theft from a contributor in Melbourne. The contributor sued the superannuation fund for restoration of the stolen amount plus unspecified but hopefully hefty damages to assuage his agitated ego on the grounds of reckless negligence of the Trustees. A PI engaged by the lawyer for the Trustees compiled an epistle of evidence that established the incautious contributor lived in a form of a commune in South Kensington, an inner Melbourne suburb. His possessions were stored in a turned sideways polystyrene banana box. Statutory Declarations attested that when a superannuation fund statement arrived in the mail it was opened and the statement and envelope were dumped onto the floor of the shared kitchen. One of the numerous transient males of roughly the same height, weight, colouring and stylishly unshaven facial features picked up the superannuation statement. When later his drug addled brain descended to normality he read it, saw dollar signs and coveted the cash.

The unidentified transient male, whose name no one could recall, helped himself to the passport, driving licence, bank book and whatever other details of the contributor he needed from the open polystyrene banana box. The transient remained in the overcrowded, odoriferous, dope drenched dwelling for about a month then disappeared with the superannuation of the incautious contributor. At a pre-court hearing it was assessed that the incautious contributor could not claim reckless negligence against the Trustees given that his own negligence clearly contributed to him being ripped off. His case against the Trustee did not get to first base. A few years ago the alcohol and drug induced indiscretions of the incautious contributor would have been treated almost as advantageous attributes and guaranteed him a win. Additionally, had he whinged about having an unhappy childhood he would most likely have been awarded heaps of dollars as damages. Reward for irresponsibility reigned rampant. But ID theft imposes a focus on added personal responsibility.

Australia's retirement reserves are not the only funds under attack. Shanghai's social security fund in 2006 managed ten billion Yuan and about one third of those assets were illegally diverted. A Shanghai Communist Chief and Politburo member was accused of illicitly investing billions of pension funds Yuan and abusing his position to the benefit of family members and also of accepting bribes. He got 18 years in prison.

As for DIY superannuation, more popularly known by the letters, SMSF any fraud is likely to be disastrous to the owners who self manage. A colleague tells me that most SMSF superannuation schemes are ripped off by one of the members, with a high proportion being spouses who separate. A Self Managed Super Fund (SMSF) is hard work. If you really want to be responsible for your own retirement then be sure you have the necessary knowledge about accounting, investments and legal matters. The Australian Tax Office strictly regulates adherence to the rules for the SMSF's with one to four members. If all members participate then each is a Trustee. If the management of the SMSF is outsourced to a Corporate Trustee, then each member is a Director.

The key to success is sound preparation before you decide to transfer money from an existing fund. If the existing fund is a defined fund you forfeit the protection of the employer's guarantee. You also forfeit the ability to approach the Superannuation Complaints Tribunal to resolve disputes, and if you lose money due to fraud you will have forfeited access to any special compensation schemes. Many people are persuaded into SMSF's without appreciating that a large amount of investment capital, some say $200,000 ,is needed for the income to cover the set-up and ongoing expenditures that accrue such as audit, taxation and financial advisors fees, to name but a few. Some professional organisations dispute this. But perhaps the most serious shortcoming of ill-prepared SMSF Trustees is the failure to comprehend that frauds are adept at tailor making scams that appear genuine to the inexperienced. Fraud against superannuation funds and contributors manifests itself in many guises. Some attempts to rort are simple, others complex and some involve cupidity of a contributor willing to bend the rules a bit.

Two crooks, a father and son, were jailed for promoting a big superannuation based fraud and for Contempt of Court. It was not the fund that was ripped off but greedy, gullible or desperate ex-fund members.

How much money they ripped off is not clearly known. Andrzej Janusz Michalik aka Andre Tomaszewski aka Stanislaw Knostantly Krawczk and his son Martin Michalik acquired a waterfront property in Oyster Bay, other property at Coledale NSW, motor vehicles including an MG Roadster, a Jaguar, a Range Rover and a Toyota and a ten metre power cruiser plus a luxurious lifestyle on the proceeds of their frauds on superannuation members. In local Southern Sydney newspapers the Michalik frauds used headings such as "Superannuation Cashback" and other words to imply they could obtain early release of preserved superannuation benefits. An objective of superannuation is to prevent access to accumulated benefits before retirement age but two unlicensed financial advisors devised a scheme to exploit the legislative porthole allowing early withdrawal for genuine hardship or compelling compassionate causes.

The Michalik scam involved, inter-alia, them setting up SMSF funds for contributors and arranging a rollover into that SMSF from the contributor's previous legitimate fund. The fraudsters would clean out the cash from the SMSF, deduct a sizeable commission from the illegally obtained money and hand over the balance. It is alleged that some of the gullible ended up with nothing and that the total value of the scam approximated $10 million.

Despite surrendering their dual nationality Australian /Polish passports, the Michaliks managed to acquire another passport each and, in breach of a NSW Supreme Court order, left that State and were caught in Perth, WA, International Airport intending to board a Qantas plane to Singapore. They had over $70,000 in Australian notes in a body belt and cabin bags. I wonder about the AFP Officer who apprehended them when they were so close to a clean getaway. Did the Michalik's associate the name of one of their dodgy companies with that man? The name of their dodgy company was Kilahim.

I also wonder what is the benefit of my country of allowing dual nationality. Is it necessary for medical reasons? Are the people with dual nationality closet schizophrenics? Or do they regard Australia as a safe haven from their dysfunctional homeland during a time of troubles. A tolerant country to be exploited at their convenience with no regard for the values of Australia? Does their homeland offer them a bolt hole into which they can escape with stolen Australian money? Abe Goldberg did just that, to name only one.

Polish born Abe, Australia's then biggest bankrupt being chased by ASIC about $1.5 billion missing from his business, escaped Australia and submerged himself in Poland. At the time of his departure, extradition of a Polish citizen was strewn with hurdles. In Warsaw he became a property magnate, owning dozens of buildings. According to a magazine report he was unrepentant about exploitation of his country of opportunity and is quoted as saying "I don't care or give a damn for them". If we must permit dual nationality then we must insist upon reciprocal extradition.

I am constantly amazed at the feeling of euphoria some people have when telling me they have just set up their own SMSF. When I ask if they understand the regulations that they must now comply with, Australian Prudential Regulations Authority (APRA) Australian Taxation Office (ATO) and Australian Securities and Investment Commission (ASIC) and Superannuation Industry Supervision Act (SIS) they seem confused. I was appalled that seven of the ten owners of SMSF's I spoke to did not know that their financial advisor must have an Australian Financial Services licence. Not one of them told me that they know what the letters SPAA represented. (Self-managed Super Fund Professional's Association of Australia). Not one of the ten knew failure to abide by SMSF rules can result in a jail term. A dangerous combination, euphoria and ignorance.

So after several diversions into aspects of superannuation frauds we finally arrive at the answers to the question "How secure is superannuation?" If you contribute to a big superannuation fund, Retail, Industry, Corporate, you have a big amount of security against the fund suffering from a fraud. If you contribute to a medium sized fund you have a medium degree of security and if you only have a little one, your own SMSF, then you only have a little degree of satisfaction. When it comes to superannuation, size does definitely count.

Remember though, wherever the size of your superannuation you carry the risk of rip-off if someone steals your ID. Be responsible with your superannuation records; treat them as you would your passport and bank details. If you have an SMSF consider that the installation of a combination lock home safe is inexpensive insurance. Check it out, it may be tax deductible. Keep all your personal information secure and protect your superannuation. ID theft is predicted to be the epidemic crime of the next few decades so don't be a soft target and give the thieves as easy time. Ensure you are a hard target, defend all of your personal details. Get a safe and be safe.

THE LAW

Earlier in this tome I candidly confessed to being dill when it comes to many aspects of the laws of my beloved Australia and its States.

Generally there are four main aims of Criminal Law:-

- Punishment – community's retribution for an offense against itself an individual, or property.
- Deterrence – discouragement by penalties to instill fear.
- Isolation – to incapacitate of put out of action to protect the public.
- Rehabilitation – to reform a convict.

Many people, far more knowledgeable than I, hold that the effectiveness of criminal law depends more upon the certainty that criminal conduct will be detected and followed by conviction, than it does on the magnitude of the penalty. I'm not so sure about that because from my experience many frauds attempted against superannuation funds seem based upon the premise that, although a perpetrator may be detected, the penalty for superannuation fraud is so ridiculously lenient its worth giving it a go if the opportunity arises. Many bitter and twisted individuals have successfully avoided well deserved conviction because of the reticence of Trustees to implement criminal proceedings.

The superannuation industry likes to project the image of a pristine pure white iceberg floating in a serene azure blue sea beneath a golden sun in a cerulean blue sky. It abhors anything that tarnishes that image on the grounds that public confidence may be diminished. Publicity about losses of assets are an embarrassment to any industry and the superannuation industry seems particularly sensitive.

Whether the relative insignificance of the penalty for superannuation fund fraud is still applicable is an open question in my mind. Maybe the reluctance to prosecute will diminish with more accumulation funds replacing defined funds. But what is not an open question is the persistent perception held by many in the conman community that penalties are microscopic compared to the reward. Fraudsters love lenient sentencing. The public perception that the weight given to mitigation is excessive compared to the weight attributed to the crime adds to their audacity. Some feel that extensive, untested, pleas for mitigation outweigh victims' impact statements.

Similarly, the conman community regards their ability to shelter from criminal conviction to be enhanced by laws such as the Privacy Act 1988 and the Victorian Charter of Human Rights. Again, whether this situation is, in fact, true, is not the issue. What is the issue is that conmen have told others that they perceive it to be true so others are positively attracted to give crime a go. Lately, improvements in Civil Law statues and the imposition of larger financial penalties together with custodial penalty options (particularly for repeat offenders) seem to be strengthening the four aims of the law in punishment, deterrence, isolation and rehabilitation. What is still missing is publicity within the superannuation industry about these added strengths. It is reluctance due the iceberg theory.

The superannuation industry needs to reinforce the legislative improvements by a constant drip-feed of information to Trustees, management, employees, contributors and beneficiaries. ASIC enforces the Corporations Act that regulate financial services and regarding superannuation it considers reports of misconduct and breaches of the Act. Maybe ASIC could examine the prospects of a regular column in major industry magazines. Conmen read them just as assiduously as members of the industry. Emphasis on deterrence will significantly diminish temptation should an inadvertent administrative event create an opportunity. ASIC is to be commended for its efforts in publicising penalties for superannuation maladministration and fraud, especially via its www.moneysmart.gov.au information data base. Based on that well-presented information, the industry could advantageously consider implementing a positive deterrence program, with an industry rewards system for employees who identify and report systemic weaknesses.

Regrettably, the industry generally seems to avoid mentioning anything that may cause contributors and potential contributors to infer that superannuation is anything less than a monolithic edifice of security. The iceberg again. Community priorities toward the four pillars of the aims of the law, punishment, deterrence, isolation and rehabilitation vary from time to time. Increasingly the public seem now to be focusing on the magnitude of the punishment penalty across the entire spectrum of criminality. I support that view and confidently assert that prison sentences for frauds will at least ensure that recidivists are kept out of circulation.

From my observations, reading and discussions with various law enforcement officers, it is clear that many conmen fear losing their hidden stash of stolen money more that they fear a term in prison. A trio of conmen bragged to a colleague of mine that a short prison term is like attending a post-graduate refresher course. Loss of money hurts them to a greater degree than loss of freedom. So while I fully support tougher prison sentences, a linked effort to more vigorously recover stolen money must be pursued. Mentioned above was the comment that caught conmen told me that they feel shielded by some parts of the law. They readily slip into bankruptcy mode to protect assets acquired evilly. Some are experts in phoenix companies, using insolvency laws to avoid paying creditors thereby adding to ill-gotten wealth.

Included in their protective shield is the perception of conmen that superannuation provides a haven. The conman pays ill-gotten millions into a superannuation fund then declares bankruptcy. He thereby maintains his multi-million dollars of investment within the sanctuary of his superannuation. After a leisurely stay in a minimum security prison the conman emerges to collect a billion dollar lump sum. While he keeps the cash as a lump sum it is inviolate. Only if he takes a pension can creditors stake a claim.

To preserve its well-deserved image with the public, an initiative is needed from within the industry to remove, "superannuation sanctuary". Unless an informed industry takes a greater role it may find legislators arrive at decisions which could impose provisions that prove more difficult and costly. That action needs someone young and enthusiastic to curb the thieves. I'm too old and as I frankly admit, when it comes to the law I'm a dill. Who will accept the challenge to be the "White Knight" in the industry? Someone who believes in Meliorism.

QUO VARDIS SUPER?

Four interlinked actions will greatly enhance our country's unique superannuation industry. Each alone will bring a benefit. Together they will marvelously advantage Australia.

Firstly, the industry regulations need to be simplified with model rules applicable to every fund and with a maximum standard tax rate of 10% throughout. This important concession will stimulate increased contributions. Any actuary will calculate the estimated massive increase of inflowing subscriptions that will compensate the Government for any short term tax losses.

Secondly, the Federal Government needs to re issue Government Bonds, with a Reserve Bank interest rate coupon, being a fixed base rate of interest payable half yearly with investment related to RBA rate variations, to bona fide superannuation funds only. Superannuation funds will leap at investing in secure bonds with a guaranteed interest rate. It insulates part of their income from extreme volatility. No investment in that sphere of suitable magnitude has been available for decades, so contributor's benefits have deteriorated in other, mainly foreign, investment as Trustees chase yields overseas with higher risk profiles.

The Treasury should use the cash inflow to reduce our enormous balance of payments deficit and the interest paid thereon to overseas entities. Why pay interest overseas? Pay the interest to Australians! Advantage ourselves first. That's what national advantage is about. The Treasury will find it far cheaper than paying interest to foreigners on our deficits. Currency fluctuation volatility will be reduced. It benefits Australia to look after the retirement benefits of Australians as a priority. In both short and long terms it advantages Australia within the world economy without upsetting the so called "level playing field" of international free trade. It needs to be done now before international interest rates rise. Stability and its confederate, confidence, will restore credibility to an industry seriously deficient of that attribute for over a decade.

When I first proposed the re-introduction of Commonwealth Bonds strictly for superannuation funds, detractors scorned what they claimed was the low level of the return. However 2014 research shows that the typical fund has fallen more than one percent as a result of global share market volatility. The detractors would today be pleased to have the return on their funds of the bank rate, compounded over the last five years. At least it would be positive not negative. Let's issue the super bonds while the Aussie dollar remains relatively high against most overseas currencies.

Thirdly, increase protection for contributors by simple clear and punitive punishments for people who steal, negligently waste or misappropriate the contributions of workers to superannuation funds. The personal assets of the thieves should not be immune from recovery whether they be in Australia or secreted overseas. We learned a lot, at a cost, in trying to recover the money that disappeared when Christopher Skase fled. We need to use that experience, not let it lapse. Protection afforded to recklessly negligent or criminal operators who shelter behind two dollar proprietary limited companies, bogus asset transference schemes and overseas transfers should be smashed. Many of the "protective" protocols belong to the age of button up boots not to the age of the computer.

Superannuation must not be allowed to remain a secure haven for thieves. A crook steals money, puts it into his superannuation fund, and then declares he is bankrupt. The stolen money is not recoverable from his superannuation fund – that is wrong, it is immoral, it must be changed. It is absurd that convicted criminals have access to free legal aid to protect their stash of stolen money for later lawful retrieval. We need to stop financing the fight against ourselves.

Historically, Commonwealth Government bonds have been the security least attractive to frauds, swindlers and conmen. Keep it that way by updating the issue regulations from the punched card era to that of the computer. If a limit on the magnitude of any issue or subsequent redemption date be required, then allocate that advisory task to the Board of the Reserve Bank. But don't distort the system by making the Reserve Bank the issuer of the Bonds. That creates a conflict of interest which is undesirable in my view. Issue the Bonds though any reputable financial institution on a bid basis. Probably we have twenty institutions of a size and degree of competence to place bonds with genuine superannuation funds in semi-annual issues.

Fourthly, Superannuation is a giant industry and needs its own regulatory entity. The Australian Taxation Office, a revenue raising entity, is an inappropriate regulator. I wonder whether the superannuation industry cross subsidies the activities of the ATO. An independent entity would seem to be less costly. Such an authority may incorporate the Superannuation Complaints System.

Obviously this four point plan will require fine tuning by lawyers, actuaries and administrators. Beaut! But ensure it complies with the KISS* principal – otherwise Aussies will not support it. Start today by issuing Commonwealth Bonds, then phase in the other points. Don't knock it until you try it!

*KISS = Keep it Simple Stupid

Chapter Twenty

WHEN WILL SUPER BE A TERRORIST TARGET?

THE QUESTION IS "WHEN", NOT "if". Terrorist organisations Al-Qaeda and Jemaah Islamiah are running low on funds due to the massive effort in tracking and curtailing the sources of terrorist finances by the United States FBI, the British Police Special Branch and the Australia Federal Police to name only the agencies more popularly known. The traditional source of money for terrorists is from drug exports and more latterly from oil sales. Wealthy religious donors sponsor religious sects but even that source of donations is drying up. Identification and publication of Saudi Arabian donors, in particular, has an embarrassment element causing severe curtailment of direct donations. The United Nations must maintain sanctions against the countries supplying munitions to terrorists. Indirect donations are becoming more difficult to hide. Blocking of money transfers from fake charities further restricts cash flow to terrorists. The bogus businesses identified by law enforcement authorities are having assets frozen so cash transfers are also drying up.

The FBI's chief financial crime expert advises that Al-Qaeda, Jemaah Islamiah and ISIS do not need vast sums to remain active because each is decentralized and "unstructured". Main expenses are for munitions, establishing safe houses for terrorists, paying for training camps and remunerating the families of suicide bombers. That expert also advises that the terrorists are adapting to the choking of their finance sources by moving into new areas of fund raising such as credit card fraud. But credit card fraud is the province of numerous established and powerful fraudsters. Competition from terrorists may be resisted at a level up to and including terminally fatal.

Technology and increasing law enforcement focus on credit card fraud will undoubtedly limit the magnitude of net gains to terrorists, particularly as cooperation to defeat terrorists may come from the criminal element that dislike being drawn into the centre of law agencies' intensive efforts. Probably the terrorist movements will gravitate towards the enormously popular type of frauds perpetrated by the well organised Nigerians. In terms of online fraud, Nigeria runs second to the former USSR with the USA and Canada as joint thirds and Australia quite a few rungs down the ladder of deceit.

Terrorist financial generals are looking for soft targets with big, quick rewards. A democratic country with a legal system that bends over backwards to be fair and just, appears to offer terrorists a diminished risk of long term or intolerable incarceration if their financial soldiers are apprehended. And it's cheap. The terrorist simply pretends penury and Legal Aid pays all expenses. A stiff prison sentence in Australia is a trifle compared to a stiff sentence in many other less enlightened countries. A few years in an Aussie prison with TV, computers, libraries with books in their own language, gymnasiums, swimming pools, access to education courses, access to counsellors and food prepared to comply with various alleged religious affiliations, may be classed as luxury living compared with some Pakistan, Iran, Palestine or Afghanistan prisons.

Rather than volunteer to be a suicide bomber, terrorists may make a sacrifice that allows them to rip off a few hundred million dollars for their cause and spend some time, if caught, in the comparative comfort of an Australian prison. It could prove to be an acceptable alternative contribution to a cause. Even the Japanese in 1945 were running out of kamikaze pilots when it was appreciated that their supreme sacrifice contributed nothing to their cause. Religious or perhaps more properly, tribal superstition still attracts martyrs. Organisations declared to be terrorist under the Australian Criminal Code include Abu Sayyat Group,

Al-Qaida and its many offshoots, Jamait ul-Ansar and Jemaah Islamiah. Lately ISIS and its convoluted branches were added to the proscription list.

Superannuation in Australia is a trillion dollar industry. One massive fraud could yield a stupendous reward to an intelligent and fanatically driven terrorist team. Already evident is the mastery of the media by sections of terrorists using sophisticated computer systems. There is no computer barrier that they will not try to penetrate. Rewards are high the risks are low. Experience in the 1980's of banks chasing high risk ventures to unload their bulging vaults of surplus cash with disastrous results is a memory that time is erasing. Currently our superannuation funds have many characteristics similar to the banks of the 1980's; a continual inflow of capital with too few outlets that enable them to make reasonable returns, so pressure towards higher risk investments is beginning to build. With pressure comes error. Errors give access to assets. Conditions are looking propitious for an intelligent, resourceful group to pull off a scam. The CSS Fraud mob nearly got away with $160 million at Christmas 2003 and they seemed not over-endowed with brilliance. They were caught within days and $147 million was recovered.

What form will a new attack take? I do not know, but predict that soon a relatively small operation will be mounted against a medium sized retirement benefit fund in a medium sized country, maybe in Scandinavia maybe in South America or maybe here. If the fraud is successful it will become the template for simultaneous frauds against the enormous retirement funds of five or six of the Western democracies. Co-ordinated attacks are one of the trademarks of terrorists. Another trademark is that of incredible brutality so expect a clever electronic foisting of finance combined with an act of barbarity designed to distract, attract maximum publicity and delusional recruits. Time frame? The trial run before 2015 ends and the big scam 2016/17. This chapter began with the word "When" not "If".

Should any reader think multi, multi-million dollar losses impossible, please pause and contemplate the HIH $5 billion loss, or Mr Upul Anthony who pleaded guilty to illegally taking $16million from a former AMP subsidiary. These were not scams by terrorists but they demonstrate that huge losses have happened. A Federal Court judge made restraining orders on Royale Capital Pty Ltd and Active Super Pty Ltd and their directors, Justin Gibson and Jason Burrows, to inter-alia, prevent them dealing with superannuation accounts of their current SMSF clients. The companies had raised $4.75 million from over 200 investors and ASIC were concerned about connections with companies based in the United States of America and the British Virgin Islands. A Filipino, Mr Nestor Ching is wanted by Police over serious fraud offences involving the loss to superannuation funds of $5.5 million. Another Filipino, Dana Joyce Delos Santos is also on the Police wanted list for laundering money stolen from superannuation funds.

Halssam Safetli pleaded guilty to the murder of Michael Loch McGurk. The murdered man was alleged to be a director of 28 failed or deregistered companies. Bentley Smythe Financial Services was one of his trading entities. McGurk, not the name given to him at birth nor is it the only name he used, is alleged to have defrauded superannuation funds between 2003 and 2005. Police say he was the mastermind of a superannuation fraud that used false drivers' licences, birth certificates, and Medicare cards to fraudulently obtain early release of superannuation investments from unsuspecting members of the public. Millions of dollars were sent overseas. Police also claim he was a money lender of last resort and that his list of defaulters featured Maurice Terreiro the brother of Matthew Terreiro, the man who made the error that led to the CSS Fraud unravelling. An associate of McGurk said he flew first class to Indonesia and Thailand to transfer stolen money. In March 2005 he claimed to have transferred $350,000 to an account in Jakarta. An Ethiopian-born Sydney Accountant Robert Aguis along will associates Kevin Zerada and Debbie Jandagi were convicted of a tax fraud involving money transfers to Vanuatu. A judge described the $100 million scheme as "crude, inept and haphazard".

None of the above were connected in any way with terrorism. I list them purely as examples of massive money movements overseas. If one "crude, inept and haphazard" scheme transfers over One hundred million dollars overseas, imagine what a competent terrorist group could gain. Never, ever, underestimate the enemy.

The world is at war, indeed a world war. Although I stop short of calling it World War Three, later historians may name this period World Terrorist War Three. The duration of the war is uncertain and is highly likely to continue for decades. It seems ironical that terrorists, who fight to revert to a Dark Ages tyrannical, theocracy, utilize the most up-to-date technology to achieve their retrogressive ends.

Despite my gloomy prediction of overseas terrorist attempts to steal superannuation from a major fund I remain extremely confident that the industry will robustly thrive in defiance of those attempts. I believe in the concept of superannuation and I believe that Australia's superannuation system is the best in the world and managed by the best people in the world.

Regards to my readers, a healthy and prosperous retirement to all.

www.ingramcontent.com/pod-product-compliance
Lightning Source LLC
Chambersburg PA
CBHW070546160426
43199CB00014B/2398